T0374220

# CALMING CLASSROOM CHAOS

An Educator's Guide to Strategies and a
Different Perspective on Behavior

Kristin Martinsen Robison, MOT, OTR/L

CALMING CLASSROOM CHAOS
AN EDUCATOR'S GUIDE TO STRATEGIES AND A
DIFFERENT PERSPECTIVE ON BEHAVIOR

iUniverse books may be ordered through booksellers or by contacting:

iUniverse
1663 Liberty Drive
Bloomington, IN 47403
www.iuniverse.com
844-349-9409

Illustrations by Bekah Rosas
Editing by Betty Christianson Martinsen
Cover Design by Trish Sagare

ISBN: 978-1-6632-2474-3 (sc)
ISBN: 978-1-6632-2475-0 (e)

Library of Congress Control Number: 2021913032

Print information available on the last page.

iUniverse rev. date: 08/14/2024

# INTRODUCTION

*Happy* matters.

When kids struggle, it is hard on everyone. *The Secret to Happy- A Parent's Guide to Helping a Unique Child Thrive* was created to help parents better understand their unique children and the challenging behaviors that prevent *Happy*. But families often turn to educators for guidance and support because educators are a huge part of a child's life, and these behaviors also happen outside the home. We have more and more kids whose parents are stressed or absent, so the support at home may be inconsistent or non-existent. All of this puts a strain on the relationship between school and home. Parenting is hard enough, but "parenting" a child who is one of your students is borderline impossible, yet many educators find themselves doing essentially this.

Behavior is a vital communication tool that influences how we engage with one another. We can often figure out what is going on by reading behavior, but this can be affected by our perception. If we wish to change the aptitude of our students, we must begin to see their behavior differently, through a new lens. When a child acts as a bully, disrespectful, out of control, or lazy, this behavior can define how we see this child, which often alters our response to them. If we slow down and ask *why,* it allows us to consider the human behind the behavior, and maybe this will increase our compassion so that we react differently, leaving space for us to help. Solutions don't work if they aren't targeting the true reason behind the behavior and for this, we must understand the problem from the child's perspective. Often this is translated through their behavior. Children may still exhibit attention-seeking or extreme behaviors to attain goals or display habitual responses that don't match the situation when their needs are not met. However, when a child feels heard and their nervous system is ready for engagement with the world around them, behavior becomes more adaptable and manageable.

It is pretty easy to pick out "that student" who is the source of stress in a group. The child who has trouble making friends and acts like a bully to avoid anyone knowing they are actually very much alone. The child who unexpectedly reacts to anything new or unknown. The smart student who is failing despite their intelligence. And the toughest of all, the child you can't reach no matter how hard you try- the one who struggles with social rules, can't find success with academic challenges, and who finds themselves in trouble or going to the office all the time. This child's behavior prevents them from actively engaging and learning, but it also affects the social and emotional climate in which everyone would love to thrive. Often, these kids go home only to find more stress, more difficulty, and little support. Gaining a better understanding of these kids is the purpose of this book.

Social-emotional development is critical for happiness. It is the foundation for resilience and cognitive growth. Emotional intelligence is as important as academic intelligence, yet it is easy to overlook the pieces involved in the development of regulation and *Happy*. We are enduring unprecedented times with extreme behaviors seen on social media daily that erode our perception of community, togetherness, and common ground. Tough kids often experience strained relationships; sometimes the only support is a teacher, coach, or other outside adult. Our kids need relationships and support in new ways to navigate the constant stress and trauma of their world. They need to be heard and understood. Relationships provide the roots for growth but kids are especially vulnerable in relationships because they don't have the experience or self-understanding that comes with age.

Our educational system was designed to support kids; sometimes it works, and other times it doesn't. The process of supporting and educating children has become very complex because many state and federal guidelines determine much of the programming requirements impacting behaviors; not all content is appropriate for every student, yet every student must complete the given content. When a student can't, poor behavior usually follows. Another force- technology- is utilized daily and serves as a wonderful tool, but it also changes how the brain works, alters attention, and often negatively influences behavior when kids can't effectively balance screen and real-life time. Consequences for poor behavior have become harder to implement, and many teachers feel that their hands are tied when they try to manage complex behaviors, so when consequences don't change behaviors, we need to know how to adjust- adjust our approach, and more importantly, adjust our perspective of *why* this behavior occurs.

This book is designed for any educator. The obvious are teachers and paraprofessionals working with kids in the school setting; it also extends to anyone responsible for discipline and classroom management, and everyone dealing with a unique student or challenging behaviors. Maladaptive behavior can prevent us from seeing someone for the gifts they possess, and our assumptions can prevent us from finding anything positive to hold onto. If you are struggling to understand a child, I hope this book will help you see them differently.

Understanding and exploring the *why* behind various behaviors can increase our tolerance and acceptance of the child behind the behavior. When we can remember that every child is amazing, even during a challenging moment, we might have an easier time discovering our own gifts that can completely change the course of a child's life.

**\*\*Instructions for the Use of this Book\*\***

Each section of this book will review information to meet different needs, and all of them are valuable because classrooms today have almost every type of student sitting at a desk and none of these kids come with an instruction book. Some educators need an explanation of nervous system function to better manage behavior in the classroom, and others might want to better understand a specific disability. Many are in survival mode and need immediate strategies to rediscover the joy and reason they chose education in the first place.

To be an effective educator with classroom management skills that support *all* types of students, each section of this book can be relevant but not necessarily in the order it is presented. This is not a cover-to-cover read. It is intended to provide quick strategies to try with specific behaviors and references that provide potential explanations for *why* these behaviors might occur. You will see repetition of strategies because often, there are different explanations for behaviors that can be supported with similar tools.

- *Section One: The Cycle of Regulation* introduces all the "puzzle pieces" and summarizes how all the systems affect each other to impact regulation and behavior. Nothing happens without regulation. This section is vital to read even if you are exhausted and only want some quick strategies because it will help you choose among the tools more effectively.
- *Section Two: Specific Behaviors in the Classroom and What to Do* is the quick reference portion that includes easy-to-implement strategies. This section will also reference more detailed information within Section Three, including additional strategies to try if the quick tools aren't enough. This section is broken into three parts: work production, writing, and behavior.
- *Section Three: An in-depth look at the Puzzle Pieces and Tools* goes deeper into the specifics of the nervous system and brain functioning to interpret why we see the behaviors that prevent success. There is some repetition throughout this book, but as

educators know, repetition helps with assimilation. More tools with specific strategies are listed in each of these segments, so if you keep seeing the same references, you will now have additional resources to try. For instance, if the quick strategies repeatedly send you to the executive functioning segment, spend some time reading through the details of this chapter and try the additional strategies specific to this topic listed in the *Practical Stuff.*

- *Section Four: Specific learning types or Disabilities* covers details you might need to manage a specific student or disability. It outlines the general concepts related to special education with terms critical to individualized programming. More special education students are participating in the general education environment today, so this segment gives valuable information about disabilities and other issues that impact a student's access to academic programming.

# CONTENTS

# SECTION ONE

## THE CYCLE OF REGULATION SUMMARY

We must consider many necessary puzzle pieces to understand and affect behavior. It is crucial to appreciate the nervous system's role because there are factors that we cannot change, but we can still help a child achieve regulation despite maladaptive functions. The effectiveness of sensory processing *signals* and executive functioning *skills* will determine if an adaptive response can be achieved (Fig 1). If growth is to occur, there must be some way to monitor the entire process so the system can adjust. Success means finding more of what works and eliminating what does not. The environment can impact this cycle at any point. It is a huge factor for all people, but children are especially vulnerable because they do not yet have the experience to handle or compensate for an environment that is not conducive to their growth and self-actualization.

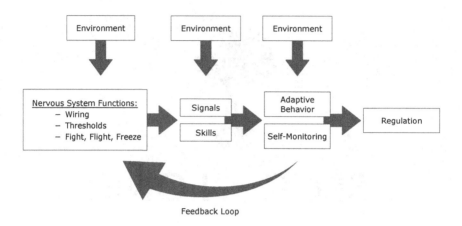

*Fig 1. Cycle of regulation with the various factors that
affect the feedback loop and behavioral outcome*

***Regulation*** is the ability to self-manage, a key area of competency for social and emotional learning. Regulation means a child can focus even when there are distractions. If a child is regulated, they can learn, realize their potential, and find success. They can handle plans that change and recover after a disappointment. Regulation can come easier for some because of the complexities within the nervous system and the balance of signals and skills. Executive functioning and sensory processing are interdependent; we need signals and we need skills for regulation to occur. If you want to know the *why* of behavior, you must be aware of both. When signals come in, skills determine the response. No response or a delayed response can look like intentional behavior, defiance, or a lack of motivation. There are numerous areas of the brain and neurotransmitters that are essential for regulation to take place. If there is an imbalance in the system, dysfunction often ensues.

The ***Environment*** is a key consideration in this entire process because the details of our world affect every single part of the system and ultimately behavior. The environment can include anything a child is exposed to such as people, stress, physical objects, and sensations. Factors such as time (i.e., the pace of an activity), intensity (or interaction with others) and expectations are other critical aspects of an environment that will impact this cycle. It is important to remember that the nervous system depends on the environment and that children function according to their environment; nothing is static and behavioral responses are affected by many ever-changing forces.

Sometimes we cannot do anything about the environment so perception or looking through a different lens is now vital. When kids don't have the skills to adapt successfully or when they go home to a place that undermines all we have tried to do at school, the environmental factor is huge in understanding and guiding the intervention and interaction we have with this child. When a child is merely surviving in an out-of-control environment, a significant point of intervention is to provide the opportunity for control somewhere in the world we help to create for them. Control can affect a seemingly impossible piece of the regulation puzzle.

There are three major environmental influences to consider when assessing what can be addressed to improve regulation.

- Behavior is significantly affected by our *emotional environment*. If a child feels supported, their behavior will be different. Abuse, neglect, and poverty create an environment that impacts *everything*. Subtle feelings you have about a child can also affect an emotional environment; this can include mere chemistry between two people. If you don't click with a child because they are difficult, or if you feel they are lazy or disrespectful, this affects the emotional environment in which they function.
- The *Developmental environment* looks at a child's developmental level, which might be very different from their age, especially if they have any special needs. Developmental milestones, exposure to drugs or alcohol in utero, and even birth-related factors can significantly affect development and the overall system at any point.
- The immediate *physical environment* also alters behavior. We need to consider noise levels, visually busy spaces, and even the objects that provide comfort or serve to support a need. Our expectations or demands for a task are a considerable aspect of the physical environment that can determine if success is possible, and all of this will influence behavior.

> "When a flower doesn't bloom, you fix the environment in which it grows, not the flower."
>
> Alexander Den Heijer

*Self-monitoring* is the ability to examine internal signals and communicate these findings to the brain. The first step to regulation is knowing something is off so you can adjust behavior which results in self-management. Self-monitoring draws attention to the fact that something is out of balance which creates a problem to solve so the *why* of behavior can be assessed. When this self-awareness is not intact, it is difficult to adapt. Young children or kids with special needs can have difficulty self-monitoring and sometimes need adult help. Understanding the adult role in this situation can change everything. When kids don't know *what* they are feeling or don't have words to describe these feelings, they won't be able to adjust their behavior, ask for help, or regulate. Teaching how to self-monitor can be one of the most significant life skills a child can learn.

*Adaptive Behavior* occurs throughout development and largely depends on exposure to various experiences. When adaptive behavior is positive, this contributes to regulation and creates positive learned skills. When something does not feel right and a response is negative, we see maladaptive behavior that prevents regulation and increases avoidance. Self-monitoring contributes to the feedback loop to communicate what is working and what is not (see Fig 1). We can affect adaptive behavior through awareness of different portions of the regulation cycle, including signals and skills.

## Signals and Skills

*Sensory Processing Signals* communicate what is going on inside us. Basic sensations such as feeling tired or overwhelmed, hunger, thirst, temperature, or

pain affect the regulation cycle. Signals also relay what is going on in the outside world, such as the pace or intensity of the outside world. Signals communicate with the brain, which responds to this input, so a skilled response will occur. If the signals are not communicating effectively, kids cannot figure out what they are experiencing and won't know how to respond. Too many or too few signals affect the process of planning, starting, and staying focused. They cannot figure out what is wrong and have no idea how to get help. The interpretation and balance of signals allow us to make good choices and stay safe... to regulate.

- Too many signals means the brain is in protection mode.
- Too few signals means the child doesn't know they even need to respond.

***Executive Functioning Skills*** are necessary for behavioral regulation and become effectual when the brain can analyze, process, respond, and learn. However, this only happens if the signals reach the brain's thinking part, so both must be discussed. Executive functioning skills are developmental in nature, which means they improve with exposure, practice, and time. If you push too hard before they are developed, you will see frustration, poor behavior, and lots of failure. When we allow kids to try safely, they will *do* more which improves their ability to navigate the demands of childhood and increases proficiency with the complexities of adulthood. We may find that a lot of support is required at first when these skills are underdeveloped. The *art* of support is knowing how much to help, when to back off, and how to advocate for a child who may have unique needs that require temporary scaffolding to assimilate skill development and increase independence.

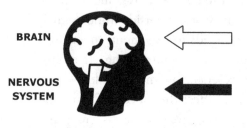

**BRAIN**

**NERVOUS SYSTEM**

Executive functioning skills are in the thinking part of the brain and what we use for execution or to make a response.

Signals of sensory information come in from the body and nervous system. They are the connection and communication between our body and our world.

## Nervous System Functions

Many factors are unique to the individual and related to genetics, environment, and exposure. Some will not change without chemical intervention and others can be positively influenced if the child is given the proper support. Understanding the complexities of the nervous system, which includes sensory processing and executive functioning, should provide more explanations for behavior. This can be a significant part of the *why*. Understanding why behavior happens will determine where the breakdown occurs in the cycle and where we can provide strategies. Nervous system functions include individual wiring, nervous system thresholds, and fight, flight, or freeze responses.

*Wiring* is an innate nervous system function and what many refer to as personality. It is how someone comes into the world and is the static piece of the puzzle; it does not change with strategies or time. When there are issues, especially related to brain chemistry, pharmaceuticals can alter the function and appearance of behavior, but it really will not change who this person is. Since we cannot change the chemical aspect of the brain without medical intervention, it is enough to simply understand the role that wiring plays in behavior. If someone is wired busy, they often do better when they can move. If they are asked to sit still and listen, they will likely have trouble regulating focused attention. If someone is wired quiet, they might not like too much going on around them, which will impact behavior. Some people are wired in certain ways that make self-awareness challenging, so they may struggle with "reading the room" or knowing how they feel inside. Wiring should influence our expectations for an individual student's behavior because when we observe behavior knowing how wiring affects it, we gain a new perspective of *why*. This awareness and altered perspective can now help us assist a student in finding success.

*Thresholds* are nervous system functions that determine if and how we respond to our world. We need to hit this threshold to engage, attend, and focus, but we also do not want to hit it too often (Dunn, 2007). People are prone to a certain threshold because of their wiring, but thresholds can be affected by using strategies to alter behavioral responses. Behavior directly results from a person's threshold at that moment, with that activity, and with potential strategies in place. Behavioral responses can appear similar but differ in origin; some reactions can be due to overstimulation, and others because of understimulation. When we acknowledge wiring and begin to see trends in behavior, it becomes easier to determine which tools will work.

- Exercise, caffeine, and fidgeting are all strategies that help someone reach a high threshold that is understimulated. People who are wired busy need to move a lot and if they do not get enough input, they might under-respond because there are insufficient signals to tell the brain what to do.
- Taking a break, finding some quiet time, or meditation can help someone who is overstimulated and had their lower threshold hit too frequently. People who are wired more sensitively don't need as much input, and when they get too much, they might over-respond because too many signals bombard the system.

*Fight, flight, or freeze* is our physiological response to stress and another important nervous system function. When our system gets flooded with too much input, like when signals go astray or we struggle with a low threshold moment, it can quickly put us into fight, flight, or freeze. This is our most primitive system, and we tend to end up here when we experience repetitive or extreme stress. We do not have to go through an actual "life or death" experience because our perception of danger can be enough to trigger this response. Controlling behavior, learning, or regulating is impossible when this mechanism is engaged. A child's wiring and threshold for input will determine when this function kicks in and how they will respond. Some tend to fight, while others might be more prone to flight or freeze. Recovery is the goal when kids hit this point; engaging and problem-solving (even with the best intentions) can quickly worsen behavior.

# SECTION TWO

## SPECIFIC BEHAVIORS
## AND WHAT TO TRY

When we improve our read of behavior we can help
a child adjust, adapt, and find regulation.

**Quick Reference Section**

Specific maladaptive behaviors seen in the classroom can be challenging to manage, especially in the moment. Because behaviors stem from various sources, it is important to have different tools to address the dysfunction's potential reasons. Pay attention to *Why We Might Be Seeing This Behavior* column in this section because this will guide you toward what to do first and direct you to further chapters with more detail and additional tools.

Another piece of critical information concerns strategies and more specifically, *when* we utilize them. Many of the strategies that kids need must occur *before* work can happen. When a child needs input to respond but we use strategies as rewards for work, behavior often can't improve. If you put a reward out there but a child doesn't respond, you must consider *why*. If this child is wriggling around and struggling to do work and you offer the yoga ball to sit on *after* they get their work done, certainly they would do their work, right? But if their system needs movement (that they would get from sitting on the ball) to focus and do work, they will never get the work done, no matter how much they want the reward. Their nervous system needs the input of movement to perform. This can explain why rewards and consequences don't always work.

> Fuel can't be the reward if it's vital for the engine to run.
>
> It's like turning the key in your car and not understanding why it won't run when there is no gas.

This section has been chunked into three main sections but because behavior is cyclical, many areas will overlap. For example, difficulty demonstrating knowledge often comes from writing issues and certainly ends up with behavioral issues. Try to determine the primary source of difficulty when choosing your tools but be aware that you may need to use multiple sections until you find something that works. This section is designed to provide quick, easy-to-administer ideas that address multiple explanations for behavior.

## Demonstration of Knowledge

- Preparation for Knowledge: Getting to class on time and having the learning materials.
- Non-Engagement and Avoidance: Poor participation and engagement during learning.
- Work Production: Starting, staying on task, and focusing on completing the work cycle.
- Application of Knowledge: Not working to potential, poor demonstration of knowledge, or difficulty with independent work.

<u>Writing Issues</u>

- This section covers the various reasons we see writing difficulty. Some are occupational therapy issues, others are more related to regulation and executive functioning.

<u>Behavior Issues</u>

- Tier I Behaviors: Disruption in class, creating distraction, or poor response to requests.
- Tier II Behaviors: Dysregulation, more intense defiance, and behavioral responses.
- Aggression: Self-injury and extreme emotional blowups.
- Anxiety: Difficulty with change, transitions, and behavioral regulation.

# DEMONSTRATION OF KNOWLEDGE: PREPARATION

## WHAT DOES THIS LOOK LIKE BEHAVIORALLY?

- Always late or absent
- Computer isn't charged or it is at home
- Doesn't get or have materials needed for class
- Poor organization and no plan for anything

## WHY MIGHT WE BE SEEING THIS BEHAVIOR?

- Executive functioning deficits: planning, organization, time management, delays
- Attentional deficits
- Sensory issues impacting regulation
- Gifted students with inconsistent skill development below assumed level

**Overall Objective: Shift our support and energy to focus on when they DO arrive on time or have the necessary items for learning.**

## WHAT CAN WE DO?

- Focusing on the positive means more success. You may have to start with a lot of support and lower expectations initially, but eventually, you will be able to remove some of the scaffolding and they will be able to *do* more.
- Assist in the plan for execution: how to start, how to organize their thoughts or materials, and what this looks like done. Catch them using the steps of the plan and positively reinforce their effort even when success is minimal. Little achievements are critical to point out because they often don't recognize this as growth so there is no motivation even to try.
- Check in at the end of class for a quick, verbal review of what is next, where they are going, and what materials they will need.

- Create a routine with their team of teachers to include a quick check-in before this student is released from class; the more they practice planning, the better it will become.

- Remember that planning is a developmental, executive skill and a lack of performance might be due to this delay. Try to focus on skill development instead of consequences for behavior (especially if previous discipline approaches have not been effective). Coaching and reinforcement of a plan and execution is a great way to build these skills and can be done while other kids work on a warm-up activity or exit ticket. Frequent check-ins should review a plan for their day and how they expect to accomplish it; your guidance is critical if they are going to find success realistically. They also get great feedback from you in the moment of plan development and you can acknowledge their growth in these unique skills.

- Focus your energy on the kids who DO show up on time and are prepared to learn instead of giving a student attention when they are late. Negative attention can be better than no attention.

- Utilize a visual that shows a list or images that show what is next or help them create a plan for what is next.

# DEMONSTRATION OF KNOWLEDGE: AVOIDANCE & NON-ENGAGEMENT

## WHAT DOES THIS LOOK LIKE BEHAVIORALLY?

- Daydreaming
- Forgets to turn in work
- Doesn't notice body language or subtle communication of peers so may be inappropriate or disengaged
- Avoiding class
- Finding excuses to leave class (bathroom/nurse)
- Buried and can't catch up

## WHY MIGHT WE BE SEEING THIS BEHAVIOR?

- Anxiety and fight, flight, or freeze response to stress
- ADHD, not focused in this moment because of distractions
- Weak executive functioning especially involving initiation & planning
- Demands/expectations are not appropriate for skills/regulation of child
- Need for movement or sensory tools
- Mismanaged threshold responses

**Overall Objective:** Shift our attention to focus on small moments of success or participation. Don't let them get too buried before we intervene.

## WHAT CAN WE DO?

- Shorten work or remove old assignments if mastery is demonstrated, especially if the student is on a 504 or IEP and has accommodations or modifications.
- Chunk the work (missing or current) with clear deadlines and rewards for each piece completed.

- Make a list of newly assigned work with at least one older/missing assignment. Don't hyperfocus on details, just make it easy to check off items to increase motivation for completion.
- Reward work they did versus punishing work they didn't do.
- Alter warmup activities to suit their skill level or strengths better so they can actively participate.
- Praise them when they are working or focused (to prevent elopement).
- Pushing and reminding often don't help. If you have already ensured they know what is required, double-check that they know *how* to do what you're asking. Remember that many kids don't want their peers to know they don't understand, so the more discreet you can be, the better your chance of sharing practical tools with them.
- Provide dynamic sitting options (standing in the back, wobble stool, cushion, or ball) with the assumption that they can't reach their threshold so they cannot work or engage without movement.
- Ignore work refusal and give your energy to the kids doing what they should. If work refusal is an attempt to get attention, this is a great way to provide an immediate model for desired behavior and avoid giving attention to behaviors you don't want.
- Notice and make a big deal out of the little stuff. When they begin to work or attempt what is requested, notice this effort (small as it may be) to increase momentum for additional success.
- Create a just right challenge by altering demands/expectations or helping to supplement skills.

# DEMONSTRATION OF KNOWLEDGE: WORK PRODUCTION

## WHAT DOES THIS LOOK LIKE BEHAVIORALLY?

- Homework score affects the overall grade more than content mastery (because of late/missing work)
- Frequently not finishing work
- Difficulty starting work: sitting and staring or fidgeting and moving around
- Can recite information they can't get on the page

## WHY MIGHT WE BE SEEING THIS BEHAVIOR?

- Threshold issues impacting *how* they are working: too low or too high
- Executive functioning skill weakness or ADHD: poor planning, organization, time management, or initiation
- They don't know what to do or how to start but don't ask for help
- Sensory issues that prevent regulation

**Overall Objective:** **Shift our support and expectations from task-driven activities to mastery of learning objectives. If mastery can be demonstrated, don't focus on work completion (aka busy work).**

## WHAT CAN WE DO?

- Provide an alternative path to show knowledge other than writing: allow them to represent concepts with pictures, create a slideshow, or grade them by what they can explain to you for times when they are struggling.
- Many kids with attentional deficits don't hand in work because it isn't complete. Work out a deal for the missing work to have them show you they understand the process or content versus completing the whole page, and then let them check off that assignment.
- Turn activities into a game. Time activities to see if they performed it as quickly as *they* thought.

- Use or create a binder system (see www.secrettohappy.com for examples) or visual planner page unique to their needs.
- Ensure that they understand what is due and when. Sometimes an additional visual (like on a post-it note) is needed to get their attention for deadlines even 10 minutes from now. Notes of different colors they choose for each task can help increase their attention, which might increase the likelihood of it getting done.
- Check in with them at the beginning of instruction to ensure understanding and confirm or support their plan for production.
- Help them with organization, prioritization, time management, and a *plan*. Point out their specific success or independence with each of these areas.
- Adjust demands or chunk requirements to see if they can find success; add more only when they have achieved the goal.
- Have a timer and visual checklist showing work *and* fun time/reward time.
- Provide *Sensory Diet* tools that are built into the schedule and visually available at all times. Oral sensory input can include gum, snacks, water, and ice. This list should also include movement and heavy work activities (see p. 119, 140 for additional Sensory Diet ideas).
- Have areas of the room with more color, lighting, and stimulation so students can utilize what they need to work. Create "centers" with different learning opportunities: texture center, manipulative center (fidgeting, fine motor activities), reading area with all levels of books (including picture-only books and books requiring flaps to open, buttons to push, etc.), a motivation center with activities to help motivate kids to finish work (see p. 171 for visuals that show time chunks and rewards).
- Incorporate breaks or movement tools for when focus has been lost.
- Use proprioception tools. Heavy lap/shoulder pads give passive input, and heavy work options, especially before work, can help with regulation. Have them carry their backpack with their arms (not on their shoulders), take the stairs, erase the board, or write on the board instead of at their desk with paper (standing gives big input, especially when they make huge letters or words).
- Work for 5 minutes, then move, repeat.

- Create new and ever-changing activities or stimulation with structure built into a program or routine, and cues for direction and consistency (try "pass the page" or other activities on p. 130, 152).
- Use sentence starters to help with ideas and momentum for work.
- Chunk work to make realistic and achievable completion possible (success usually brings more success) and use Post-it notes to separate problems or topics to write about. Put an idea or topic on each Post-it note and ask them to make a list. Check back in frequently but subtly.
- Use backward chaining. Sometimes kids don't have the motor or executive skills to complete all portions of a task but we want them to experience successful completion of this task, so we skip some of the steps at first. For instance, if a student is struggling with a science project involving cutting to create a learning tool, provide them with already cut pieces that allow them to keep up with their peers. For students struggling to find sources to support a writing activity, provide the sources and have them write their content based on the list you provide them.
- Create a just right challenge by adjusting the activity/task to make it more manageable.
- Remember processing time and the potential wait time needed for a response (up to 10 seconds, depending on regulation). Don't continue to talk before letting them process.
- Sing or play a "work" song that ends when work ends or during a transition time.
- Have students dictate as much as they can when they struggle to get content on the page so they can edit it later. Working memory deficits can significantly affect work completion because content is often forgotten before it is written down.
- Examine your expectations. Are they appropriate?
- Teach students how to chunk their time and use a timer to track progress. Have them look at each section of work and estimate how long they think it will take; use the timer to see how accurate they are. This is good for classwork because they will be more competent and accurate when it comes time to test (this can be a full class activity too).
- Highlight the instructions before having them start so they don't spend extra time processing what to do.

# DEMONSTRATION OF KNOWLEDGE: APPLICATION & INDEPENDENCE

## WHAT DOES THIS LOOK LIKE BEHAVIORALLY?

- They know the content but don't do well on tests or papers
- Test scores are good, but homework scores are failing them in the class
- Lots of unfinished or late work
- Engaged during activity or group work but can't demonstrate mastery independently
- Refusal to participate or complete work that you know they have mastered
- Trouble working without someone right next to them (like an adult)

## WHY MIGHT WE BE SEEING THIS BEHAVIOR?

- Difficulty with regulation; too much or not enough appropriate input
- Executive functioning weaknesses prevent organization and planning for writing essays, completing homework, turning in work, and prioritizing what to study (see p. 142)
- Gifted students can have trouble demonstrating knowledge despite cognitive ability or potential (Gifted p. 214)
- Poor monitoring of time prevents completion
- Boredom or attentional deficits

**Overall Objective: To provide a method for successfully demonstrating content mastery.**

## WHAT CAN WE DO?

- If mastery is demonstrated through test scores and/or they can tell you the process or correct answer, allow them to move on to the next learning target without doing all the work when they are struggling. This may not be the time or assignment to further develop their ability to sit and complete a long work page.

- Be that one person who believes in their ability to perform and succeed and let them know this.
- Allow for personally interesting and *fun* topics or different ways to demonstrate content mastery. Mix up the media they use to demonstrate their knowledge. If you notice a student does well with slides and technology, this might be better than paper and pencil.
- Teach in various ways: videos, lectures, social/group work, individual writing, research using pictures, or creation of projects.
- Create an urgent timeline or deadline for chunks of work due soon and include rewards.
- Build in control and let them choose math or English, or the number of problems before a break or reward (that is timed).
- Coaching techniques can help students more easily meet the current demands of this task or moment. This type of support allows an opportunity to assess issues from the child's perspective so that adults can address executive functioning weaknesses or provide ideas for regulation tools (see coaching section on p. 160).
- Use a timer with a clear visual of work and reward times. This can be adjusted according to what they can get done (less work, means less reward time… check out cognitive connections 360 thinking app).
- Modify how the work should look. For instance, if a warmup involves vocabulary words but this work is rarely completed, have them draw a picture or pull up a picture on the computer that meets similar requirements for learning without the writing piece. Use manipulatives or hands-on learning to demonstrate the application of content to real-life scenarios.
- Help students understand their wiring and threshold needs so they can use tools that help them get the appropriate type of input: maybe they need to stand, sit on a wobble stool or swivel chair, or maybe they need a different and quieter space to work independently.

- Incorporate activities or topics that are interesting, kinesthetic, and engaging to catch their attention and enthusiasm for learning. Sometimes just letting them choose part of the topic for a non-preferred subject can be enough to allow them to show you their knowledge of the writing process which can snowball into more work completion.
- Another person (peer or adult) can aid in regulation through check-ins during independent work time, or try sitting them near a peer who can focus and perform.
- Consider the environment the child is testing in. Many kids with attentional deficits need a smaller testing setting with fewer distractions.
- Have a visual that shows all students what the current "work mode" is.. independent work, focus on the teacher, and transition. This allows for kids to know what is expected for that moment even if they missed the instruction or read of the room.

# WRITING ISSUES: HANDWRITING, SPELLING, CLASS NOTES, PAPERS

## WHAT DOES THIS LOOK LIKE BEHAVIORALLY?

- Illegible handwriting, poor spacing between words or letters, writing too small or large for space provided
- Spelling and grammar issues
- Can't keep up with notes in class during lecture
- Notes or summary of lecture is missing key concepts necessary to study later
- Overall organization of writing is poor: random information throughout or repeat of the same information
- Writes too fast for legibility

## WHY MIGHT WE BE SEEING THIS BEHAVIOR?

- Dysgraphia (see p. 231)
- Executive Functioning issues with organization, planning, and production
- Motor issues affecting hand endurance or strength
- Poor kinesthetic awareness of the hand so writing isn't automatic and takes a lot of effort and concentration to form letters or words
- Poor focused attention or working memory so content is forgotten before it gets on the page

**Overall Objective:** **To help the student demonstrate their knowledge. Different ages have different goals (elementary focus is on the motor aspect of writing versus secondary school, where the focus shifts to typing, dictation, and other ways to get thoughts on the page).**

## WHAT CAN WE DO?

- Help the student get more proficient with typing and technology and set fun typing goals.
- Teach kids how to utilize apps and grammar/spelling checkers to support their work. Some apps help with note-taking so the

student can type a word while their computer listens and records what is said. The student can later click on the word they typed to hear the audio recording for that portion of the lecture.

- Provide notes for students to follow along with a highlighter or add to their notes.

- Encourage a picture search to help with ideas when writing content and details.

- Utilize picture organizers versus word organizers when planning what information or detail goes into which paragraph (see p. 166 for example).

- Try cursive versus manuscript; often kids with dysgraphia will do better because it is more fluid and less segmental.

- Make a plan with the student for the organization of writing. Provide sentence starters that get them thinking about what the content should be covering.

- Consider alternatives to paper/pencil writing such as creating Google or PowerPoint slideshows, orally dictating, video recording, drawing pictures instead of words, or doing pair work with one student writing. These alternatives can also help you see where the breakdown is in the writing process; often it is with the organization of their content which is an executive function.

- Examine the environment in which the student is working. Are they distracted? Do they have the things they need in that space to be able to focus on writing?

- How is regulation? Maybe they need to stand or move more throughout the writing process. Are there things related to regulation making it hard for them to attend to their writing?

- Do they write too fast? Often bright or impulsive kids will write so quickly that it is illegible. Use a timer in the opposite manner, having them slow down.

- Provide spacers or have them use a finger to place between words to increase spacing and improve legibility. Show younger kids how words in a sentence can look like houses on the street (each word is a neighboring house) with driveways separating the homes. This provides a fun way to verbally cue them when there is nowhere to park because there is no space between their words (or houses). For older kids, have them draw boxes around the words to determine if there is consistent spacing between the boxes. This provides a different way to visualize the spatial aspect of writing and can be done with math and number concepts too.

- Try various grips for pencils or different types of pencils (rocket pencil, larger diameter, mechanical pencils, triangular or squishy grips).
- Slantboards make writing easier for some students because the page is more upright. This can be a commercial product or a 3-inch binder that is closed and sitting with the spine away from the student.
- If they hold the pencil in too much of an upright position, put a rubber band on the end of their pencil and around their wrist. This little bit of tension can help position the pencil in their hand.
- Optimal hand position for writing means a stable base on the page; have them hold a penny or small, flat object between their pinky finger and palm while writing. This will help make their hand more stable so their fingers can move and keep the pinky in by the hand versus on the pencil or "detached" from the hand.
- Are they sitting in a good chair with their feet firmly on the floor? This is the base from which all writing occurs so sitting options can be really important.
- Writing can occur in different positions which can be fun but also helpful for some kids. Have them lie on their stomach with a dry-erase board, or they can stand at the board to use their entire arm for letter formation.
- Provide paper with raised lines so the child can feel when they have touched or crossed the line.
- Turn lined paper on its side or use graph paper for kids to use during math when they have to show multiple lines of numbers that must be aligned vertically and horizontally.
- Hand writing actually increases the learning process but this is not always practical for every student. Encourage typing, manuscript and a combination of cursive-type letters to help with fluidity of writing. The letters do not need to look like cursive letters but can be manuscript letters linked together.

# BEHAVIOR ISSUES: TIER I (DISRUPTION)

## WHAT DOES THIS LOOK LIKE BEHAVIORALLY?

- Distraction to others
- Not focused on the task or instructions
- Blurting, talking to neighbor, making noises, humming
- Silly, constant fidgeting, playing with anything they can
- Always getting up: sharpening pencil, getting a drink, wandering the room, tipping in chair
- Trouble with transitions in the hall
- Not responding to requests or questions
- Getting in trouble in class and during recess

## WHY MIGHT WE BE SEEING THIS BEHAVIOR?

- Threshold isn't appropriate for the task or their current environment
- Sensory processing is inadequate: understimulation or overstimulation
- Behavior might be communicating a need such as attention, a tangible item or a sensory need
- Other brain-based issues (ADHD, Autism, Anxiety, or Gifted)
- Expectations are not realistic for the child's ability or regulation

<u>Overall Objective:</u> **To help students meet their regulation needs for emotional control and engagement in academic programming and during social interactions.**

## WHAT CAN WE DO?

- Remember processing speed times: maybe they are still thinking?
- Prep the student before so they have more time to respond. Have a visual schedule to show what is next or a timer to show how long they will do this activity.

- Provide a different work method: oral recitation, highlighting or fill-in versus essay.
- Chunk the work, and reward for *effort*.
- Focus on the positive. If they aren't working, ignore this but catch another student working.
- Consider that they might need a break or more stimulation. Acknowledge sensory issues and allow for independent seating options that get them some distance from peers or distractions.
- *Replace* maladaptive behaviors rather than telling them to stop because kids often engage in behavior to regulate. Try giving them an alternative that is similar to the behavior you see. Encourage the use of *tools, not toys* which means if they aren't listening or working with this new tool, it is clearly a toy at this moment and not supporting regulation.

  o  If they are tipping in their chair or constantly wiggling, have them stand in the back while working, sit on a yoga ball or wobble stool, and use a Thera band around chair legs to push, pull, and bounce their feet.
  o  Difficulty sitting still on the floor might mean they need to sit in a chair with a back, or lie on their stomach instead of criss-cross on the carpet square.
  o  Fidgeting or tapping hands, feet, or objects provides proprioceptive and tactile input so replacements can include non-distracting fidgets, deep pressure into hands, a vibrating toy, heavy work before working, or dynamic sitting options.
  o  Times of listening with poor retention or focused attention might be improved with doodling or anything they can fidget with that isn't too interesting or involved.

- Teach kids how to *self-monitor*, then use tools for over-stimulation or under-stimulation (see page 69).
- Utilize a *Sensory Diet* or heavy work before quiet or independent activities to prime the system so kids who can't hold still or be quiet can succeed with more sedentary activity time (see page 119, 140).

- Confirm understanding and/or provide a list of things to do so they know the sequence of upcoming events.

- When a consequence is needed, try an exercise break or job to help the teacher instead of a "time-out" that forces them to sit still. Have them help rearrange the furniture because they are so strong and you really need their help (and now they are regulated because their muscles feed the nervous system for regulation).

- Think about the environment they are struggling in. Is it quiet? Visually busy? See if the student can identify what isn't working and problem-solve how to make a learning space that works for their wiring and learning style. Empower the ability to affect their surroundings for success. Sometimes we need to add more, other times we need to simplify things (see page 96, 153).

- Provide dynamic sitting options such as standing, wobble stools, dynamic cushions, or lying on their stomach for reading and listening.

- Keep things interesting. For the kids who need to move, have them get up, sit down, stretch, or move around. For the more sensitive, quiet students, try increasing the structure and consistency by letting them doodle while the more active kids move. Awareness of threshold needs and ways to help find balance can prevent much of the disruption that comes with maladaptive behaviors.

- Expectations or demands that don't align with a child's skills or ability to regulate can be one of the biggest roadblocks to success. Try to adjust these by creating a just right challenge. Make things easier, shorter, and more frequently rewarded. When they experience success, add in a little complexity. Challenge students to take on more but make it fun, not a baseline expectation.

- Standing or walking in line can mean being bumped into and boredom with waiting and walking at a pace that might not work for their system. Stretching and breathing techniques or having kids touch their arm to their opposite leg can keep them busy during stationary wait times. Create distractions and shift the focus to a quiet game of "I Spy" (finding words or colors in the hall) or counting steps to the library so they are too busy for poor behavior.

- Humming, verbal processing, and blurting are common sensory anchors or ways kids might try to self-regulate. They may like how the vibration feels in their mouth, or the sound might be alerting or drowning out other noises in their space. Oral input such as water bottles, gum, or things to suck or chew on are appropriate replacement items.

- Social stories or comic strips can review specific behavioral details or skill sets, especially for younger or non-verbal kids (carolgraysocialstories.com). These stories or comics show how to navigate a challenging situation while presenting options for recovery or managing powerful feelings. They can also present ideas for how to get through difficult situations that exceed the regulation ability of the child.

# BEHAVIOR ISSUES: TIER II (EXTREME DYSREGULATION)

## WHAT DOES THIS LOOK LIKE BEHAVIORALLY?

- Repeated detention or consequences
- Challenging authority and defiance
- Not following instructions
- Extreme, repetitive, and maladaptive behavioral responses

## WHY MIGHT WE BE SEEING THIS BEHAVIOR?

- Unrealistic expectations or demands
- Inadequate skills for the situation (executive functioning weakness, ADHD)
- Using behavior to get out of a task or to avoid doing what they don't want to
- ODD (oppositional defiance)

**Overall Objective:** **To help students meet their regulation needs for emotional control and engagement in academic programming and during social interactions. Recovery may need to be addressed first to prevent further escalation.**

## WHAT CAN WE DO?

- The most important thing that affects *your* perception of a child's behavior involves the concept of "Kids Do Well if they Can" (Greene). When adults believe a child's performance is intentional, these kids often lose motivation to impress the adult or adhere to the rules because they perceive that their efforts are futile, even when they genuinely try. Lazy, disrespectful, unmotivated, or oppositional are terms used to describe the behaviors of kids who can't regulate and have given up. When a child feels like an adult accepts them and is trying to help find roadblocks versus labeling behaviors and sending them to the office or calling home, it is amazing how much more success a child can find. Problem-solve signal or skill deficits that might be primary factors behind the behavior you are seeing.

- Telling a child to "STOP" does not allow them to fulfill their need for the type of stimulation necessary for regulation. If kids can problem-solve replacement strategies when they are regulated, they can be more easily utilized during times of difficulty.

- Assess the expectations. If you expect that a child with ADHD is going to sit quietly and focus, then it isn't the child's behavior that is the problem, it is the unrealistic expectation. There are usually negative behavioral repercussions when there is a large gap between demands and ability.

- Are the consequences making an impact? If the same consequence or disciplinary approach is not affecting the behavior, it is time to adjust. Sometimes the perception of losing a reward is enough to put a child into explosion mode. Focus on the times when they find success and ignore when they aren't. The real world is about working hard and earning the good stuff so modeling this similar to real-world behavior approach helps them see that effort can result in a reward. If we don't show up to work we don't get paid, but we don't lose the pay we earned last week. Our behavior approach should be similar.

- Ensure the instructions are understood and that a child has the skills to do what you ask. If they missed the instructions, they may not know how to start and that might be the discipline issue you are dealing with.

- Assess the environment to determine if something is putting them into fight, flight, or freeze; the chemistry between an adult and a child can be enough to prevent success.

- Consider the time of day and if it is relevant to the ability of this child to regulate. If kids struggle in core classes at the end of the day, maybe a schedule change to morning is a simple fix. Kids with anxiety, ADHD, or any learning or social difficulty are often exhausted by the end of the day making math or English during 6th period really hard. Consult with the school counselor to adjust when class demands can best be achieved. Electives or physical education classes might be better at the end of the day or this child might need more input early in the day to find success with core classes later. Extreme behaviors often require an individualized approach based on your observations of how they respond to stimulation at different times. Talk to the child for their perspective because often they will know what helps them feel good and when.

- Don't forget that many of the behaviors we see in kids at school are a direct result of how these kids are treated at home. Whether by parents, siblings, or peers, if a child is neglected or abused, they often lash out with similar behavior. Many of these kids are in survival mode because of their home life which might be why they are so tired or don't have homework done. Working with this child individually, and considering these specific factors might make all the difference in their perspective of school, learning, and adult support.

- Breaks and movement or sensory-based tools can help kids better regulate, which means they can better manage their behavior. Teaching them about how their nervous system works, how to self-monitor to figure out what is happening right now, and what they can do about it can be a lifelong benefit.

- When kids are sent to the office, they often return to class with little feedback for the teacher regarding why and then what to do next. Communication regarding what was discussed, strategies and goals, and a plan for future behavior management is something the entire team should be involved in so there is consistency with every interaction. Adopting an office form that covers the various *why* explanations to behavior and problem-solves the *what next* can be really helpful templates for success. This must be shared with the teacher and any team members or parents if all the adults are going to be able to support this child (see page 284 for Refocus, Reset, & Re-Enter Form).

- Try to determine the child's signs of distress and encourage a break or tool *before* they get too far. Many kids refuse to use tools because they are way beyond the point where that tool might have been effective. You may have to "self-monitor" for them until they can understand what distress looks and feels like. Prevention is easier than recovery so catching behaviors early and while their thinking brain will still work is critical.

- Many school discipline programs focus on motivation: provide rewards and children will behave. But for kids who can't regulate, this is really hard because they likely don't have the regulation to earn the reward. If we can assume that maladaptive behavior is a signal or skill deficit rather than a motivational choice, we might be able to get to the core of the problem. This conversation must include the child because the adult's assumptions of behavior might be missing the real problem which means consequences or discipline won't address the actual *why*. You can find more information from Dr. Greene at https://livesinthebalance.org with tools and assessments.

- Count to 5 on YOUR fingers (quietly) when a child is challenging you or you are waiting for a response; this allows you to remember and be aware of the necessary wait time needed in many situations. Many kids need extra processing time or just silence for a few seconds after a request is made.

- When a consequence is needed, try an exercise break or an activity to help the teacher but only after the recovery time.

- Be sure to communicate as a team so that all teachers and adults this child might encounter are aware that this child needs acknowledgment for positive behavior in even the smallest of moments. This can be the difference between a great day and a rough one.

- Don't forget that kids with ADHD, gifted brain types, and high-functioning autism can appear typical but all three of these issues affect performance. Potential and performance are two entirely different things and behavior plans should support performance. Adjust your expectations, catch them using their tools for performance, and see what this positivity can do.

- Utilize a behavior or safety plan ensuring that all team members, the family AND student are involved in creating this plan. See page 263 for an example of how this can look.

- Often extreme behaviors can be an indication of anxiety. When kids have no limits, they often misbehave in a subconscious effort to get them. Big behaviors get big attention and usually limits are enforced. Use a firm, no-nonsense tone and set limits for behavior *before* eruption; be specific with your demand/request, use very few words and don't back down until they have complied. Be consistent and have key phrases that all staff members use and remind the entire academic team to follow through. If there are tears that's ok because many of these kids feel a huge sense of relief from knowing how far they can push things.

- Kids who feel no control inside, or who have no control at home, act out because they feel out of control. Providing two or three options can help them with buy-in, motivation, and initiation. When they find even small successes, this will encourage more production.

# BEHAVIOR ISSUES: AGGRESSION

## WHAT DOES THIS LOOK LIKE BEHAVIORALLY?

- Issues on the playground or during unstructured time
- Playing too rough or fighting
- Behavioral outbursts
- Self-injury
- Trouble resolving conflict with peers
- Severe behavior when asked to perform a non-preferred activity, transition, or when they don't get their way

## WHY MIGHT WE BE SEEING THIS BEHAVIOR?

- Fight, flight, or freeze response in the nervous system (p. 87)
- Over-stimulation or under-stimulation
- Expectations aren't appropriate for the needs in this moment
- Inadequate skills. Do they know how to play or engage with others? (Executive Functioning, p. 142)
- Inability to know "how" they feel inside so they can't adjust arousal level (Sensory Processing, p. 121)

**Overall Objective: Recovery is the critical first step to prevent further escalation or self-harm. Provide a space or opportunity where they can have less stimulation, less engagement (with adults, peers, and academic content) and a chance to recover before problem-solving strategies for regulation.**

## WHAT CAN WE DO (before escalation or after recovery)?

- If you've "threatened" negative consequences with little or no success, present challenges or, "I bet you can't ....(get in line or put away your computer before everyone is in line, etc.)" and walk away. Allow for time to respond and remember it may take up to 10 seconds for processing to occur (but this is a great amount of time to allow them to watch all the energy their peers are getting for doing what you have requested).

- Try not to give much energy to negative behavior. Ignore the maladaptive behaviors you can and focus your energy on the behavior you want (which might be displayed by one of their peers). When you point out the positive choices being made around them, kids now have a model of what is expected and a potential reason for doing what you asked because they aren't getting any attention for misbehaving. **Never ignore behaviors that cause harm to themself or others.

- Create "thinking spaces" in the back of the room that limit engagement with peers, and distractions from noise and visual input. A study carrel or barrier encloses kids so they can control the input they are getting while still being physically present during instruction.

- Refrain from talking a student through the moment because when their system is in fight, flight, or freeze they can't use the logical part of their brain. Allow for a break or change in scenery before talking.

- Picture prompts and simple "first/then" commands can help the child redirect or utilize a strategy for resetting their nervous system.

- Try to create organized, clutter-free environments, with dim lighting and calming, quiet music as options for students to utilize as needed.

- Tell kids what TO DO, not what they shouldn't do. Some kids get stuck with the last thing they hear and might not know how to find success.

- Consider that poor behavior may be due to not knowing *how* to do something. Even play is complicated for some kids. Giving them something specific to focus on or instructions for something that seems easy might be all they need to decrease their frustration. Give the child something to do like a focused activity during unstructured time. Scavenger hunts, play equipment like a ball, or sticky note "challenges" that give them ideas for what to do during recess can help prevent maladaptive behaviors.

- Have a reference sheet for students to refer to so that if they miss instructions and their behavior is to avoid doing what they don't understand, they have something to prompt them that isn't an adult intervention, nagging, or further engaging the child in a negative direction.

- Give warning at least 5 minutes before a response is expected and do check-ins to ensure attention and comprehension.

- Have a visual of what is coming next in addition to (or instead of) auditory instruction.

- Set a visual timer so they can see how long they have until the end.

- Catch the student being good. This is especially important when they are trying a tool or strategy, have appropriate behavior, or when they follow instructions.

- Help the child learn to self-monitor when they aren't distressed so they can use this strategy when they are struggling.

- Increase opportunities for breaks or movement during work or dysregulation.

- If you provide rewards for good behavior, consider that these rewards must be immediate (not at the end of the day or week), motivating (chosen by the child, agreed upon by the adult), and positive.

- If a behavior program takes things away, many kids just give up because they feel they have already lost the reward, which can result in shutdown, outbursts, or aggression. For kids with extreme behaviors and short attention spans, try using small chunks of time to *earn* a minute at a time toward a reward that they can redeem within a couple of hours. Instead of losing time for poor behavior, they simply don't earn it.

- The back and forth of social interactions requires many skills. Role-play conflict resolution, starting a conversation, responding to someone's negative comment, or ideas for joining a group.

- Many kids need extra time to process; make sure you have given at least 5 seconds of processing time before assuming this child is being defiant. When kids can't respond quickly, they can go into fight, flight, or freeze and much of this looks like aggression or defiance.

- Be aware of responses with kids when you call them out in front of others. Putting kids on the spot, demanding a response, or forcing engagement in a group setting can put the nervous system into protection mode. Find different ways for these kids to respond: write on a whiteboard and hold it up, have them give you a thumbs up/thumbs down, or ensure comprehension by having them quietly whisper to you as you roam the room. If they need to answer aloud in class, prepare them by telling them beforehand what you will be asking and when.

- Always remember your goal: If it is learning, maybe simplify the environment by not having them work in a group until they are competent with the content. Many kids can only be challenged in one area. If the goal is social, give them something fun and easy to do together.

- In the teaching process, consider that some kids don't need the practice that others do, so be willing to adjust the amount of work if they can show mastery. When kids are bored, overwhelmed, or overstimulated, aggression can be the end result.

# BEHAVIOR ISSUES: ANXIETY

## WHAT DOES THIS LOOK LIKE BEHAVIORALLY?

- Head down on the desk (shut-down)
- Behavioral outbursts for no reason
- Wearing a hoodie, or using headphones
- Violence or destruction
- Difficulty with transitions between academic demands or locations/classes
- Bullying behavior

## WHY MIGHT WE BE SEEING THIS BEHAVIOR?

- Over-stimulation
- Fear of the unknown
- Previous failures
- Fight, Flight, or Freeze
- Ineffectual attempts at social engagement

**Overall Objective: Preparation is a critical first step for the prevention of anxiety-based behaviors, but when kids are in the moment of stress, recovery must be addressed first. Consider the following ideas as ways to support a child, but adult awareness and perspective are usually the best ways to help a child find success. Consequences and disciplinary action during extreme behavioral episodes escalate behavior because the primary force in this situation is the nervous system's protective mechanism of fight, flight, or freeze.**

## WHAT CAN WE DO?

- Increase consistency and structure and ensure the child understands and can *see* what the task or day looks like. Create time to review anything new or any areas of concern.
- Enforce limits consistently and have all the adults using the same terminology.
- Allow for recovery space and time when things escalate.

- Understand that the brain doesn't work when it is protecting so engagement isn't appropriate in these moments.
- Decrease the amount of stimulation by adjusting their <u>environment</u> (headphones, seating, or lighting). Section off a child's space with a study carrel or cardboard divider. Sometimes just decreasing the amount of visual stimulation a child has in their workspace can increase focus and help them control the many overwhelming signals.
- Consider the <u>social implications</u> on the nervous system. Is there something affecting them that we have missed? Anticipation for a social situation in the afternoon can affect a child's behavior in the morning, or days before. Help them figure out where the stress lies and come up with tools or ideas they can use when they are in the moment.
- Assess the <u>task demands</u>. Is the request or expectation too high for the ability or regulation of the child? Where can you adjust the task? How can you improve regulation?
- Take pictures of anything new or the multiple steps of an activity or day. Visuals are easier to process and remember than words so this can be a soothing (and even fun) way to support anxiety. When kids go out for recess, or in the morning before the bell, take this child around the school to take pictures of classes, teachers, or things they will be doing that day. The distraction of taking a picture paired with the exposure during a *safe* and supported time can help increase what their nervous system can handle in the future.
- Use distractions for transition times or moments that can result in poor behavior: count the number of breaths as they walk, find all the different green things as they transition or break to lunch, create "I spy" type distractions, or count steps to the library.
- Visual timers help kids see how long they have until their next transition or break.
- Some kids who have trouble with noise or visual stimulation struggle at assemblies and sporadic special events at school. These may not be appropriate for them to participate in, especially if it hasn't gone well in the past but if this is required, review ways to

distract when input is becoming too intense. Maybe they shift their focus to count how many people are wearing pink in the audience, or have headphones or a quiet distraction tool they can use in the moment. Any time we can just get this child into an environment that is hard for them without extreme stress, their nervous system gets the exposure that helps integrate future experiences and input, but only if we support the process. This integration *will not* happen if we don't appropriately support the process; if they are pushed past the success of their tools, ensure you have an exit plan in place (even 10 minutes of an assembly can be enough to support future participation).

- Simplify their world. Use very few words, reduce visual clutter, move to a different space, and allow quiet time and time to just *be*. Give them permission to focus on *recovery*.
- Utilize breathing techniques, visual imagery, or calming music (see vagus nerve techniques p. 47).
- GoZen offers amazing online resources and cartoons that address all areas of anxiety. There are strategies and many amazing in-app things you can do with a child who is struggling to come up with ways to manage their worries and other behavioral challenges.
- Discuss with students that mistakes are wonderful opportunities for learning and expanding their knowledge. This will help kids who have a lot of anxiety about being wrong begin to feel like mistakes are good starting points for a different approach.

**For more strategies or details, refer to the section on fight, flight, or freeze (p. 87).**

# SECTION THREE

## THE PUZZLE PIECES AND ADDITIONAL TOOLS

Understanding the various puzzle pieces involved in regulation will help make behavioral dysregulation more transparent and solutions easier to find. Regulation is dependent on many things, and so is perspective. This section further details the many pieces that impact behavior and regulation. When the pieces aren't fitting and life is hard, what then? How can you make them fit? How can you explain what is causing the behavior you are seeing?

All of this is possible with a slightly different perspective and more in-depth information.

Segments Included in this Section that Directly Affect Regulation:

1. The Brain

    a. Ways the Brain Influences Performance
    b. Foundations to Learning and Play
    c. Unique Brain Types and ADHD
    d. Brain Development and Expectations
    e. Other Brain-Based Issues that Affect Performance

2. Wiring
3. Self-Monitoring
4. Fight, Flight, or Freeze
5. Thresholds
6. Sensory Processing (signals)
7. Executive Functioning (skills)
8. Self-Esteem and How to Focus on the Positive

**\*\*The Easiest Way to Use this Section\*\***

Each section segment provides additional information to better understand behavior. When you get to "The Practical Stuff" within each segment, you will find additional strategies, tools and things to consider that are specifically related to that topic.

# 1. THE BRAIN

When discussing the legitimacy of regulation issues that impact behavior, it is important to acknowledge that all behavior has a background based on neuroscience. There are specific chemicals and areas of the brain and nervous system that will impact behavior, arousal (or attention) and how everything feels inside. Information enters the nervous system through the spinal cord (central nervous system) or sensory receptors (peripheral nervous system) and travels to the brain. Appropriate input is required or the brain can't analyze anything. We depend on sensory neurons to relay information from our senses about the noises we hear, the things we see, and how things taste or smell. Interoception, our seventh sense, involves messages from organ systems about hunger, thirst, knowing when to use the bathroom, and even impulses that change heart or breathing patterns based on activity demands. Touch or movement signals are detected through receptors in muscles and joints. Dysregulation will impact success if there are issues along any of these paths or in how the brain interprets input. Understanding where the breakdown occurs can help with our approach to dealing with behavior because it can affect how we engage with a child, solve problems, and guide us to the appropriate tools or strategies.

Once the information comes in, we depend on the brain for a response to occur. Various parts of this system must also be intact to get an organized, purposeful response.

- The <u>Reticular Activating System (RAS)</u> filters incoming information and is critical for regulation because it activates other systems for organized responses and arousal levels. If too much input comes in, we see shut-down behavior or over-stimulation. If not enough input enters, we will see delayed responses or an inability to do what is requested. The amount of information allowed through this filter, or gate of the RAS, depends on a person's wiring, the demands of a situation, the sensory aspects of an activity, and the current threshold needs of this child. We see poor regulation when this system lets through too much or insufficient input for the situation. Strategies can affect regulation or arousal levels and alter the way the gate works so this is why the RAS is important to understand in the management of regulation and behavior. Some strategies can inhibit or decrease the amount of information coming in, and others that facilitate or alert the system to allow for more input. All of this will improve regulation, attention, social engagement, behavioral management and self-monitoring.

- The <u>limbic system</u> is our emotional brain and is very important in the process of regulation. When our emotional system activates, information travels directly to the amygdala and this is when the brain engages the threat analysis functions of fight, flight, or freeze. When this happens, the cortex or thinking part of the brain is bypassed and nothing logical can occur. When kids experience extreme stress regularly, this pathway becomes easily traveled, so very little input prematurely activates this threat analysis system. When this sympathetic system is triggered, behavior is complicated to control and little problem-solving or cognitive thinking can occur.

- The <u>insular cortex (IC)</u> is located next to the limbic system and frontal cortex so it is critical in self-regulation because of the connections between sensory processing, emotions and executive functioning. When we are mindful and receive appropriate sensory stimulation, there is more activity in these areas that will help with regulation. The IC is a big player in socially appropriate behavioral responses, responsivity to pain, and the awareness of our interoception system. The interoception system monitors the organs and communicates internal needs such as when to use the bathroom, when you are hungry, and other internal signals that tend to be more automatic. The IC also sends signals of pleasure related to empathy and making good choices or making others happy (Gibbs, 2017).

- When we aren't stressed, we function more from the parasympathetic nervous system through which information travels to the frontal areas of our brain where most of our executive functioning skills reside. The brain develops over time, so when information reaches the <u>frontal and prefrontal cortex</u> for analysis, our response depends on brain development, which can occur at very different times for each individual. If there are delays in skill development, we will see this in specific maladaptive skill performance. Making decisions, inhibiting certain behaviors, planning, problem-solving, and goal completion are only a few skill issues that might impact behavioral responses.

- The last critical area to consider is the <u>vagus nerve.</u> This nerve is a key player in the parasympathetic nervous system of "rest and digest" and is connected to many organ systems. When kids have trouble with behavioral regulation it is usually because they spend a lot of time in the sympathetic state of fight, flight, or freeze. The vagus nerve can help to shift the nervous system response to a calmer state for improved recovery. Recovery is critical for kids to achieve expectations and appropriately respond to the demands of a social situation.

Often kids will have trouble with regulation or balance. Some are too hyperactive in class to sit still and listen, while others may daydream and completely miss content. Stimulation of the vagus nerve is a crucial strategy for regulation when these techniques are used in the appropriate setting and incorporated into daily life. This nerve is the longest in the body, connecting the brain to important organ systems like the intestines and stomach, which is why we get stomach aches when we are stressed. It talks to the heart to increase and decrease heart rate, influencing how quickly or deeply we breathe. All of this impacts balance, mental health, and regulation. When we spend too much time in a sympathetic, protective state, it can be hard to find this balance. Research indicates that stimulation of the vagus nerve creates a positive feedback loop that decreases stress and helps our students find success (Horeis).

> Think of all the anxiety responses we see and the constant stomach aches when kids struggle; all of this can be related to the vagus nerve.

# THE PRACTICAL STUFF:
# HOW TO STIMULATE THE VAGUS NERVE

- Exercise. Walk, run, or start with any activity to increase the heart rate.
- Deep and slow breathing. Take six breaths in one minute (versus the 12-14 we usually do). Put your hand on your stomach to feel the rise and fall while breathing, making the exhale longer than the inhale.
- Laughter or being around people reduces cortisol levels, our primary stress hormone.
- Singing, humming, and gargling affect the vocal cords which connect to the vagus nerve.
- Progressive relaxation: In a relaxed position, squeeze fists as tight as possible, hold for 5 seconds, then relax. Shrug your shoulders as high as they will go, hold, and then relax. Scrunch your face as hard as you can...press your toes into the floor as hard as you can...etc.
- Mindfulness practice: Shift the focus to *now*. Have kids acknowledge something that might be stuck in their head or that is bothering them, feel that, then feel it float away. Focus on what they can hear, the darkness (because their eyes are shut), how their body feels against the chair or floor, the smells around them, and how their breathing feels (fast/slow, deep/shallow). When thoughts surface that are not related to *right now*, have them visualize putting these thoughts into a box that can be opened later... just not now.
- Meditation supports the neurofeedback loop. This can be yoga, progressive relaxation, breathing exercises, mindfulness, or any way to promote relaxation.
- Gut Health: While we can't always affect this system in the classroom, just being aware of its importance can help you support parents or give you some things to try for yourself. Since many neurotransmitters are produced in the gut (90% of our serotonin, the 'feel good' neurotransmitter, and 50% of dopamine, the 'motivation' neurotransmitter), it is important to prioritize gut

health and digestion to improve overall emotional health critical to reducing anxiety and stress, and improving mood, learning capacity and regulation (Bonaz et al.).

o Omega-3 fatty acids (from fish oil) are essential for nervous system functioning.

o Probiotics support gut health through the management of bacteria.

o Good nutrition, healthy snacks, and plenty of water help with blood sugar, protein consumption, and hydration.

o Activities that promote relaxation techniques support gut health.

• Reflexology allows us to tap into our parasympathetics with techniques that can be incorporated into a daily schedule.

o The Movement Paradigm (Missimer) demonstrates three simple points on the inside tip of the pinkie finger (the side facing your ring finger). Hold pressure on this point for 30-60 seconds, do small circles in this spot for 30-60 seconds, and then feather light strokes for 30-60 seconds.

o The ear has many points that stimulate the vagus nerve. Whole Body Revolution (Baxter) shows three places to try in and around the ear. Find the space just above the ridge of the ear canal and massage in a circle for 30 seconds. Next, make circles inside the ear canal, near the back, moving the skin gently for 30 seconds. Finally, behind the ear and in front of the hairline, push the skin up toward the top of the head and hold for at least 30 seconds, then down for the same amount of time.

o The foot also has many points that stimulate the vagus nerve and decrease blood pressure. Rotating your ankle, rubbing the sole of your foot and gently stretching your toes back and forth are all massage techniques that work really well ("5 Ways To Stimulate Your Vagus Nerve – Cleveland Clinic").

o   Cross your arms to give yourself a tight hug, grab the lower part of your ear lobe with thumbs facing forward and gently pull down and hold for 10 seconds, do three times (Gibbs, 2017).

o   Inversion is getting your head lower than your heart to increase oxygen and blood flow, and it also increases relaxation. Rolling forward over a large yoga ball, leaning forward in a chair, or any other creative way kids can get their head lower than their body will activate the vagus nerve (Gibbs).

•   Cold stimulates the vagus nerve and allows for the parasympathetic nervous system to take over while the body is adjusting to the temperature change.

o   Have ice packs to put on the back of the neck or wherever the child may want them (especially for kids who frequently have severe behaviors). They sell ice packs that activate without a freezer so they are easy to transport and have anywhere.

o   Splash cold water on face, back of neck.

o   Go outside for a brisk walk when the temperature is cold.

# WAYS THE BRAIN INFLUENCES PERFORMANCE

Brain development must be pivotal in our expectations and how we program our academics. We've determined different ways to test and evaluate our kids but behavioral regulation seems to be getting worse. We've been unable to adapt, as a system, to meet the needs of children today and this is significantly affecting our youth's social and emotional health. This impact on the longevity of professionals who work with these kids means fewer teachers and less adult support available for our schools. Suicide, depression, and violence continue to plague our communities at alarming rates and many people ask if we have done enough.

Prevention of these issues might be the answer, yet we have a fairly archaic educational system that hasn't evolved with our kids. Not all kids are college-bound, but success and self-esteem are affected when all kids are required to be exposed to the same school curriculum. Kids who explode behaviorally, and are possibly presumed to be "broken" or defiant, might just be responding to inappropriate expectations in their academic programming. Bookkeeping, parenting, and basic budgeting are no longer a consistent part of the mandatory curriculum, yet *every* student will encounter times when knowledge of these *will* be necessary. When we are getting extreme behaviors during classes that might not fit the needs or ability of a child, maybe it is time to look at the environment or the expectations we have for our academic programming. Perhaps added knowledge and research related to our expectations and child development will allow us to better identify the why behind various behaviors so that these children with poor stress response might not be so quickly labeled or written off. Maybe there is something more we can do as educators to help these kids.

Every child is unique and much of this is related to brain development which will affect their behavior and ability to effectively engage in everything. Holding every child to the same standard means that some will find success and feel good, but not all will find this. What about the kids with little or no support at home who may never grasp algebra no matter how long we expose them to the content? Brain development is one of the most important considerations when assessing behavior because when maladaptive behavior is no longer viewed as volitional or something a child can control, we can begin to uncover the real problem and maybe even help this child further develop their skills *and* self-worth.

# FOUNDATIONS TO LEARNING AND PLAY

People ask why kids today seem to struggle more than they did twenty years ago despite the new and abundant educational information and research. What is often forgotten in the creation of amazing educational programming is that brain development only occurs so fast and is related to many foundational requirements that might not be prioritized in daily lesson plans. Building with blocks, making letters out of clay, play involving movement, and even cooking pretend food are all foundational skills that are slowly slipping out of our academic classrooms only to be replaced by higher-level learning concepts. If we ignore the foundations of learning, we will eventually see the effects and much of this will translate into maladaptive behavior due to regulation and skill deficits. Sometimes just returning to the basics of play can help refine these skills so more complex demands can be met.

While knowledge of development can help with the understanding of behavior, consider how play affects regulation and behavior. What do kids do in their free time? Video games and computers are even in schools now and are required for most assignments. Technology has presented an incredible opportunity, but it also replaces much of the active outside play that was happening twenty years ago. Our nervous system molds according to our experiences, and these are very different for children today. Play is the primary occupation of children because so much happens in the nervous system with active play that is critical for development. Imagination, movement, integration of input through all the senses, and building of executive skills through planning, trial and error, and impulse control all occur with play. Often this happens in a social environment which provides an even more complex, yet fun, foundation for learning. Riding bikes, building forts, and inventing goofy games with evolving rules all contribute to brain development. The nervous system and brain receive input from all the senses with these wonderful, varied activities so that they can handle more information. Yet much of this isn't happening, at school or home.

Screen time versus outside time is affecting the experiences kids get from their world which in turn influences the kind of input their nervous system will build on for further development.

When we are able to support critical concepts of play (and fun) in our academic programming, we will not only get better engagement and attention, but we will also provide opportunities that can enhance brain development, social interactions and later learning potential. Fun means lower stress levels and higher levels of feel-good neurotransmitters that flood the nervous system and brain for regulation, skill development, and confidence for later learning.

# UNIQUE "BRAIN TYPES" AND ADHD

Behavior is often viewed as a way to get or avoid something; a child's tantrum may be to get a toy or avoid something they do not want to do. But behavior also communicates vital information about how the brain is functioning beyond seemingly obvious volitional factors. Behavior is dependent on regulation and regulation is dependent on many things. Certain *brain types* can result in an imbalance that easily prevents success and skews our read of behavior and resultant engagement. The critical structural parts of the brain and chemicals that help the brain function (neurotransmitters) present roadblocks between ability and performance with these certain brain types. Sometimes tools and strategies are often not enough to effectively override unique, genetic brain traits so having a better understanding of how they influence function and behavior can be important in altering programming and demands for success.

Dr. Thomas Brown, a researcher and creator of The Brown Model of ADD/ADHD, uses the metaphor of an orchestra playing without a conductor to describe what is going on in the unique brain of someone with ADHD (Brown, 2021). This brain type will affect how a child responds to various environmental and situational demands because of how the different parts of the brain work together. Various distractions might prevent them from paying attention and focusing on what they are reading because suddenly a different part of the brain has now taken over and the sound coming from the hall is more captivating than the words on the page in front of them. These kids get really good at hiding that they are distracted so when it is time to shift to the writing portion of an activity and they fail to get their pencil, it can be more related to not knowing what to do or how to do it than defiance or even avoidance.

Often verbal instruction is lost because of the many distractions that hit the brain of a student with ADHD and they may not let you know that they missed what you said. Understanding that missing instruction is a common and fairly typical issue seen with this type of brain can help the adult to alter the way this instruction looks. Maybe as the steps are being discussed, they are also being written on the board. Or maybe this particular student just needs a quick, brief list written on a post-it note detailing the steps of this next task. If you have a child who won't start when work is assigned or is disruptive when work is happening, it might be a good idea to think about whether they got the instruction in the first place.

Research indicates that cortical brain development can be developmentally delayed by several years in individuals with attentional deficits (Shaw et al. 2007, Shaw et al. 2012). This can mean a 12-year-old is actually functioning at a 9-year-old skill level. This significantly affects performance and is an important factor to consider when assessing *why* a child is struggling. If there are delays in the brain's prefrontal region, this can affect the signals and the brain's response to input. This child might be extremely bright (which we often see in the gifted population), but developmentally they don't have the skills to effectively write *and* listen so this is why they sit and take no notes. They might not have mature visual scanning skills so they don't remember content they just read. This under-developed skill paired with attentional deficits means they might *never* remember what they just read. They may be smart but can't navigate the complexities of social interactions and therefore have no friends. All of this can be developmental in nature and related to how their brain is wired and their developmental skill level.

Brain chemistry is also important in the analysis of behavior, especially with ADHD brain types. Hormones and neurotransmitters in our body influence regulation and these chemicals are all related to wiring. Forgetfulness, disorganization, and difficulty with focused attention are some of the trademark signs of ADHD and these are affected by the neurotransmitter dopamine. Neurotransmitter levels and the effectiveness of receptors for these chemicals are often related to genetic factors predisposing individuals to certain behaviors or clinical conditions. ADHD brains tend to have less dopamine meaning memory, mood, and motivation will be affected. Individuals with anxiety or depression tend to have less serotonin and GABA which is needed to produce a calming effect in the brain and improve mood. All of this will impact the success of academic programming, behavior, and it is all related to skills that often develop asynchronously due to variations in the developmental timelines of our students.

I was in a second-grade class, observing a child who reportedly "never wanted to work". He clearly had attentional issues but watching more closely it was clear there was more going on. He was looking at the pictures, flipping quickly and randomly through the pages of his book. When it came time to write about what they just read, this child got up and began wandering the room. He wouldn't do anything the teacher asked.

This student was seven years old. If he had an attentional deficit and a developmental delay of three years, this would mean we have expectations that a four-year old student would be able to independently read a story and answer questions about the content. This was not realistic for this student. This is where programming and expectations become critical. Are there ways to adjust this reading/writing task? When kids aren't doing what we are asking, it is up to us to figure out *why*.

# BRAIN DEVELOPMENT AND EXPECTATIONS

It is hard not to hold our students to certain expectations for behavior and performance, yet often these expectations are the very thing preventing success. Behavior communicates what the nervous system can handle. When we see smiles, work completion and engagement, we know this child has the self-management needed for the demands requested and for current expectations. But when regulation isn't supporting performance, the demands and expectations must be considered as a point of intervention.

The ability to meet an expectation or demand depends on regulation which is influenced by wiring or threshold needs. If the expectation is too high, this child will rarely meet it on their own. If a child is wired busy yet the expectation is to come and sit for a lecture, the behavioral response might appear disruptive and certainly not what was requested. The goal of an activity is important to remember; if the goal is listening, a child must be regulated to focus. If this child is listening but standing in the back or pacing, have they not achieved the goal? If they need to move or doodle while listening to regulate, maybe this is a strategy, not maladaptive behavior. Acknowledging how a child is wired and then exploring how this impacts their performance will allow for more realistic and achievable expectations because it can help define the behavior we see.

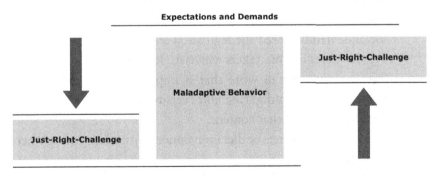

If we can do something to affect the signals or skills, or if we can adjust the expectations or demands, we will narrow the gap between ability and performance. This point of intervention creates what is often called a "just right challenge." This phrase, originally conceived by the Sensory Integration Pioneer, Jean Ayers, suggests that we can utilize tools and strategies, or alter our engagement and expectations to support a child in finding success. This means that one day may require more adjustment than others, but only when a child can meet the demands of a task or situation should we begin to push harder. Never before.

Adjusting the gap to create a just right challenge can be individualized for a child's specific needs. Altering this gap means finding ways to modify work, their work environment, or how the work is done. Some ways you can do this include:

- Have the child do fewer problems or grade what they do with the option for additional points with additional work later when they are better regulated.
- Increase time for a task or adjust the timeline so they can do some work, take a break, and then continue with more work.
- Chunk work with frequent deadlines with rewards after completing each section.
- Adjust the environment they are working in. Provide a less intense, quieter space or allow headphones with music or noise-canceling capabilities. Have sections of the room with different lighting or visual interest for different threshold needs.
- Let students work independently instead of in a group when the social demands exceed the regulation ability during an activity.
- Provide notes or note-takers where students fill in answers versus figuring out what to write that is important from the lecture. Sometimes just highlighting notes versus writing will increase the comprehension of that content.
- Allow for oral answers or dictation options instead of writing when they struggle.
- Provide ways to adjust input through the sensory system with dynamic sitting options such as large yoga balls, wobble stools, cushions, or options to stand or lie on their stomach.

- Adjust the intensity of the task by allowing independent work versus group work, moving the student to a quieter place, or allowing them to work in the hall.
- Adjust the task by modifying the demands. Make it shorter, allow for fill-in versus writing a complete sentence, have a buddy who helps, or provide notes to follow along with.

> When the demands of a situation exceed the skills
> of the child, behavioral regulation is difficult.
>
> Holding a child to expectations that might be appropriate for
> a peer doesn't necessarily mean that these expectations are
> appropriate for *this* child and *their* developmental ability.
>
> Respect for this timeline allows a child to try without judgment,
> fail without fear, and gain knowledge from experience.
> Everyone fails and everyone gets scared, sometimes.

## The Spatial-Temporal Window of Development Influencing Expectations

Skills mature as the brain develops and this generally drives our expectations for performance. But if our assumption of a child's developmental ability is inaccurate, this will shape our perspective on their capabilities, performance, and behavior. The just right challenge means a child can find success because the activity is appropriate for *their* developmental level. When an imbalance prevents success, we begin to see that this child's current ability may be nowhere near their potential and this can significantly impact their behavioral responses.

For effective execution, there must be a plan and usually, this occurs in a different space and time than the execution. This is the spatial-temporal window (Ward and Jacobsen). Spatial refers to the space where the plan is made and executed (i.e., the plan is made on the bus and executed at school). Temporal refers to when the plan is made, and the execution occurs (i.e., the plan is created in the morning and executed later that day). The spatial-temporal window represents how far away from this space and time effective execution *can* occur.

- When we teach a toddler a new skill, we plan, demonstrate, and monitor the execution of this skill in the same space and time because, developmentally, this toddler has a small spatial-temporal window. This is a just right challenge because we have acknowledged this child's developmental ability and created our expectations based on this knowledge. If the expectation involved independent execution from instructions given to this toddler yesterday, task completion would look quite different because the spatial-temporal window was not accurately considered when determining our expectations.

Expectations for an older child would assume a higher level of proficiency because we know what a child *should* do at a certain chronological age. But executive skills develop with time and are unique to each individual, not each chronological year. This is why some kids can't ever seem to meet the demands of their world.

- The expectation for a seventh-grade student might include coming to class on time with the materials they need to work on. For this to occur, a plan must be made *before* class starts if they are going to have proficient execution when the bell rings. If this child knows what they need from their locker and which class they go to first, execution is possible and efficient. But if a child's brain has a different developmental timeline, as seen with ADHD, our expectations and assumptions might be mistaken because planning and execution are *developmental* skills. This child may not be able to navigate this task successfully because their spatial-temporal window is not as we expected. The gap between ability and demand is too large. This awareness can affect your perception of this child's behavior when they continue to show up late to class. It is also a huge factor in the determination of appropriate expectations. (Dündar-Coecke et al. 2020).

# OTHER BRAIN-BASED ISSUES THAT AFFECT PERFORMANCE

**Screen Time:** Research studies are examining the association between screen time and behavioral regulation issues (Tamana et al. 2019). Some researchers and clinicians believe that ADHD symptoms are being created by screen time due to how this type of input affects the brain's responsivity. We know that the nervous system evolves according to experience; screen time is definitely a different experience than outside time. One could assume and conclude that even the gate in the RAS (reticular activating system) would be affected, which could explain why the brain needs more input just to respond. Suddenly listening to a story and looking at the pictures aren't enough to captivate attention since the brain is accustomed to quick, visual details that come with every screen-based application. The implications regarding effects in the classroom are endless and engagement requirements might be impossible to meet in the school setting without addressing regulation needs.

- Researchers found that by age 5, kids who spent two or more hours per day looking at screens were 7.7 times more likely to meet the criteria for a diagnosis of ADHD than kids who watched for 30 minutes or fewer per day (Tamana et al.).
- 3-5-year-old children exposed to over 2 hours of screen time a day showed more externalizing behaviors and attentional issues similar to those diagnosed with ADHD (Tamana et al.).

**Processing Speed:** Processing speed affects our assumption of behavior because if a child does not respond in the time we expect, we might conclude that they are lazy or not trying hard enough. The reality is that kids who struggle with slower processing speed are anything but lazy; most of the time they are actually trying harder than other kids. If a child could, they would (Greene 2014). Processing speed can affect verbal, visual, and motor responses, and we know that school requires all of these and often all at once. Visual motor skills are needed to copy notes from the board and reading aloud requires a visual, motor, and verbal response. Successful execution of these skills is based on the structural integrity of the brain and the effectiveness of neurotransmitters, which is unique to each individual regardless of cognitive ability.

The concept of time is not only something children need to learn, but also something adults need to understand when assessing appropriate response times. Similar to the spatial-temporal window, an adult's assumption of appropriate processing time will affect the expectations of a child who might not be developmentally prepared for the demands put upon them. Multiple sources indicate that the wait time between instruction and a *typical* child's response is between 3 and 5 seconds (Rowe) (Stahl 1994). This can feel like an exceptionally long time. If a child has learning or attentional issues or trouble with signals and skills, they may need up to 7-10 seconds because of the many processes that take so much extra time in their nervous system (Barry 2011). Many adults make a request with the expectation of an almost immediate response, so seemingly maladaptive behavior might simply be the time this child needs to process what was requested. This can markedly exacerbate other issues that affect their ability to find success.

- Faster processing

    o Pro: This child might not need extra practice or repetition for mastery.
    o Con: This child might impulsively start and miss critical details such as due dates, critical steps, or instructions.

- Slower processing

    o Pro: This child might catch details, attend to instructions, or weigh options due to additional time spent assessing what is required.
    o Con: This child might need more time to make a response and this can make people think they're not listening.

There are instances where processing speed can be affected by exposure and repetition because as a child grows, their nervous system evolves. Experiences mold how this child will receive, interpret, and respond to these experiences. A child sitting and looking at a screen is experiencing very different input than the one moving their body, creating various sensory-based play opportunities. The nervous system becomes accustomed to the experiences it is exposed to and this determines how effectively the body communicates with the brain. When more senses are used, more of the brain is engaged and more neurological synapses are created. These synapses are used later for learning. It stands to reason that the more we repeat an experience, the better the pathway between the body and brain. Our wiring and threshold for input determine how much balance we can find to learn from the experiences around us, and subsequently process sensory input.

When our tools, strategies, or instructional practices don't alter the behavioral or academic outcome, it does not mean this child isn't trying or is broken. Much like ADHD brain types, there will be times when kids continue to struggle despite our attempts to support their individual needs. Processing speed can also be a static force related to brain function. Whether a child has a cognitive deficit or simply a genetic predisposition to processing speed that impacts successful learning engagement and retention, there are still ways to support this child. Sometimes all it takes to help a child grow is an understanding adult who sees them for their strengths but helps them figure out ways around their weaknesses. This is when we adjust. We adjust our expectations, our perspective, and engagement with this child because they are doing everything they can with the facilities they have.

# 2. WIRING

Wiring is similar to personality; it is how people come into the world and it is a relatively static piece of the regulation puzzle because it is hard-wired. We don't want to change this child; we want to highlight that their wiring is something to be proud of but sometimes it prevents them from succeeding in certain situations. We need to understand wiring because it influences how a child might respond to the demands of their world. We must also consider special needs or pre-existing conditions because we can't change these things. Because every child has a purpose, we aim to better understand wiring to see why, how, and when they respond. This is how we can help them make their wiring work *for* them instead of *against them.*

The more you understand a child, the easier it is to help them. Some are really busy, talkative, and require a lot of input. Others are more sensitive and require way less input. This can be tricky to determine since we have no instruction book and often don't know much about our students outside of school. If a child is wired talkative and busy, how can they find success in the library or during quiet work time? If a child is wired sensitive, this will affect their ability to handle changes in routine and faster-paced activities. When a child's personality or wiring is working against them, is there something we can do to help them find success?

> Think about a toy bunny that jumps fast when you put
> in the battery. This toy is *wired* to jump and go fast. If
> you make it jump up a steep hill, it won't go as fast.
>
> Now think about a turtle. Put the battery in and there will
> be no jumping and very little will happen quickly because it
> isn't wired for speed, it is wired for this slower pace. If you
> make this toy turtle go down a steep decline it will likely go
> faster, but it will never jump or go at the pace of the bunny.
>
> This is how wiring can influence behavioral responses.

Aside from learning about their wiring, one of the first steps to supporting a child is to help *them* understand it too. You can do therapy with a child every day for a year, and at the end of that year, you won't have changed this child's wiring. You can affect their skill level, performance, and overall awareness, but they will maintain that same energy, or wiring, no matter what you do. Knowing and sharing this with a child is the most critical first step to helping them become successful, realistic, independent individuals who are comfortable in their own skin regardless of the setting. Acknowledging, respecting, and adjusting to a child's wiring will also help you in your relationship with this child. Sometimes all it takes to change an entire classroom dynamic is awareness. When a child feels that you see and accept them for *who* they are, but that you also have tricks that can make life easier for them, this can promote self-confidence and pride in traits that others might define as problems. Suddenly their constant talking can be seen as a sign of intelligence; we just need to help them figure out when to verbally share this intelligence.

When wiring is considered in the analysis of behavior, there is
a lot that can be learned. Not only will we be able to better
understand a tough kid, but this tough kid might actually
realize they have something to offer *because* of this wiring
that has long been perceived as a flaw. If we can change our
perception and stop expecting everyone to be "normal"
and the same, we might catch a couple of these kids, or
people in general, who would have slipped away from us; we
might even open a door so they can find their true path.

A lot goes into the analysis of wiring. Trends in behavior can help with
understanding. You can actually figure out how kids are wired by watching
how they respond to things, what they are drawn to, and how they behave
in various situations. Do they always do the same thing? Can you figure
out what came before or after the behavior? Is this behavior more than
wiring and something that might need to be addressed? Can you change
something through a subtle adjustment to the environment or the activity?

Wiring also determines the strategies that work and when they should be
used. Just an awareness that there are static forces impacting behavior can
help us problem-solve ways around their difficulties instead of constantly
needing to "remind" them *how* to behave. Some kids need to move, so
activities and ideas to support this wiring will help them find success.
Others need less, so this might result in your creation of a quieter space
with less intensity for a child to work in.

Talking to kids about their wiring can result in lots of questions too and
these kids might desperately need help reconciling these issues.

- Why am I always getting in trouble?
- I can't start anything...does that mean I am lazy even though I
  try really hard?
- Why, if I'm smart, am I failing?

This helps put a few pieces of the puzzle together. For instance, if they are
wired busy, this is why they are loud and constantly moving before big

tests or in the middle of the day when it is time for quiet desk work. They might need frequent trips to get water, sharpen a pencil, or they may create noise and distractions during quieter activities. This wiring isn't a flaw, but it will affect how people see this child and how well a child can perform in a given environment. They might be labeled as obnoxious, disruptive, or inconsiderate when they are really just wired busy, and busy means certain things have to happen to keep this kid regulated. When behavior isn't working, regulation is *always* relevant.

> Understanding that maladaptive behaviors might be related to wiring rather than a volitional behavioral choice can change how we approach an interaction with them.

Figuring out ways to discuss wiring with a child, or even a group of kids, can be fun because many of these kids have never had an opportunity to think of the complexities of their behavior. I love when full class discussions encompass this kind of information because kids begin to see that everyone has times that are hard because of their wiring. These questions or ideas don't have to result in immediate answers or solutions, but just exposing kids to the process can be very powerful and help them discover more about their wiring and how to make it work for them. The process can also help them find empathy and try to see someone for more than the irritation they might be dealing with on a daily basis.

Sometimes, depending on your relationship with a parent, you can also help *them* better understand their child's wiring because certainly, these challenging behaviors are present at home too. One way a child can begin to see behavior differently encompasses introspection and many questions.

- Talk about what they love about their world. Where do they find success?
- Next touch on what is problematic in their world. What has been really tough?
- It is essential to review times of the day that are tough and the different environments that seem to be most challenging; what is it about that time or place that results in difficulty?

- You can even talk about different people and how their personalities, or *their* wiring, affect the environment and their success. Often the chemistry between an adult and a child is a critical factor in the success and self-esteem of that child.

- See if you can determine what motivates them and what makes it hard to focus. Remember, this is their system and *they are the experts*. The adult is only a *guide*. This child has to figure it out but sometimes they need help getting the ball rolling.

- I also like to share a little about *my* wiring; kids love it when they realize we *all* have things we are working on.

Many kids today are slipping through the cracks because their behavior is all people see. When poor behavior is the primary defining factor in *who* this child believes they are, it can be very difficult to convince them that they have much to offer the world. Many kids have been written off as not caring when they are actually doing everything they can to make their brains work so they can do what we are asking. It can be difficult to help a child like this reconcile anything positive about their wiring when all they see and feel is the struggle. Life isn't always geared for all types of wiring, so kids need to learn how to change how they handle things or utilize specific tools to help them adapt. Helping a child learn that they have some control over a situation or their responses can be a life lesson unlike any other.

Our own wiring will explain our view of the world, the people in this world, and how we feel about all of it. Your read of behavior is based on *your* wiring and experiences. Your response to behavior will often determine if a child can get through a situation and adapt. How many times do we see the same kids in the office, or in detention? These frequent fliers experience consequences or responses from adults that clearly do not support their emotional needs. If the consequence is inappropriate for the developmental or sensory needs of this child, their behavior will not improve. So our perspective about what this child is feeling will affect our expectations and often the outcome of a situation. We have to assess *our* assumptions based on how we are wired and always ensure our emotions are in check no matter what behavioral response we are dealing with.

# 3. SELF-MONITORING

Regulation starts with the ability to monitor what is happening both around and inside us. When self-monitoring occurs, it allows for regulation because we have a better idea of what isn't working or doesn't feel right. Self-monitoring and regulation are big pieces of the behavioral puzzle because they allow for adjustment and behavioral management which feeds social and emotional health.

- Self-monitoring is the ability to monitor signals and then communicate the findings between the body and the brain.
- Regulation is what happens when self-monitoring occurs and we can adjust.
- Behavioral responses communicate whether regulation is occurring or not. If someone is laughing, we know they are happy and regulated. When they are crying, they need help. We can often adjust and adapt if we know things aren't right. We must have some sort of indication that there is a problem or we won't know that this child needs help.

When kids are young and don't yet have words, we depend on their behavior to tell us what they need. Sometimes when kids are older and able to communicate, they don't or can't at that moment. Regulation is completely irrelevant of age and entirely dependent on the child's ability to monitor what is happening inside.

> Math today is hard, even though it was not a problem yesterday. The math skills may be there, but the regulation in this moment, is not. Figuring out how to help requires this understanding. Focusing on math facts might not help at all... especially if it is the focus and attention that is preventing success. If a child struggles with regulation and then doesn't know how to monitor how they are feeling, nothing related to learning can happen right now.

Signs and self-monitoring affect regulation and self-monitoring, so we must discuss both.

- <u>Sensory processing</u> depends on the signals coming into our system and these are important to monitor; if too many or too few signals come in, nothing will make sense, and there will be no adjustment and likely an inappropriate response.
- <u>Executive functioning</u> drives the skills behind behavior, but it will be difficult to behave and succeed if the skills aren't mature yet. If you can read the room, then you should be able to adjust your behavior to be more appropriate. If you can think before you talk, you can often keep friends, laugh, and not hurt feelings.

> Have you ever had those moments where you're moving fast or on the go, only to come inside and find that you're practically yelling? Your nervous system is still in "go mode". Adjusting it to a new, quiet environment can take some work. We know the body needs to send signals to the brain to get moving or to slow down. Sometimes a strategy can make a behavior worse; this is an out-of-sync strategy. Many kids have trouble getting their nervous system where it needs to be for the expectations in their world.

*The first real step to regulation is knowing something is off. If you aren't aware that your tank is out of gas, you can't figure out how to start the car. This is self-monitoring.*

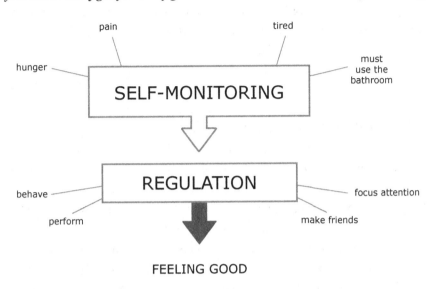

You must know what is wrong to communicate, respond, or adjust behavior. Self-monitoring is not easy; even some adults haven't mastered it. The problem with certain types of wiring or various conditions that affect behavior is that self-monitoring is essentially not happening. If the sensations within the body are not the typical, "I need to use the bathroom" or "I'm hungry, tired, sick or thirsty," then how does this child communicate what is wrong?

Brain functions and structures are also required or this communication simply won't happen. Maybe this child doesn't have words to describe these feelings. In many cases there are no words, so behavioral dysregulation becomes a daily occurrence.

> Sadly, negative behavior or tantrums are what begin to define this child. Suddenly the sweet, curious, funny child you know so well, is replaced by one that is moody, whiny and essentially uncomfortable in their own skin.

When brain development isn't at the same level as chronological age or cognitive ability, the skills of planning, starting, staying focused, or turning off a bad mood don't support adaptive behavior. Not only can they not figure out *what* is wrong, they have no idea how to get your help in figuring it out. It won't matter how many words a child can say if they can't figure out *what* is wrong to tell you. If they can't self-monitor, there is no way they can self-regulate.

To increase self-awareness, body scans encourage the child to slow down and focus on each body part to determine if they feel too many signals or nothing. It also tells you *where* they might be feeling these signals. If they feel it in their head, they might be over-stimulated and need less going on around them. If they notice something in their stomach, they might need to think about how they feel emotionally. If they feel nothing at all but they are also not responding appropriately to the cues around them, they likely need more input so signals can talk to their brain. All this valuable insight can be obtained through an all-class or individual approach and can be used immediately to create strategies. Kids can also apply this knowledge to better understand the behavior they observe around them to further enhance relationships and encourage mindfulness.

There are different ways to introduce body scans. Older kids may respond to a progressive relaxation approach where they tighten each body area, hold this tension, and then relax to notice how that area feels. It doesn't matter if you start at the feet or the head, just make sure they pay attention to each area as they tighten the muscles and relax.

Younger kids love the magic wand technique where they hold an imaginary wand just above their head, moving it slowly down the body, paying attention to every part the wand moves over.

- Maybe your head hurts, or your eyes are blurry.
- Are you thirsty or hungry?

- Next is the chest. Is your heart racing or pounding?
- How is your breathing... slow or fast?
- Then the belly. The belly has a lot to focus on because it can be upset, hungry, have butterflies, be too full, or tell you to use the bathroom.
- Legs and knees are next... toes, and so on.

Go slowly and focus on each part as it passes under this magic wand. If the child is older, have them visualize or focus on each part of their body from top to bottom until they figure out *what* they feel, or at least *where* they feel it. Introduce this activity when a child is *not* upset. If they can get good at this strategy *before* they are uncomfortable it will be easier, more automatic, and effective when they *are* upset.

Kids who have trouble with regulation and need help with self-monitoring, usually benefit when an adult can help them with the process. Many kids depend on the adults in their world to help them regulate because they can't yet access the tools independently. Kids are really perceptive and I often refer to them as sensory sponges. They know when we are stressed, when we are anxious, and when we are frustrated. They soak up all of our negative energy and it can prevent them from finding regulation. As adults, we have to ensure that *our* emotional energy is in check to support this child's regulation needs when they are struggling.

We must remember... *IF THEY COULD, THEY WOULD.* If they don't have the right kind of input to make an impression in the nervous system, there will be no signals to let the brain work. There will be no regulation, no behavior management, no work production, and eventually, no self-esteem.

> *When we use the same consequences repeatedly with*
> *no change in behavior, we have to re-assess the why to*
> *find new and different solutions to the problem.*

Many programs help individuals visualize and conceptualize what is going on inside their bodies. Knowing if you need more or less input is the critical first step so you can begin to use tools to feel balanced and happy.

The Zones of Regulation (Kuypers 2011) uses colors that are highly effective in determining feelings before and after movement-based strategies are used.

- The green zone is a calm, ready state that enables learning, social interactions, and participation.
- The red zone is used to describe heightened awareness or intense emotions.
- The yellow zone indicates intense emotions but with a feeling of having more control than the red zone.
- The blue zone describes low levels of alertness and sad, tired, or bored emotions.

The Dragon Phenomenon is similar to the Zones of Regulation in that colors still indicate the intensity of emotions. This technique utilizes an external character that can be trained through problem-solving to find tools or strategies that affect regulation (Robison, 2021). It provides a fun way to talk about behavioral difficulties without blame and encourages movement-based, sensory strategies to change the problem dragon that is currently visiting.

- The green, trained dragon is the goal. Signals are effectively shared between the body and the brain so regulation is intact.
- The red, fire dragon shows up when too many signals bombard the system, resulting in extreme responses, shut-down, and often initiation of the fight, flight, or freeze mechanism.
- The sleepy, blue dragon fails to provide appropriate signals to the brain so this low level of alertness often results in poor responses to requests, boredom, daydreaming, and difficulty with reading a situation or engaging appropriately.

The SAM program (Self-Regulation and Mindfulness, Gibbs 2017), uses stories, a visual figure, and strategies to identify and manage when emotions are out of balance.

The Alert Program (Williams and Shellenberger, 1996) compares the body to a car engine. Sometimes it runs too low or too high but the goal is to use tools that optimize how the engine runs.

Ultimately, it doesn't matter what system you use, it matters that there is a way to notice, discuss, and solve regulation issues. Each of your students will have different regulation needs so everyone must have the same vocabulary to communicate when things are out of balance. Each student will come up with a different result from their self-monitoring, and then a specific tool can be used to address the imbalance. Each student will also present with different tolerances to input and starting points for stimulation; they are the experts of their system and different tools might be required for different times or issues. None of this is possible without self-monitoring. Our nervous system is designed to help control our energy, thoughts, movements, and all the automatic functions that keep us alive; it is designed to help us find balance so the brain can do its job. First, self-monitoring must occur, and then we can figure out what tools to try that will either add or reduce the signals to find this balance. Once you've tried the tools, it is important to check back in to see if you feel better. Are you in the Green Zone? Did you train your Dragon?

When consequences don't change behavior, we know we need to modify our approach, and self-monitoring is a huge part of this process. If they still aren't doing math after two days of detention, consider that maybe they don't know how to start. If they are talking or humming during quiet work time, maybe we need to replace this behavior with oral input like gum to help them focus. If we don't solve the potential *why* of behavior, we end up with diminished self-esteem and no effective tools or strategies to change behavior or regulation.

- If disruptive behavior can be ignored or redirected to a strategy, adjustment may be possible.
- If attention can be given to the child who is demonstrating appropriate behavior, they are caught attempting improved regulation and it will make a clear impression of what desired behavior looks like.
- Recovery after a disruption or poor choice is important to focus on after a mistake. We can briefly acknowledge the bad, but focusing on recovery and a plan for success is often more effective.

# THE DRAGON PHENOMENON

The Dragon Phenomenon was created to provide a different way to talk about signals and self-monitoring with kids. Dragons communicate with fire signals so this can be a fun way for kids to visualize how input works in their nervous system and brain. Dragons are also a fun way to talk about dysregulation; they give words to emotions that some kids might avoid feeling. The presence of this creature provides a problem to solve instead of a failure to focus on. Taming a dragon is a safer endeavor for those kids who struggle to analyze internal and often traumatic emotions that influence behavioral regulation. It is a starting point for communication, problem-solving, self-monitoring, and regulation through the use of tools that work for their system, or the dragon issue they are currently facing.

- When kids imagine flames everywhere, it helps them understand why they have been so emotional, sensitive, or annoyed. This might be why success can't be found.
- If there are no flames, only smoke, this might be why they missed the instructions or read a cue incorrectly from their friend.

If kids learn to monitor signals, they will better understand how to respond with strategies when things are out of balance. Visualizing the dragon and his signals begins in the brain. Imagine a dragon who lives in the limbic system or center of the brain. This dragon cave sits at the base of all our thinking power which is where the skills develop. It is where the signals from the body are conveyed to the brain for analysis and a response. It is easy to see that even a smart thinking brain can't work if the signals coming from the cave are inaccurate. Signals and skills are both needed for regulation.

Thinking brain (skills)

Dragon Cave (signals)

The dragon who lives in this cave is critical because we count on their warning or signals to keep the thinking brain informed, to stay safe, and to find regulation. But balance is vital; we need the right amount of signals.

- Fire dragons send out too many signals so the thinking brain doesn't know what to pay attention to. It is impossible to respond appropriately when signals are flooding the system.
- Sleepy dragons don't give any signals at all. It is impossible to respond when we don't know there is something to pay attention to.

When the dragon is in check, children can work their magic. They can laugh with friends, listen, and figure out what they need to do. We need to be able to handle dragon problems so we can be safe, logical, successful… *and regulated.*

- If a child continually forgets their supplies or homework, do you think it could be due to signals? Is their dragon reminding them to pay attention, finish, and focus?
- If a child resists working in a group, going to recess, or specials (like PE or music) or if they are erupting behaviorally, do you think it might be due to too many signals? Is their dragon convincing the thinking brain that protection is critical and nothing else matters?

Dragon power can be managed and in time, any child can tame their dragon. While it might take time for the dragon to evolve or to calm down, just helping a child understand how this character works in their system can help them begin to problem-solve and feel better. This dragon concept encompasses everything related to thresholds, sensory processing, and executive functioning so it is an effective tool for the identification of arousal levels and it also provides a fun way to address the many ways we can control our arousal levels to feel better.

One of my favorite sessions involving "dragon talk" was when I was working with a kindergarten student who had repeatedly torn up the classroom and just could not play school… even the fun stuff was a disaster. We took a walk and I told him about the world of dragons. I shared which one I usually deal with and then we talked a little about his dragon. Apparently, it had 8 heads and huge claws (pretty telling information from this little guy!)

We decided to draw his dragon, but first we needed to trace *his* body. Using a long piece of colorful butcher paper the same length as he was tall, I traced his body and he marked all the places he felt the dragon: his belly, his head, and his chest. We practiced doing body scans on this flat, paper version of him and made a plan for dragon taming.

The next day I came into his classroom and his entire class got to hear about the amazing world of dragons. He got to share what his looked like and even taught the class how to do a body scan; it was the first time you could see him proud and engaged. His peers were asking him for help, and he was regulated! This is when we came up with the "Master Dragon Tamer" title because so many of these dysregulated kids needed to celebrate success too.

I was the therapist, and I introduced the dragon concept to this amazing kid, but he taught me so much more. Every time since, I have had many "aha" moments by letting the kids take the dragon idea and run with it.

# SLEEPY DRAGONS

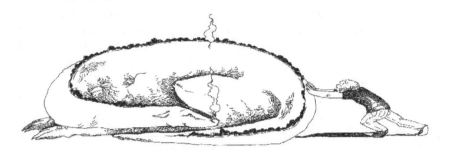

A child dealing with a sleepy dragon is usually pretty clueless about their surroundings because they aren't getting the signals they need to create a response. A visit from this sleepy dragon represents a time of low arousal or a moment with a very high threshold that has yet to be reached. All of the resultant behaviors can appear to be volitional: lazy, unmotivated, disinterested, or non-compliant. When there are no signals, kids miss instructions, forget to do homework, forget to hand in homework, and many adults assume this is because they don't care or won't bother. Reading the room and a friend's non-verbal communication is important in making and keeping friends, but this requires signals.

The Sleepy Dragon seems to be common with many kids, especially those who are highly intelligent. One of my first sleepy dragon experiences was with a gifted student whose teacher saw her struggling to follow *any* instructions or complete work; she was convinced this child wasn't trying hard enough because she clearly had the intelligence to succeed.

Observations of this student made me realize she was getting NO signals. The teacher prompted students to hand in work but she sat and didn't move. Kids would walk by her and still, she sat. Watching her facial expressions and reading body cues indicated she wasn't being defiant; she had truly missed *all* the instructions. When it came time to respond, or work, she not only didn't know what to do, often she didn't know there was something *to do*.

Helping this student understand this about her system guided us toward strategies that helped the signals make an impression on her nervous system. It gave her a problem to solve and something to focus on besides the failure she constantly felt. She wasn't ignoring the teacher and she *did* care about her grades, but she genuinely didn't know how to do better. She now could find a solution.

# FIRE DRAGONS

When there are too many signals and the dragon is always shooting flames, this indicates a high level of arousal or a low threshold that has been hit too much or too fast. When there are too many signals, kids might miss what is happening around them because their system is trying to protect them from danger. This feeling inside can keep kids  from interacting with new people, or experiencing anything new. Anxiety is widespread among people who commonly experience too many signals, and these constant worries can be exhausting... for everyone. Anxiety might mean these kids *do* have their homework done and they *can* follow instructions because they are actually worried about their performance. But other issues that are not typically associated with anxiety or worries can become problematic. Aggressive and loud behavior, or the "class bully", can actually be due to insecurity and fear because their behavior is being used to counteract the feelings inside. When the brain switches into protection mode, more and more stress hormones are released and this vicious cycle can create erratic and often misunderstood behaviors.

If a child can visualize a silly dragon shooting flames for no reason, they can begin to manage those flames without their system trying to instantly protect them. This is our goal!

Things to consider with fire dragons:

- If kids are not sure how something will feel at any moment, they will try to control it through behavior, which might appear obsessive-compulsive, aggressive, or like they are avoiding things.

- If everything makes fire, you can be left with a kid who overreacts and seems emotionally fragile.

Remember, we don't want to problem-solve or strategize when the system is in protection mode!

# WHY TALK ABOUT DRAGONS?

## <u>THE NUMBER ONE REASON WE TALK ABOUT DRAGONS IS TO PRESERVE SELF-ESTEEM!</u>

The dragon allows a judgment-free way to discuss how a child behaves in the moment. It can help a child understand how the signals work in their brain. They might even find that they have some control over this *temporary* issue that makes them feel awful inside. Now they can figure out which dragon is hanging out, which may lead them to strategies that can tame a fire dragon or wake up the completely useless sleepy dragon. When you discuss a child's difficulties as a dragon issue, there is something to solve, not something wrong with this child. They just have a dragon issue to deal with, and the goal is to find balance.

Children who struggle with the sleepy dragon are often asked:

- "Why didn't you get that done?"
- "Why are you talking when it is supposed to be quiet?"
- "Why didn't you hand in your homework?"

Children who struggle with those fire dragons are often asked:

- "Why won't you participate in your group discussion?"
- "Why aren't you playing during recess?"
- "Why were you late to music class?"

The dragon concept can help us talk about tough behavior, and it even provides fun ways to explain the negative feelings that come with poor regulation.

*If we can teach our children that people, all people, deal with dragon or signal issues, it might help them to remember that the PERSON is still valuable and worth knowing. This person might be working through something that is affecting how they appear or behave.*

Teaching children to be thoughtful, insightful, and happy people requires self-reflection, which means they must take responsibility for their actions. Dragons aren't excuses. They allow kids to think about their mistakes or poor behavior in a way that doesn't cause them to be defensive or completely shut down and give up. The dragon concept introduces baby steps that will eventually allow a child to see what is going on with their system. When kids continually fail, their nervous system is so shut down that they are often incapable of taking responsibility and turning a negative experience into something positive for future learning.

Talking about dragons with kids is fun! They come up with all kinds of dragons, and even ways those dragons can be real stinkers. Discussing ways to tame a dragon encourages kids to self-monitor and begin the process of self-regulation, which we know is critical for happiness in life. There are certainly times when a child has a dragon you don't expect, but overall, they are pretty consistent with this child's wiring and threshold needs. When they have balance where they need it, they feel good, can pay attention, and can engage with the world. They are *regulated*. It really doesn't matter which dragon a child is more prone to as long as they can figure out what is going on inside so they can counteract those feelings with *functional* strategies.

Some kids don't like dragons, or maybe dragons aren't a useful tool for their communication or developmental level. There are many other ways to explore how things feel inside that directly impact behavior. The key is finding something that is fun to use when solving problems related to signals. This will depend on who this kid is, their interests, and where they are developmentally.

- A young child might love Disney characters, animals, or princesses.
- Children with special needs may be older but at a different level developmentally than their peers. If they come up with the character, it will be more powerful for them, and their imagination will take over. Don't worry about age-appropriate characters… focus on relatability.
- Some kids respond to a computer because they can lag and prevent us from getting the information we need, just like the sleepy dragon. They can glitch or overheat when too much is going on or they have been on too long, just like the fire dragon.

Don't forget that it is almost impossible to self-monitor and develop strategies in the moment of fight, flight, or freeze. Self-monitoring should be introduced and practiced when no one is upset or it won't work during moments of dysregulation or stress. The same goes for dragon taming. Dragon talk allows the child to think out of the box at a time when things can be fun and the nervous system isn't trying to protect. No one is in trouble and they haven't screwed up again. Their dragon may have some issues, but this child can still be in the driver's seat, and their brain will work for them as long as they don't feel threatened.

Kids can come up with ideas or try out your ideas. For times when the dragon takes over and their brain doesn't work, they can refer to pictures or visuals that show which dragon is visiting and the tools that might tame that pesky creature; we don't want to make things worse by talking to them or attempting to problem solve during stress. The goal is to empower kids to make good choices. When they demonstrate successful and positive behavior, the dragon balance is working, which means they are Master Dragon Tamers!

The goal isn't dragons.

The goal is understanding signals and finding tools to help kids feel better.

# 4. FIGHT, FLIGHT, OR FREEZE

Emotional and cognitive growth is impossible when survival mode takes over. Yet, we have all experienced times when our behavior is hard to manage and we cannot find success anywhere. Yet, recovery from these moments can build resilience, mental strength, and emotional intelligence. Stressors have increased with the speed of our present-day world, an archaic educational discipline system, and the impact of technology use. Insurmountable demands or expectations can lead to physiological responses taking over and we simply survive. When kids struggle with these issues, they begin to believe they are the problem or that they are a failure; this sets the tone for who they believe themselves to be and often results in self-doubt, more failure, and unhappiness.

Our sympathetic nervous system has a built-in threat analysis mechanism that constantly scans for danger. Fight, flight, or freeze is responsible for our survival because when anything alarms the system, this input comes into the brain and completely bypasses all the parts related to logical thinking to ensure a fast response. Our brain goes into overdrive and must quickly determine how to respond; is this a real threat or a false alarm? Ignore or react? This is how we survive.

The mechanism of fight, flight, or freeze relies on signals, so balance and awareness of how these signals work in the system is important to understand related to behavior. This system is an automatic function and it is difficult to control the extent to which a child might respond. The amygdala perceives stress and sends a signal to the prefrontal cortex to determine whether this threat is real. Signals also go through the hippocampus and limbic system so an emotional memory can be created to ensure an even faster response next time. If it is presumed that this threat is real, a signal goes to the hypothalamus to turn on hormones for a survival response. If the brain can determine that this is a false alarm, the signals can be ignored.

Problems arise when this system is always scanning and finding danger. The emotional memory from each previous threat triggers additional scans that prevent the prefrontal regions of the brain from working. The many cognitive processes that allow us to ignore false alarms are bypassed during repeated stress so school-based skills such as attention and working memory are impacted and this can make poor behavioral regulation appear intentional. A child doesn't have to be going through an actual life-or-death experience to have this system take over because the *perception* of danger can be enough to trigger this response which can be very inconvenient at school. A social situation, an expectation, or a simple request in class can be the *perceived* threat this child feels and we fail to detect. Awareness of how this sympathetic response works in the nervous system can help us in our response to this behavior. We definitely don't need to make things worse but it is easy to do this when we don't recognize the various functions of this system.

> Imagine you are walking alone in a dark parking lot and you realize you are being followed. You might not notice you stubbed your toe, and you certainly can't remember what is on your grocery list right now! You are afraid, and your senses are tuned into safety. This is a fight, flight, or freeze response that is appropriate. When a child experiences this same physiological reaction with everyday activities they are doing, we begin to see that life can get pretty exhausting.

Hormones are also released during the fight, flight, or freeze response which can affect behavior because they prepare the body for protection.

- Adrenaline boosts blood flow to the muscles and causes an increase in breathing.
- Cortisol constricts or narrows arteries and this increases blood pressure. It floods the body with glucose which is energy for our big muscles.
- Norepinephrine increases heart rate and blood pressure.

Physiological changes due to these hormones can tell us when a child is in this protective state. A change in facial color, red ears, and dilated pupils indicate that the limbic system is taking over and the thinking brain is no longer working. Clenched fists or rigidity and limp muscles that cause "noodle-like" motor responses can be related to muscle tone changes that make the behavior appear intentional. The fight response can look like aggression or defiance. Freeze is a state of shutdown where you might not get a reaction. Flight can be a little trickier; it can be avoidance, excuses, daydreaming, or blaming. Much of this is subconscious, and a child may not even realize what is going on. It all ends the same way: difficulty with social situations, listening, focusing, learning, and behaving.

> Many times, simply providing for *anticipation* will help the thinking brain overpower the excess signals. If something is scheduled that typically triggers a protective response, talk together to create a backup plan. If this child can picture what it will look like, they can discuss what it might feel like and problem-solve how to manage those feelings before they are experienced. Addressing concerns while the brain is still working helps to bypass protection mode.

Even with our encouragement, this mechanism can prevent kids from looking at anything in a logical way. The perception and *emotion* of what's coming in is very real to the nervous system so we see poor behavior at unexpected times. Something like recess, which is supposed to be fun, can be the biggest hurdle of the day for a child who doesn't know *how* that unstructured time will feel or what to do. Play should come naturally, but a lot of skill goes into successful play. It can be hard to navigate asking for a turn, joining a group, or making small talk. Sometimes kids come up with creative ways to disguise that they really have no idea how to participate and this can be why recess or fun, unstructured time can be problematic. These issues, simple as they may seem, are very real for this child. The "deal with it" approach won't improve their response to this protective mechanism which has taken over with little notice. Now we might see an exaggerated or delayed response or find this child completely unable to access their frontal lobe because their system thinks it needs protection.

One of my favorite teachers once told me she *always* tries to get recess duty. This seemed strange to me because recess is a lovely, quiet time for teachers to re-group, plan, and exhale. This amazing teacher quickly figured out that the kids in her class didn't all know what to *do* at recess and this caused a lot of stress in their day. Sure, you see the kids who go grab a ball or a swing, but there were a lot of them who truly didn't know how to navigate the unstructured time of recess. As adults, we sometimes forget that simple things like *play*, can actually be quite a mystery for some kids.

She made a point to be out there and show them games, or different ways to ask for a turn. She also loved the time to just *be* out there; she was available for them. The stories the kids shared with her in this unstructured time also helped her figure out a little more about how they were wired and how to better teach them.

Thank you, Joanna Kaiser!

When a child is already stressed it can take very little additional input to put them into fight, flight, or freeze and this can mean extreme, unexpected behaviors. Some think if we simply raise the expectations, kids will try harder and see that everything is really okay and maybe even fun. The only problem here is that they already can't do what we're asking, so raising expectations isn't the answer. If our expectations aren't appropriate for a child's ability level or capacity to regulate, we might add to the already high levels of constant stress. Our goal is to help kids begin to recognize stress and manage its effects.

It is also important to remember that what is fun for a peer or us may *not* be fun for this child. Every stressful situation carves out a pathway in the nervous system so that the next response can come faster to ensure survival. But these kids do not need better protective pathways because their system is already on high alert. These kids need balance and this can come with the help of an understanding adult who respects that even recess can result in fight, flight, or freeze mode.

## Toxic Stress

Toxic stress is a response that occurs when a child experiences intense, recurrent, or prolonged adversity without adequate adult support (Franke, 2014). Physical or emotional abuse, chronic neglect, exposure to violence, caregiver mental illness or substance abuse, and extended family hardship affect the brain in ways that can have long-term effects. It is important to be aware of the effects of constant, elevated levels of cortisol in the system from this repeated exposure to stress. When we get cortisol that's always released from constant stress, there are many dangerous side effects, and research shows how hard this is on the system. The Ph level of the gut is affected and since the gut produces many neurotransmitters like dopamine and serotonin, behavior, mood, and motivation can all be negatively impacted. Prolonged stress alters digestion and the absorption of B12 which influences energy, mood and even vision; all of these are critical for school. Long-term health issues affect the immune system and are linked to increased inflammation, heart disease, diabetes, depression and brain structure changes (Koch et al., 2017). Brain imaging from a study released in 2023 indicates decreased brain volume in individuals experiencing traumatic events, family conflict, violence, lower household incomes, and historical structural inequalities; this gray matter is critical for everything required at school (McFarling, 2023).

Imagine swimming in the ocean and suddenly seeing a shark fin coming right at you. It is the threat mechanism of fight, flight, or freeze that pumps adrenaline and cortisol into your bloodstream to help you fight harder and swim faster. This response keeps you alive. However, this stress response is only appropriate and useful if you are actually in the water with a shark. Problems occur when a child's nervous system responds as if they are constantly fighting off sharks. A child whose single working mother is struggling with alcoholism and poverty may be enough to alter how this child can manage stress so the nervous system protective responses now become toxic to this child (Barber and Phang, 2017).

Sadly, we cannot always have the foresight, communication, or ability to avoid every situation that puts a child into fight, flight, or freeze, so recovery is critical. Stuff happens. How a child responds to that stuff begins to define who this child is. It is what teaches them to endure and trust in themselves as well as others. It is important to include this in the conversation with a child. If they can try a strategy and then analyze its effectiveness with you later, you have assisted in their life-long journey of self-monitoring and regulation. Calming strategies provide ideas that can help the nervous system reset and calm down so a child can feel some control over those feelings inside.

It is also important to understand that stress isn't always a bad thing and some of the mechanisms and neurotransmitters involved in fight, flight, or freeze can be helpful and might explain behavioral responses we see in school. Cortisol assists in the process of creating an immediate response which ensures survival, but it is very effective for short periods because energy, focus, and motivation are also important for work completion. Procrastination can actually be a subconscious behavioral response because this mechanism is hard-wired into our human physiology. Awareness of the cortisol effect can lead you to strategies such as chunking work with frequent deadlines and rewards to "trick" the nervous system and tap into a little extra cortisol for a quick response and immediate attention that can support academic success.

## Why We See Fight, Flight, or Freeze

- An environment that is busy, loud, or unstructured.
- A task involving too many things: hard content that isn't a just right challenge for a child, or group work with social expectations and academic demands.
- A social situation that is too much, too intense, or too difficult to navigate.
- An emotional or physical issue that prevents them from effectively engaging, participating, or producing a response that is expected. Many kids arrive at school in survival mode due to things at home such as abuse, neglect, poverty, or other trauma-based situations impairing their ability to regulate.
- Sensory issues can quickly over-stimulate a child such as intolerance to certain fabrics, activities that involve touching others (holding hands, etc.) or messy substances, peers too close to them, or various smells (Scentsy or plug-ins, perfume, body odor, or cigarettes). Some kids struggle with activities that stimulate the vestibular sense (movement) such as when their head is below their heart, spinning, or climbing.
- Fear or anxiety because of an unknown: substitute teacher, new activity, working with a peer they don't know well, class changes, or transitions during the day that involve different people, places, and new activities. Not knowing what to expect can be very scary.
- Expectations that are unrealistic for this child, this task, this environment, or this moment in time (some kids are better regulated in the morning versus afternoon so more challenging activities or group work in the afternoon might be enough to trigger over-stimulation).
- The child might be too active or excited to adjust to the demands of a task. Coming in from recess can be a hard adjustment; they don't know how to come down to a regulated state for work because their nervous system is still in "run mode".
- Overstimulation can be physiological and we can see it in behavioral responses but it can also be mental which means it is harder to see. When the mind is in overdrive it can feel similar

to when you are getting sick, where you notice every little thing and everything is too much so tolerance for anything is decreased.

• The brain *does not* work when overstimulation occurs, so allowing for recovery is critical if they are to get anything out of your teaching or interaction. Don't stress over missed instruction when they are in the recovery phase because they would have missed the content anyway. If they can have some time to recover, then their nervous system will be primed to learn and regulation will come easier.

# THE PRACTICAL STUFF:
## STRATEGIES FOR FLIGHT, FIGHT, OR FREEZE

<u>Simplify or alter the activity</u> they are struggling with so they can feel successful and maybe begin to perform as their peers are. Possible ideas for times of stress can include:

- Take out the social piece and let them work alone when content is new or difficult.
- Allow them to use a calculator for the first half of the problems to decrease the amount of math required in their head in conjunction with demonstrating the mathematical process.
- Try dictation into their computer or to an adult/peer that can scribe.
- Allow oral answers to questions instead of writing responses when they struggle.
- Let them write just a word instead of a sentence.
- Prepare them through pictures or front-loading instructions. When there will be a new task demand, a new or different person, or a previously aversive activity, talk to the child beforehand and show them pictures, tell them details, or share tools that they might be able to use to handle any anxiety that comes. When a child realizes you understand the things that make them uncomfortable, they are often more open to trying. If you can continue to refer to a visual schedule, kids can mentally prepare for what is coming which helps them feel in control of their world and their body (p. 13 or see www.secrettohappy.com for example of a visual schedule).
- A step-by-step visual representation of an activity can help a child whose brain has turned off because of over-stimulation. They can use this list or visual to increase independence but they can also cross off the items as they are completed which helps them to feel progress and possibly improve focused attention and motivation for task completion.
- Provide communication tools that allow them to tell us when they need a break so they don't have to get our attention with poor behavior. Include break opportunities that match the

communicative and cognitive levels of the student such as with a break card or "signal" between the student and an adult that other kids don't know, etc.

- Build in an opportunity for control. Have them challenge themselves with how many problems they can tackle or which ones to do first. Present options for the use of colored pencils/pens or colored paper to help them feel like they have some say in how this task will look. Options for seating may help decrease anxiety because they can choose a quieter space that you might not even realize they need.
- Use a different medium such as Google Slides versus writing a paper.

Simplify or alter the environment to create different zones in their space to access when their regulation needs change.

- Create a quiet corner with very little clutter (even on the walls), and space away from others. Provide tools that decrease stimulation such as headphones (with or without music), heavy weighted objects, and visuals that show strategies such as slow belly breathing (6-7 breaths per minute), and breathing sessions with exhaling longer than inhaling.
- Create a space where they can work on regulation with pictures to show them ways to utilize tools or strategies that help them feel better. Dragon dens (for younger students) or a strategy corner with tools for signal issues allow options for regulation that don't require talking or further engagement that is dysregulating. This can become an entire class activity but having space for a student to access for a few minutes can promote self-monitoring, independence, and advocacy.
- Section off a child's space with a study carrel or cardboard divider. Sometimes just decreasing the amount of visual stimulation a child has in their workspace can increase focus and help them control the many overwhelming signals.
- Provide a clear list or visual representation of what is expected so they can see it and continue to refer back to it as needed.

Depending on the cognitive/developmental level of the child, these can be simple words, pictures, or sentences that help to decrease the unknown of an activity or time period of the day. Pictures, planners, calendars, and lists are great ways to help anyone anticipate what is coming. They allow for processing before the protection phase takes over. Don't think a child is too smart, too young, or doesn't care. It is surprising how helpful it is to know what the day looks like, or what an activity entails, step-by-step.

- Create structure even when there isn't any. Give a child tasks or things to focus on when entering a new or unstructured setting. Sometimes just having a plan for recess can completely change the behavioral regulation required for this unstructured and busy time of the day. Discuss with a student the things they enjoy outside or on the playground. Write out a "plan" for how they can access these things and backup activities if they cannot access what they want to play on or with. For example

  o 1. Go to the swings... if they are full, try the slide.
  o 2. Walk around the track, look for kids who might need a friend and say hello.

- Simplify their world. Use very few words, reduce visual clutter, move to a different space, and allow quiet time and time to just *be*. Give them permission to focus on *recovery* as needed.
- Be aware of the number of adults engaging with a struggling child. This "support" can be the very thing creating too much intensity or input.

Use the <u>sensory system</u> to create strategies that help increase regulation and decrease protective responses.

- Proprioception is the sense we get from our muscles and joints and it is often our most effective sensory system to use for strategies related to dysregulation. It involves heavy input into the joints and muscles which is very organizing to the nervous system during times of over- and under-stimulation. Activities of heavy work can help when a child is escalating. Try activities such as carrying a crate with books, lifting, pushing, or pulling (such as putting chairs up on the desk or erasing the board). Heavy work into the jaw and mouth can be provided with bagels (chewy), carrots (crunchy), gum, or allowing them to suck thick items through a straw (applesauce or pudding). Create warm-up activities or breaks involving stretching, moving, wall or desk push-ups, or any movement.

- Be aware of the vestibular system. This is related to motion, head position, balance, movement, and posture. Generally, vestibular input is overstimulating when a child already has too much input. Even activities like leaning over to pick something up from the floor can give too much input into this system and cause further dysregulation. If you provide movement opportunities make sure they are calming like rocking slowly, forward and back (rocking chair), or slowly swinging (without being pushed). Any kind of rotational movement provides extra input that can quickly become overstimulating. Sometimes you just need to provide a break with very little movement because they may have gotten too much vestibular input during recess with swings, spinning around in circles, etc.

- Quiet breaks with dim lighting and less sensory input help to reset the nervous system. Focus on the different sensations that don't involve vision. What do they hear right now? What can they feel? Can they smell anything? This engages other parts of the brain and serves as a great distraction as long as their brain is working and not protecting at this moment.

- Anything oral is soothing. Think about how babies tend to soothe; sucking, chewing, and drinking provide input to the mouth which is like the computer terminal to the brain.

- Deep pressure, firm touch, or vibrating massagers can be very organizing to the nervous system because it involves the tactile system, which is a root for foundational strategies. Some kids like light touch and vibration while others absolutely do not, so if something seems agitating, stop and try something else.

- Some kids respond to smells so essential oils may help.

- Use programs such as *The Zones of Regulation, The Alert System,* or "Dragon Training."
- Find a way to introduce activities or opportunities that create laughter. When fight, flight, or freeze takes over, laughter stimulates the vagus nerve to promote regulation.

Address <u>social skills</u> and help them begin to read and understand the social climate around them.

- Practice reading body language and working in a group only when kids are regulated and experiencing success. This might mean some kids work independently while others can be in a group activity. These different opportunities for social engagement can help decrease maladaptive behavioral responses.
- Expectations or requests that students work with others in groups can put many into dysregulation. We want to teach them how to work with others but we must be flexible and adjust our expectations as their behavior dictates.
- Desensitization is the process of starting easy and getting harder so you can help with aversive social situations. Start with watching a video first, reviewing books or social stories about how to engage with others, using role-play, and then try it live after reviewing a plan for appropriate engagement.
- If kids are overstimulated in a social setting, have them perform tasks they have previously mastered.
- Remember to respect a child's cues and preferences.
- Kids can show you very quickly if something isn't helping. What might work for one child may be awful for another.
- Pre-teaching, practicing, and role-playing help students feel calm, centered, and capable because they know what is coming or how to do something.
- Have a plan for social interactions. Help them come up with one-liners they can use to ask if they can have a turn or join a game. Many kids don't know *how* to play or socially engage, so helping with initial ideas can give them the opportunity to increase their exposure and build confidence.

## Strategies for Auditory Overstimulation

- Provide headphones for noise-canceling or listening to calming music that a child can choose.
- Use very few words. Pictures are effective, but always remember to utilize a communication device if necessary. Don't underestimate the power of quiet.
- Talk in a calm voice, with low intensity and volume that allows time for students to process.
- Have a space away from others that is quiet with few demands.
- Plan ahead for activities that will be noisy; avoid these entirely or bring tools to help them cope.
- Provide distractions or purposeful activities in noisy environments.
- DO NOT HAVE MORE THAN ONE PERSON ENGAGING WITH A CHILD AT ANY TIME WHEN THEY ARE ESCALATED. For safety, we often need multiple adults with one student and this increases the amount of stimulation and intensity this child is exposed to. Additional adults can assist the person engaging with the child but try to have one adult dealing with the child with the other adult prepared to get needed items, remove items to keep the child safe, and observe the immediate environment to prepare for escalation.

## Strategies for Visual Overstimulation

- Provide spaces with different lighting: bright light, sunlight, blue glare shades, lamps, and complete darkness (using a fort or separate space) are options.
- Adjust visual detail on the page: make the font bigger, use a different colored page, or copy fewer problems on the page (i.e. 3 problems per page instead of 9).
- Use a timer that is easy to show chunks of work time with reward time that is visually represented (see p. 171 for an example).
- Be aware of the proximity a student has to another child/adult, and provide the opportunity to sit/lie in a different space of the room.

- Use a divider or study carrel to block the visual input allowing the auditory to remain available.
- Utilize a visual schedule that shows them what their day looks like or steps to the activity they are doing (even if you think they understand).
- Incorporate a visual checklist to mark off items when they are done.
- Provide various sensory-based visual tools such as bubble tubes, fiber optic strands, alternative lighting, or mirrors.
- Allow for flexible seating so a child can choose where in that visual space they feel best.

## Strategies for Tactile (touch) Overstimulation

- Fidgets, heavy balls, resistive tubing to manipulate, and various textures can provide opportunities for input that can be calming to the nervous system.
- Provide soft play options with mats, bolster cushions, bean bags, and blankets.
- Create sensory tactile walls with different textures that can be felt and incorporated into various games (guessing with eyes shut, labeling how this feels, etc.).
- Applying deep touch pressure to the upper lip can be calming (see p. 111).
- Give slow, consistent, firm pressure down the spine (with permission from the child) and NEVER light touch unless it is requested (see visual example on pp. 279, 280).
- Seat a sensitive or overstimulated child away from places where they might be accidentally touched as kids walk by.
- Respect a child's dislike for touch and activities that involve touch or holding hands, etc. They might approach you for touch because they have control over this, but your approaching them may put them directly into fight, flight, or freeze.

## The Creation of a Recovery Space

- Adjust lighting options such as dim lighting or dark, fiber optic strands, bubble tubes, objects that light up when touched, or mirror balls. Projectors can display calming scenes on the wall without concern for breaking expensive technology and it creates an entire environment vs. watching a video or TV.
- Soft play could include pillows, bolsters, tunnels, wedges, wall panels with different textures, weighted items (blankets, stuffed animals), or vibration items (pillows, toys, massagers).
- Scents can be Scentsy wax in small containers, or various essential oils but be aware of sensitivities and smells that are intrusive or difficult to adjust (like plug-in options).
- Include noise that drowns out the environment they need a break from; try calming music, noise machines with a heartbeat, nature sounds, or a metronome.
- Pictures or PECS can show how tools are used and prompt the use of strategies (deep breathing, shutting eyes, use of weighted blanket) without adult engagement. This child likely needs recovery first to prevent further escalation or aggression.
- Give them space!

# 5. THRESHOLDS

A threshold is the point at which our nervous system can respond to input or signals. When we can effectively manage our threshold needs, our brain can do what it does best. Experience and exposure to various input will change how our nervous system receives and interprets this input and this affects our response, focused attention, and ultimately molds our perception of the world around us. We need to hit this threshold to engage, attend, and focus, but we also don't want to hit it too often.

Thresholds can change with different activities or environments, and while wiring will affect where that threshold usually lies, strategies *can* change the threshold. Have you ever noticed how different you feel or behave when you are getting sick? This is because your threshold is so low it is being hit repeatedly, and all these signals bombard the system making you miserable. The gate is letting too much in. But if your threshold is too high, it can be difficult to reach, making you feel miserable too. Imbalance means we *cannot* regulate.

There are different ways to manage our threshold. Most adults have figured out socially appropriate ways to control their threshold because they have been exposed to various sensory experiences throughout the years. Adults also know through self-awareness what helps them regulate and they can usually get, *or avoid*, input without disturbing others. Children lack experience, so they often have not perfected the skill of gracefully managing input demands and this may be the only reason you see the behavior you do.

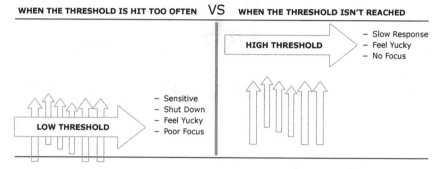

**WHEN THE THRESHOLD IS HIT TOO OFTEN   VS   WHEN THE THRESHOLD ISN'T REACHED**

HIGH THRESHOLD
– Slow Response
– Feel Yucky
– No Focus

LOW THRESHOLD
– Sensitive
– Shut Down
– Feel Yucky
– Poor Focus

The goal is to hit our threshold no matter where
it is because then we can regulate.

**The goal is to hit our threshold no matter where
it is because then we can regulate.**

We need *appropriate* input to focus, learn, read the room, and interact effectively. It is really important to be aware of threshold needs because the behavior may simply be an attempt to manage and balance input.

- Is the behavioral rigidity and dysregulation occurring because they are simply surviving in this moment of a low threshold? They may not verbalize it, but they cannot do what we ask if they cannot regulate.
- Is out-of-control behavior or constant disruption happening because they are trying to provide their own input to focus? The gate won't open if their threshold isn't hit.

## WHY DOES THE THRESHOLD MATTER?

How do we know threshold needs are impacting behavior? Is the current maladaptive behavior due to a high threshold or a low threshold? While this can be tricky to determine, it is important to remember that the goal is regulation so this is where the adult can be effective in supporting a child's regulation needs.

- If a child's behavior is maladaptive, it is safest to initially assume that they are overstimulated and that their behavior is an attempt to limit input, or a response to too much input. Help them by controlling aspects of their environment or adjusting the demands of a situation; if they can recover and re-engage, you have effectively helped them manage their threshold needs.
- If they don't respond to this change, this may mean their behavior was actually an attempt to get more input to reach a high threshold. Try to utilize tools that integrate more input into their learning process. If this was the *why* behind the behavior, then the behavior should improve. They should be able to show you that something is working; perfection won't happen immediately but something will change with their engagement, work production, or behavior.

Since individual wiring affects threshold needs, in time you will likely see trends in behavior for a specific child. This will give you a starting point for tools; you may know that manic behavior is not an attempt to get more input but actually a response to the many signals in this moment. In this case, recovery must occur before anything else. Strategies will always need to be a moment-to-moment experiment, but knowledge of thresholds and wiring help us find a starting point for intervention.

# DESCRIPTION OF THRESHOLDS

Winnie Dunn created the Sensory Profile to assess sensory processing patterns based on neurological thresholds and behavioral responses (Metz et al. 2019; Dunn 2007). The following chart shows her theory with an explanation of thresholds and how they can be applied in behavior analysis. Examples of behaviors we might see with both high and low thresholds are included. Understanding and identifying where a child's threshold is at this moment can help you determine if strategies should provide more or less input for behavior and threshold management.

| Affected Sense | High Threshold Behaviors | Low Threshold Behaviors |
|---|---|---|
| Touch | - frequently touch people or objects<br>- tend to get into others' personal bubbles<br>- put things in their mouth<br>- chew on shirt or shirt cuffs<br>- display very high pain tolerance | - overreact when people are too close<br>- hate messy things<br>- avoid situations that involve textures they don't like<br>- avoid certain foods<br>- display an overreaction to pain |
| Taste or Smell | - crave strong, spicy flavors or odors<br>- smell objects that others might not<br>- taste, or put things in their mouth that you wouldn't expect | - avoid flavors or odors more than others and may not know why |
| Sound | - make noises or talk through and verbally process everything<br>- seek out noises that distract them from what they are doing | - strongly dislike certain noises<br>- startle easily, cover ears<br>- difficulty working in groups<br>- assemblies or lunch cafeteria can be a time of behavioral outburst |
| Vision | - need a lot of visual stimulation such as with bright lights<br>- continuous distractions from movement or visually stimulating objects like TV or video games | - overstimulated by visual detail<br>- behavioral outburst at the beginning of long homework or work tasks<br>- can't find objects hiding in detail |
| Vestibular (related to balance and space) | - constantly jumping, swinging, bouncing<br>- always drawn to activities involving movement | - car sick, avoid play equipment like swings or slides<br>- poor behavior after transitions that involve tipping the head, such as bending to get something |
| Proprioception (knowing where your body is, how things feel) | - need to crash, push/pull, hit, or bite more than others<br>- play too hard and not understand why a peer is hurt by their high-five or tag | - sedentary play choices that are quiet, with little movement<br>- overreact to pain<br>- seems weak with easy activities |

# LOW THRESHOLDS

When a threshold is hit quickly and repeatedly, the signals can be so strong we may see extreme behaviors. Everything is too much: the lights, the noise, how things feel inside. Requests for a response, an encouraging pat on the back, or even a "fun group activity" can result in overstimulation and repeated surges *way past* threshold. There is an internal battle, and the intensity we see will depend on how this incoming information is managed. Very strong preferences may make a child appear stubborn and rigid. If we respect their words or preferences, they may be able to push through. If we challenge their "no" we may see extreme behavioral responses that are very hard to manage. When we assume their response is a volitional choice, we may be missing an opportunity to help; a consequence at this moment may be ineffective because what they need is less input, not a consequence. It's important to identify when behavior stems from a low threshold response because the behavior will need to be managed appropriately if things are going to get better.

> When we can view behavior differently, our response might be different than our initial instinct; we don't want to make things worse. The goal now becomes recovery rather than disciplinary action.

## Examples of low threshold behavior can include:

- Avoiding eye contact or always wearing a hoodie.
- Oversensitivity to touch or avoidance of touch from others, and displaying behavior issues during group activities or when a task involves touching textures they don't like.
- Sensitivity to noise or loud spaces means they may avoid noise or show extreme behavior anticipating a noise they know they can't handle.
- Difficulty with transitions, big events, or unexpected changes like assemblies, parties, last-minute changes, or new people.
- Extreme tantrums or constant disruption occur when kids overstimulate because some kids respond to counteract what

they feel. Self-injury can mask overstimulation, elopement can get them away from input they can't handle, and creating huge distractions can mean they get out of something they do not want to experience.

- Poor engagement can be the result of shutdown so they may appear lazy, sleepy, distracted, or disrespectful when really they are in protection mode and their wiring sets their behavior to fight, flight, or freeze.

- They may show extreme reactions to pain or different types of input. Light touch, small bumps from others who walk by, or someone sitting too close can result in an unexpected reaction that is difficult to make sense of.

# THE PRACTICAL STUFF:
## STRATEGIES TO <u>DECREASE</u> INPUT

**Pay attention to the *delivery* of stimulation; focus on slow, even, consistent, and lower-intensity input. Always have permission from the child or tell them before you attempt a strategy or enter their "bubble." Any of the techniques discussed in the fight, flight, or freeze section would also be appropriate to decrease input:**

- Apply slow strokes down the spine. Put a finger on each side of their spine at the base of the neck. Slowly move down the spine to the waist pressing firmly. Before lifting your hand off their back, have the other hand at the base of their neck ready to repeat what was just done so that you always have a hand on their back.

- Linear rocking. Have the child sit on the floor and pull their knees into their chest, holding and squeezing for 10 seconds. Then have them rock slowly, forward and backward while still squeezing their knees.

- Apply slow, rhythmic deep pressure into the shoulders. Maintain pressure with weighted blankets, vests, or lap pads for increments of 10 minutes on, and 10 minutes off.

- Practice calm, focused activities such as marching slowly, or stopping to slowly stretch with arms reaching high to the sky with deep breaths.

- Create consistent routines they can see in a visual schedule (see p. 163).

- Slow inversion increases relaxation, improves sleep, supports immune function, and increases blood flow and oxygen to the brain. Ensure there is no fear of this activity or aversion to this type of vestibular input. They can roll over a large ball on their tummy or sit in a chair and lean forward so their head is lower than their heart and they can breathe deeply.

- The use of a metronome can introduce rhythm and speed that you can adjust for them to follow. It can be used with movement and breathing activities to adapt the amount of input produced (try 60 bpm, then 120, then 45). There are various metronome apps available online.

- Foster calmness. Speak with a low volume and pace, and model slow breathing patterns to help a child realize they have control over their breath.

- Have them apply firm, constant pressure into the upper lip (see image). Hold for 10 seconds with deep breathing.

- Provide input into jaw muscles by eating crunchy or chewy snacks, sucking a thick liquid through a straw, chewing gum, or sucking on hard candies.

- Avoid fight, flight, or freeze. When you notice a child has hit this point, take a deep breath and help them find a quiet place to take a break and recover until they can control their body and begin to utilize other tools or strategies.

- Look for additional problems such as being sick, tired, hungry, or irritated by a tag on their shirt. These make everything harder and can quickly be addressed once identified.

- Control is critical. Build in as much opportunity for the *perception* of control. Provide a couple of options, ask them where they feel they work best, let them choose which problems to do first before a visually cued break, etc.

- Provide distractions, or focus on one aspect of an activity that might be silly or fun. This is similar to concepts used in therapy; kids afraid of heights may tolerate the swing if they have to count how many kids are playing basketball while they are swinging. Distractions allow the nervous system to process new input, which makes it easier the next time it is attempted.

- Utilize a timer so there is a visual cue showing how much longer to work or attend.

- Warn in advance to allow the child to anticipate intense sensory experiences and then discuss ways of preparing for certain input before their nervous system takes over. Lunch, recess, or assemblies can be easier when they know what is involved and what strategies they can use at that moment.

- Seat the sensitive child so people don't brush against them.
- Give space (take two steps back). Always respect the bubble around a child.
- Create spaces they can independently navigate to meet their regulation needs. Provide recovery spaces made from mats or under a table covered with a blanket. Have a corner carrel and various seating options such as rocking chairs, bean bags, and blankets (fluffy or weighted) for them to choose from.
- Environmental changes can include calm music or noise-makers with nature sounds. Tactile input with textures or cold/hot can alter nervous system responses. Lavender is a calming smell that can be easily introduced to a space. Time in the dark, or even dim lighting, is a great way to let the brain have a break.
- Decrease the number of adults engaging with a student. Be aware of the space's intensity, which often involves people, noises, and movement.
- Structure helps because if a child knows the general sequence of the events in their day, they can better anticipate and prepare for it. Structure can be really calming for some kids.
- Visual schedules provide cues for what is first, second, etc. This tool helps channel energy and gives a "light at the end of the tunnel" that provides enough motivation to muddle through the stuff that's hard for their system. When they know they get a break after ten math problems, it makes the math more manageable.
- Consider the social implications of working with peers. Some kids do better with adults because adult behavior can be more predictable than kids so it is way less scary.
- Decrease demands for times when students are overstimulated. When the social environment is more complex, have them perform tasks they have already mastered and are good at. If the content is new, don't add in the group work just yet unless the child feels they are ready.

The following techniques are great for *you* and your students, so try them out and consider doing them as a whole group when kids need to transition to desk/quiet time (the following SAM box techniques were provided in a neuroscience and self-regulation continuing education class by Varleisha Gibbs, Ph.D., OTD, OTR/L).

- Eye yoga. Close your eyes and gently inhale. Move your eyes (with eyes closed) to look up and down, then side to side. Open your eyes and place an arm in front of your face, following it with your eyes as it moves slowly in all directions (even toward the nose). Try not to move your head, only your eyes while breathing slowly and deliberately.
- The ears affect the vagus nerve to calm. Cross your arms over each other in front of your body and grab the lower half of the ear lobe (thumbs in front), gently pull down on your lobes, counting to 10. Do this three times.
- Trumpet blowing. Put the tip of your thumb in your mouth and without letting any air escape, fill your cheeks and blow, holding for 5-10 seconds, repeat x3.
- Eyelid massage. Take two fingers, close your eyes and gently press and move in a circular pattern, five times in each direction while counting and breathing slowly.
- Wall sits or wall push-ups.

Other effective techniques for addressing the vagus nerve and promoting calm regulation include:

- 1:4:2 breathing where you breathe in for one second, hold your breath for 4 seconds, and exhale for two seconds.
- Singing, changing, or humming.
- Meditation, yoga, and mindfulness to prepare kids for a quiet, focused activity following recess or a transition.

  o Try short YouTube videos such as "Bubble Bounce, Mindfulness for Children" (Alber, 2020).

- Cold ice packs or splashing cold water on your face.

# HIGH THRESHOLDS

The brain needs input to know when and how to generate a response. If a threshold is really high, more input is required. When behavior is different than expected, it can be due to "inadequate neural activation to support sustained performance" (Dunn 1999). A delayed or absent response can be due to this poor activation; more extreme or disruptive behaviors can be attempts to generate as much input as possible. Humans are driven to find homeostasis, which is that feeling of balance inside. This is why thresholds are so important to recognize and consider when assessing the *why* behind behavior and when trying to come up with solutions for success. Much of the behavior we get can be an attempt to reach a threshold demands that are too high for the current activity, so additional movement or stimulation is attempted to try to achieve homeostasis.

### **Examples of high threshold behavior can include:**

- Constantly engaging with the child next to them or picking fights
- Running their hand along the hallway wall and knocking down prized art projects in school
- Constant fidgeting and wiggling in their chair with difficulty calming down
- Constant verbal processing or noises that are loud and chatty, or constantly talking when they are supposed to be listening
- Behavior that appears aggressive or self-injurious (such as high fives that are too hard)
- Biting objects, grinding teeth, or chewing on clothes to the point of making holes
- Spinning their body, flapping their hands, or persistent self-stimulation (masturbation)
- Not engaged and difficulty focusing
- Need for sugar, caffeine, or any type of addictive behaviors such as video games or self-medication
- Constant need for rewards (because of a lack of dopamine)
- Engagement in high-risk, extreme activities, crashing on the floor, constant rough play

.

- Missing social cues
- Missing instructions or steps of a task
- Slumping on the desk and looking tired or uninterested
- Sedentary play options with little interest in movement activities or active participation

Think of that kid in class who is always distracting those around them with movement, talking, flicking objects for fun. Is it possible this child is using all this disruption as a way to focus? Sometimes added movement or verbal processing can help kids reach a high threshold but this behavior can be misinterpreted as volitional instead of functional behavior. The goal is to find a way for kids to reach their threshold without disrupting those around them.

# THE PRACTICAL STUFF:
## STRATEGIES TO <u>INCREASE</u> INPUT

**Pay attention to the *delivery* of stimulation. Rapid, uneven, intermittent, or higher-intensity application will create more stimulation. It is VERY important to monitor behavioral responses with these techniques to ensure this input is not overwhelming; behavior and regulation should improve. \*\*Always ask permission from the student before doing any of these techniques.**

- Provide vibration into muscles with a vibrating pillow or massager.
- Use Ice therapy by having them suck on ice cubes/popsicles or put an ice pack on their neck.
- Provide more intense and frequent sensory stimulation with activities that quickly change between fast/slow, stop/go, cold/hot, etc.
- Try a multiple sensory approach. Provide music or noise that they listen to while working, or full body movements to form letters with associated noises (say "zip" whenever you make a vertical line, "zoop" for horizontal lines, etc.).
- Set frequent but subtle check-ins or chimes that can increase self-monitoring and prompt the question, "Am I focused when I hear the chime?" Apps that help with focus are readily available now, and they even send reminders to see if you are focused at that moment.
- Supplement video instruction with live instruction. Pause the video to encourage participation and discuss how video content applies to their world right now.
- Use a metronome in the classroom to give the brain something rhythmic to help them focus.
- Foods or smells provide fun and appropriate additional input. Experiment with crunchy textures, intense/strong flavors, or smells like citrus, eucalyptus, or mint essential oils.
- Use a timer to create short-term deadlines. Cortisol is a neurotransmitter that is released when we are stressed (such as with a deadline). It can increase the intensity or motivation to

help with initiation and task completion. Motivators or rewards increase the amount of dopamine, which is a neurotransmitter needed for execution.

- Provide alternative writing utensils or add fun, new pencils or pens such as those with glitter or fragrant ink, or mechanical pencils with variations in lead size.
- Weight provides proprioceptive input, so try a weighted cuff on the wrist or have a student use a weighted pen or pencil. Pens that vibrate and wiggle provide tactile input and force more attention to the act of writing because they have to control a moving object but still make legible letters.
- Grips and pencils of different shapes increase the interest in writing activities. Some pencils look like a rocket, have padded grips that encourage harder squeezing, or have fidgets that cover the end of a pencil to keep hands busy during listening time.

Movement-Based Tools:

- Fidget tools or clay/resistive material to hold or fidget with during listening times will provide heavy muscle input.
- Dynamic sitting options allow and encourage different positions for desk work. Examples include lying on their stomach, standing at a table, sitting on a ball or dynamic cushion, or writing on the board vs. paper. This dynamic opportunity requires them to make small postural adjustments that allow for movement during sitting that will feed their nervous system to improve regulation.
- Sports and exercise can feed the nervous system with effects lasting for hours. Running, lifting weights, and organized sports are all vital parts of a child's world and will affect their ability to attend to a given activity even after they are done moving.
- Work for 5 minutes, then move. This is an excellent strategy for the toolbox because once you feed the nervous system with movement, a child can more easily focus to complete more work.

## Audio/Visual Tools:

- Have them listen to upbeat music to increase energy.
- Confirm that they got the instructions. Some may look you right in the eye and hear nothing, while others may look like they aren't listening, but fidgeting or doodling helps them catch everything!
- Have a visual showing images of regulation or emotions and the tools or strategies they have determined to help them regulate.
- Provide a visual list of instructions or steps to complete the given task.

## Proprioception Tools:

- Build heavy work strategies into desk or quiet time with a resistive band around the legs of the desk or chair so they can push and pull against it with their legs.
- Have them stack chairs, carry books, play hard at recess, or try out a "boot camp" or teacher's helper vs. staying in at recess when a consequence is needed.
- Apply deep pressure down the spine by quickly pushing down on each shoulder (with the child's permission).
- If they are hitting, banging their head, or biting, they might need deep pressure through a big squeeze they do themselves, or you do from behind. A weighted blanket or lap/shoulder pad can be used independently in a space they are using for recovery.
- Oral input is very organizing and powerful because the mouth is like the computer terminal to the brain, so gum can be a useful tool. When you see a child with their fingers in their mouth, chewing on their pencil, clothing, or other items, this can indicate that they do well with oral input. You can buy bracelets, necklaces, and pencil toppers designed to be chewed on.

Environmental Modifications:

- Create a space with colored shelves or surfaces designed for a specific subject or item. The green shelf might hold items for science, the red spot on the table is for math, etc. This helps them begin to visualize where things go but also activates them for more effective execution because it simplifies a previously disorganized system and creates a just right challenge with color and visual cues built into their work environment.
- Use bright paper or binders for the subjects that are harder for the child.
- During circle time or independent work time, provide a defined work area with a carpet square, tape around a seating area, or a clear, visual boundary where a child can be without disrupting others with their movement, lack of personal space awareness, or sensory needs.
- Use a slant board that puts their work at a more upright angle to increase visual interest.

Sensory Diet Tools:

A sensory diet is an activity plan designed to regulate a child's threshold (Wilbarger et al., 2002). Every child is different, so what works for one may not work for another. The idea is to try an activity and determine if it accomplishes what is needed to change arousal levels. Does it give the child the input they need to reach and maintain a calm, alert state that allows them to be successful in the given environment? A sensory diet program involves activities that are integrated throughout the day and within classes, subjects, or transitions. This input for regulation is similar to how we meet nutritional needs throughout the day. See the printable section (p. 277) for additional ideas and visuals that can be added to a sensory diet routine.

- Intense proprioceptive or heavy work activities.

  o Wall sits. Pretend you are sitting on an invisible chair with your back against the wall.
  o Chair push-ups. Sit in a chair with your hands beside your legs and push down to lift your butt off the chair and feet off the ground. Hold as long as you can.
  o Carry heavy objects or do a job for the teacher.
  o Squeezy ball or hand strengthener.
  o Desk or wall push-ups, lunges, or any muscle-strengthening exercises.

- Incorporate action songs, stretching, and yoga into group learning.
- Intense vestibular movements involve postures with quick up and down postures, jumping jacks, or jumping up and down (like on a trampoline). Try this and see how they respond, but not for too long on the first attempt.

# 6. SENSORY PROCESSING

Our brain must be able to process all the sensory information (aka input) in our body and from our world, or we won't survive. Sensory processing requires communication between the body and brain; signals come in for analysis and to prompt a response. When this occurs, we have regulation. When signals are off or thresholds aren't managed, we have dysregulation because it is hard to adapt and evolve when things aren't balanced.

Like everything already discussed with thresholds and the response we hope to get, sensory processing is another way to discuss how input is managed in the nervous system. Internal signals transmit information like hunger, thirst, fatigue, temperature, pain, etc. External or environmental features are communicated to tell the brain about pace, demands, and intensity. Every signal that comes in changes the brain and nervous system, which is how we eventually adapt and adjust... and survive.

- Similar to low threshold moments, if there are too many signals, the brain gets bombarded and overwhelmed and will not respond appropriately. The brain cannot make sense of anything because it must weed out which signals to pay attention to and which to ignore. The nervous system hasn't processed the sensory information correctly, and now protection mode takes over so nothing is learned.

- If there are not enough signals, the brain doesn't have the information necessary to make an organized response; when signals don't reach the brain, there is usually no response, an inappropriate response, or a delayed response for the situation.

Educators today are dealing with an array of behaviors from moment to moment, so coming up with the "why" can be challenging, but it usually involves sensory processing. Expectations and the social aspects of school are complex, especially compared to home, so often a parent's report will be different from what a teacher sees. This doesn't mean that the child isn't struggling at school, nor does it mean that home or school is to blame. It comes down to expectations and a child's ability to reach these expectations at school. When there are too many or too few signals, failure can quickly ensue from expectations that are not appropriate for the skill level of this child. Every part of their social and academic life can be affected if they have difficulty achieving or maintaining regulation for given tasks. Social interactions are often the hardest to navigate; the lack of structure during recess and lunch can make "fun" times the toughest part of the day when kids struggle to benefit from their signals.

There is a big difference between bad behavior and sensory overload. When a child gets overstimulated, overwhelmed, or can't focus when their peers can, it affects not only their nervous system responses and behaviors, but also their self-esteem. When teachers or parents can help children understand why they are struggling, they can more easily access tools to support times when balance is lost.

- Strong sensory preferences can be hard to control or navigate when the comforts of home aren't possible at that moment. Snacks, quiet spaces, and a comforting hug might not be possible at school. If these are things required for regulation, school behavior will be tough to manage.
- Focused attention is critical for school and this requires regulation. Thresholds affect our ability to feel good and regulate.

o   High thresholds may require more movement to reach, but what if this is hard to do in the classroom? What if a child can't explain *why* they always get out of their chair?

o   Low thresholds are at risk of being hit repeatedly in a class with lots of noise, movement, colors, and smells. Everything can send them toward protection mode so now they are over-stimulated and likely in trouble!

A lot can be done in the school setting to help a child with signal issues succeed and enjoy their academic years. Much of this has to do with understanding that the sensory world controls just about everything related to regulation. Kids may demonstrate behaviors that appear disruptive, disrespectful, or disorganized but this may just be their attempt to find success. Behavior is tricky, and while consequences are critical for molding behavior, helping a child figure out the role their signals play can be a crucial step for molding behavior too.

## The Unique School Environment

Awareness of the learning environment involves observing the visual space, the noise level, and even the schedule. Social and peer interactions are a huge part of the environment. When kids are trying to learn *and* navigate social situations, this can quickly become too much, and learning can be very challenging. Welcome to fight or flight…again. Behavioral meltdowns indicate that something isn't working. The environment is a huge part of intervention, so shifting the focus to include this can often be empowering and quite successful.

Time to talk about the dragon. Is it acting like there is something truly dangerous lurking around the next corner? What could it be? Hmmm.... let's stop for a moment. What can we do? Deep breathing? Water break? A little time in a quieter space? Good! Now... what lurks around the corner of the dreaded 2nd grade wing? What???!!! Nothing??!! Interesting!

Silly Dragon!

Modifying or changing a child's environment can be critical in addressing the problem. Reducing or increasing what's going on in a space can be determined by observing what the child is drawn to or avoids. Regulation begins with self-monitoring. Self-monitoring requires scanning the environment and also inside the body to determine what is going on. The sad thing about our fast-paced educational system is that teachers are ultimately graded by the test scores of their students, so this quickly and often inadvertently becomes the focus of education. If a child can't regulate, they aren't going to be able to learn, so regulation really needs to be a primary objective in how we educate our kids. When we can adjust the features of the environment, behavior can change, and life often gets easier.

Another aspect of the environment includes the energy that the adult often controls. If adults are stressed by the struggle a child is facing, it will affect how they engage with this child. Anxiety and the resultant lack of regulation also affect adults. When kids are dealing with an adult who is stressed, they will act like a sponge and soak up all that negative energy. Awareness of our responses can help us to change the emotional energy of a space which might be the one small change this child needs.

I worked with an amazing teacher who wanted to try the dragon taming lesson and strategies with her entire class. We made a chart that showed strategies for fire dragons and strategies for sleepy dragons. She showed them pictures to help them begin figuring out what dragon they were dealing with and how to quietly get the input they needed to tame their dragon.

One day she came into class, completely overwhelmed and a bit frazzled. She felt a little hand on hers, and looked down to find one of the toughest kids in her class helping her figure out which strategy would make her dragon feel better!

She was able to see that what she had shared with the class really worked and a student who rarely found success in school was able to be her hero!

What an amazing teaching moment! The entire class was able to see that *even adults* struggle with dragons and we can all help each other out!

Thank you, Lisa Holland!

## Understanding Behaviors through the Sensory System

You must consider all the senses when determining where the difficulties lie. The following is a list of behaviors you might see from each sensory system that can guide you to the specific sensory area and tools you can try. Pay attention to extremes because this will also determine how your tool will be used. If a child is avoiding, they need less input or slower and more predictable input. If you observe them seeking additional input in a specific area, they need more signals, so apply a tool randomly or with more speed or intensity. Some sensations are more effective than others which is why movement and multi-sensory activities are so important.

## Movement

- Seeking more input: This can be fidgeting, jumping, or standing during class. They may have difficulty calming down after recess, demonstrate hyperactive behavior, or constantly find opportunities to get up during class (sharpening a pencil, getting a drink, or visiting the teacher).

- Avoiding input: We might see a student stand on the sideline not playing, or avoiding play equipment such as the swings. They might exhibit poor behavior after activities involving a lot of movement, or go into shutdown with sedentary behavior. Anticipation for transitions or new events/people/activities may create behavioral dysregulation.

## Touch

- Seeking more input: Kids might seek out and touch everything, fidget with things near them, or constantly be in other people's space without any social awareness.

- Avoiding input: When we see adverse reactions to activities that involve holding hands or close proximity to others (circle time, group activity at one table, etc.), or trouble with activities or classes like art (with clay, paint, glue or other things they have to touch), this is an indication that they struggle with this type of input.

## Auditory

- Seeking more input: Often kids will engage in verbal processing (humming, talking all the time, creating noise during work) or seek out places with more noise or excitement to get more auditory input.

- Avoiding input: Signs that noise is too much can include times when they display a sensitivity to noise, have trouble in groups or loud settings, never hear instructions, cover their ears, or if they are constantly wearing a hoodie.

Visual

- Seeking more input: Distraction with watching the surroundings, working better in well-lit areas, or benefiting from bright colors or interesting visual supports can be ways you might determine more visual input is helpful.
- Avoiding input: When kids can't tolerate excess visual input we might see them cover their eyes or avoid light, struggle in a busy room with lots of things hanging on the wall or ceiling, or have difficulty with excess detail on the page or with a font that is small and compact.

Oral and Smell

- Seeking more input: Students might suck on or bite clothes, hair, pencils, or nails.
- Avoiding input: We might see a sensitivity to various food textures, or they may exhibit a dislike for strong flavors or smells.

## Using the detective to figure out the *WHY*

Figuring out strategies requires an understanding of *why* the behavior is occurring, but this can be really hard because kids with behavior issues often resist talking about their role in a discipline situation. This is when the detective becomes an effective tool for self-monitoring. The adult is needed initially, but the ultimate goal is to eventually pass the role of detective to the child so they can figure out *if* they need help, *what* they need, *how* to advocate for this need, and *when* to utilize their tools or strategies.

It's a process so when there is more modeling and consistency we see independence and success more quickly. The two primary objectives for the detective are the *when* and *what*.

-When do they seem to need input or help? When do you see them trying to use a tool?

-What do they seem to be drawn to or avoid? Is it movement-related? Is it visual or auditory? Is it heavy work?

## Points to Consider

- Teach children *how* to use their sensory system to get the kind of input they need. This will empower them to be independent and confident for higher levels of learning.
- Remind kids that what they discover being a detective, whether good or bad, is critical for learning how to find success. It is important to emphasize that this is a process of learning how to prevent their brain from hijacking their behavior; there is nothing to be embarrassed or ashamed of when they discover a weakness that needs to be addressed.
- Appropriate sensory input improves processing and sensory integration and has a lasting effect throughout the day. When kids get the sensory experience their nervous system is craving, they can attend, perform tasks, interact with others appropriately, and demonstrate self-control and *regulation*.
- If a tool doesn't meet the need and change behavior, it is likely not the tool for this job, and often it becomes a toy that further distracts or leads to poor behavioral choices.
- Glucose is required in the brain for focused attention and work production, but is quickly depleted. Studies have shown that memory and performance improve 20 times faster when the instruction is separated by short breaks (Thomas, 2021).

## Introducing Play into Academic Programming to Support Learning

Play is the most important job we can undertake to ensure adequate brain development because it activates all the critical areas of the brain with very little difficulty. The more senses used during play and learning (touch, smell, sight, hearing, taste, and movement sensations), the easier it is for our brain to store and retrieve information quickly. When we move our bodies, endorphins are released, resulting in energy, motivation, and increased happiness. The brain sends and receives signals that help sustain and plan other motor skills while keeping track of what our body is doing and where it is in space. The more signals our brain sends and receives through movement and play, the more efficient the synapses within the brain become for later learning.

Play influences brain development, and luckily it is one of those things that children are naturally drawn to. When things are fun, more learning happens because the system has more dopamine to improve regulation. Never underestimate the power of play. If there is any way to incorporate it into the schedule, you will see an amazing transformation in energy and you might even find yourself enjoying your day more. Moving our bodies, engaging socially, and tapping into different senses prepares our nervous system, and therefore the brain, for learning and regulation. Especially when kids are little, incorporating play and imagination into programming can make learning easier and way more fun.

But play today looks very different than it used to. Technology and video games can provide many wonderful opportunities for learning, but often at the cost of fewer movement-based activities. Many kids come to school from the world of technology play so they may not have much experience with active or social play opportunities. When kids are bored, they often figure out different things to do that further develop executive functioning; kids are rarely bored when technology is present. Helping them with the process of non-tech play can improve learning retention, executive functioning, and social skills.

Considerations and Ideas that Involve Play:

- Return to the basics. Good old-fashioned advice like "Go out and play" is critical because play is a child's primary job. In this ever-changing world where our kids are doing more sedentary work in elementary school, they need to play more than ever. Play allows the body and brain to work together. Amazing things happen when children are left to their own resources for play. They begin to develop ideas they test out or discuss with friends. These ideas evolve, are tried, changed, and further discussed which develops executive functioning.

- When kids are bored and have to come up with games, they develop executive skills.

- When behavioral consequences are needed, consider alternatives to missing the movement aspects of recess. Play and movement are critical foundational building blocks for learning, so creating jobs that still encourage movement and a cognitive break might be exactly what is needed for improved behavioral regulation.

- When kids throw objects at a target, they develop visual motor skills that help advance reading skills and copying notes from the board. Crumpling paper and shooting at the trash is a fun way to practice this skill and strengthen the muscles of the hand.

- Kids today are pushed to read and write at earlier ages, even before they are developmentally ready. In doing this, we can create learning issues that show up down the road. Children who make block figures or create playdough letters develop spatial skills and fine motor dexterity for writing, cutting, tying shoes, etc. When they tell stories from the pictures, they use their imagination and make inferences or assumptions that help with higher-level problem-solving.

- Tummy time might seem inappropriate for a classroom setting, but with the various sitting options showing up in schools today, it is actually pretty easy to introduce. Create a corner where kids can get a book or dry-erase board for independent work time. The extension of the neck and back (see photo) is very alerting for the nervous system so if you have a child who is sick of reading or doesn't want to work, have them lie on their tummy. The neck extension helps with focus and they are putting weight into their arms, elbows, and shoulders, which will help with foundational strength and stability for writing. *And* it is different, so it might even be fun.

- Games like patty-cake, playing cards, freeze tag, jump rope, hopscotch, Simon Says, and playing tag are oldies but goodies for a reason. They help to encourage listening, impulse control, fine and gross motor ability, and they are FUN.

# THE PRACTICAL STUFF: STRATEGIES THAT ADDRESS THE SENSORY SYSTEM IN SCHOOL

Internal signals and sensory processing must be considered when trying out strategies for regulation. Where most adults go wrong is with the assumption that they understand the problem based only on their observations or perceptions. Understanding all the different systems at play that determine behavior is important, but one of the most effective starting points when coming up with the "what now" is found in the child. Watch what they are drawn to and what they avoid, but ask them if they have any ideas. This information will provide insight into how to address a problem that has prevented a child from self-management.

## Using the Senses to Come up with Strategies or Tools

Our sensory system is designed to give us helpful information about our body and our world so we can stay safe and *regulated.* This same system is where we look first to come up with strategies. Three foundational sensory roots make a big impact on the nervous system so these are good to try initially when creating a toolbox for regulation.

1. **Proprioception**: This involves sensors in our joints and muscles that tell us where our body is and how much force we need to use, which helps us control our body movements. Proprioception is a good place to start because the child drives the activity and controls muscle use and force, which organizes the nervous system and improves regulation.
2. **Tactile:** This involves anything we touch which helps the rest of the system regulate. Being able to tolerate and soothe with touch is very important.
3. **Vestibular:** This is input from our body and the inner ear that tells us we are tipping, moving, or out of neutral. We need to be able to tolerate movement and changes in movement to make sense of where our body is in space and stay safe.

We may need to alter the intensity depending on whether we need more or fewer signals. Sometimes the same movement can be done quickly to alert the system, or very slowly to calm it. If you see that a child isn't tolerating something, help them come up with something different so their system doesn't go into protection mode. If a child is afraid of anything or avoids certain sensory activities, these preferences and fears *must* be respected. Kids avoid or respond for a reason.

The last thing to remember is that fair does not mean equal, and different isn't bad. Helping the entire class respect differences and embrace the *why* of certain strategies can help us remember that people need different things to feel good and this can completely change the emotional climate of that community. When a strategy works and behavior changes, this child will be able to find success.

Strategies for school must be simple and easy to implement. The following reviews some general ideas that will influence a child's ability to regulate.

- When a consequence is needed, try an exercise break instead of taking away recess. They still get movement but free time play is what they have lost.
- Share positive strategies for transition times. Have them put a hand on their belly so they can focus on their breath as they walk; they can count the number of times they breathe from class to class. Now they are calmer, potentially more focused, and can monitor their breathing.
- Position kids in line for transitions according to their needs. Kids that don't like unexpected touch might do better in the front or back vs. the middle of the line where kids could bump them from all sides.
- Jobs or tasks can make transitions easier. Have students count how many specific letters they can find on their walk, or count how many steps it takes to get to the library. They can deliver the important "teacher tool" to a different location in the school.
- Discuss and demonstrate that everyone has a bubble of a unique size. This can give a visual for why some kids get agitated or aggressive when people come too close.

- Seat buddies can help share notes and make focusing easier because they provide a good example and peer motivation.
- Don't demand eye contact or verbal responses. Allowing kids to feel out a situation before jumping in can prevent fight or flight.
- Calling on a student to come to the front of the room to do a demonstration in front of everyone might defeat the academic purpose you are trying to achieve. Try to prepare students for this activity if they have had difficulty in the past.

## Specific Sensory System Tools

Sensory root tools are great places to start, but awareness of each sensory system ensures that tools address potential areas of difficulty. The following tools are listed according to the involved sensory system.

**Touch (tactile system):** Tools that feed the tactile system are powerful; don't forget that touch in the mouth is also effective. What works for some kids, may not work for others and you don't want to utilize what you have observed them avoiding in everyday life. If you are dealing with a child who hates glue on their fingers, introducing a mushy strange textured clay or putty as a tool would not be appropriate. Observations about their preferences will help determine where to start. Do they put things in their mouth? What do they touch a lot? Do they fiddle with buttons or twirl their hair? Do they fidget during study time or while listening? Do they avoid light touch from others or react negatively when someone is too close or touches them accidentally? Do they avoid certain activities (such as art) on a consistent basis?

For kids who show that they are seeking touch:

- Provide items or fidgets to use during transitions or listening time. Ensure that all fidgets or tools designed to *improve* regulation are used as tools, *not toys*. These items can even incorporate heavy work such as hand strengtheners, resistive clay, or balls.

- Add texture or things to touch when they are reading or thinking. Put Velcro under the desk in small pieces that can be spread randomly for them to find with their fingers.
- Go outside for a few minutes when the weather is cold.
- Provide different textures that can be held in the lap like fleece, fur, or slime. Sitting in a large, textured bean bag or on a textured carpet square also provides sensory sitting options.
- Don't forget the power of the tactile system in the mouth; supply things to suck on like a water bottle or hard candy. Have them chew things like gum or a chewy snack like a bagel.
- Have a sensory box that students can access as long as it helps them focus and engage in learning without distracting others.
- Provide some time to discuss which tools worked for which dragons so kids can share the expertise they have figured out about taming their dragon. When kids feel they are the expert and have something to share with others, it increases the buy-in and pride which means this process will likely continue.

For kids who don't like unexpected touch or show avoidance of textures or touch:

- Allow a child who avoids touch to stand at the end of the line. Certain wiring or stressful situations impact "bubble size" or the space required between them and others; the end of the line provides some control over how close others come to them.
- Provide preferential seating near the teacher or the back of the room.
- Allow a child to stand in the back or sit on a chair instead of on the floor close to peers during circle time. Remember the goal of your activity; if the goal is learning, does it matter *where* or *if* they sit?
- When kids have difficulty tolerating sitting close to others, place an empty desk next to them to create a barrier or "bubble".
- Identify a child's workspace or personal area with tape or some sort of barrier.

**Hearing:** Auditory input can have both positive and negative results. It can be a distraction that creates way too much input resulting in overstimulation or sensitivities to noise or talking. Loud or irritating noises such as flushing toilets, buzzing lights, or the school bell might send danger signals that put the system into protection mode. On the other hand, noise can also wake up sleepy dragons or provide more input to a child who needs to hit a high threshold.

- Classical music with an even, slow beat can help organize and calm those fire dragons.
- Electronic music created from a computer, or hard rock with an uneven beat and loud bass works for the sleepy dragons who can't focus.
- White noise or noisemakers can drown out distractions.
- Hoodie sweatshirts buffer input. I must mention this again because kids love those hoods.
- Noise-canceling headphones and earplugs dampen sound. They sell inexpensive, noise-canceling headphones that work even if you don't want to play music, but having the option for either is nice for most kids.

- Create a quiet space in the classroom where kids can reset or use some calming tools with less noise.
- Provide visuals that might help avoid loud repeated instructions.

**Taste or Oral Input:** Taste can alter our mood and provide oral input that helps to regulate. Babies come into the world using the power of oral input for soothing, calming, and even alerting, so oral input by itself can provide appropriate stimulation that affects regulation.

- Alerting flavors can be sour (pickles or vinegar), spicy, minty, or citrus.

- Oral input that provides proprioception can be crunchy food such as popcorn, pretzels, or apples, and chewy foods like gum or bagels. Heavy work in the mouth can be accomplished using a straw for applesauce, yogurt, or other thick food because it provides powerful suction. This is good for any issue because making muscles work is organizing and regulating for sleepy *or* fire dragons.

**Smell:** While we often forget the power of smell, it is one of the most effective ways to passively alter the environment; it is also important to be aware of the smells in an environment as this can prevent regulation. Essential oils completely transform how a space feels.

- Calming smells include lavender, valerian, jasmine, or vanilla.
- Alerting smells include lemon or citrus, peppermint, rosemary, or eucalyptus.

**Vision:** This tool can be easily addressed through changes to the environment. What kids look at affects how the signals communicate with the brain. Observe if they prefer to look at bright lights, colorful pictures, or bare walls. Pay attention to what they seem to gravitate toward or avoid, and notice their response. Are they over-stimulated with too much visual input? Do they seek empty corners or wear a hoodie sweatshirt all the time? ***

- To increase signals, provide a bright light or varied colors and visual detail, or highlight with colorful pens so they notice different details within the text.
- To decrease signals, use dim lights, filter the light with colored overlays/covers or place a magnetic fabric cover on the fluorescent lights in one corner of the room.
- Use sunglasses or provide an environment with limited visual input. Kids might subtly create this environment by using long hair to

cover their faces or eyes. Hoodies create a safe space that buffers much of the overwhelming input, and the fabric dampens noise and prevents peripheral vision. Sometimes what a child chooses to wear or use will tell you a lot about what they need or *don't* need.

- Cover a portion of the page they're working on to prevent them from being overwhelmed. Chunking is also a great way to help kids break up the material into manageable pieces. Have them only do the part that is showing, then take a break or provide a reward. The content can get longer and longer, but it helps them simply *begin* when the visual demand is decreased.
- Make a clear and clean workspace. Study carrels work as great workspaces and are easily portable.

***Before demanding that a student remove their hood, see if there might be a reason behind the hood. Maybe there are times they can use it, and other times they can take it off. If they can listen and learn when the hood is on, does it matter? What is the goal? If it promotes learning or participation, maybe that hood is sheer brilliance and one of the tools this child has figured out that helps decrease signals.

**Movement/Vestibular:** This is one of those root senses, but there are specific activities that serve to calm and others that energize. Again, pay attention to a child's preferences. Do they crave movement like bouncing or crashing into objects? Do they avoid movement or fear high places or times when their feet leave the ground like swinging? Next, look at *when* their system needs different input. For instance, do they need input in the morning versus the afternoon, after math class, or right before a transition?

- To increase input, try things such as jumping up to touch the door frame, playing sports, running, somersaults, or sitting on a large therapy ball or dynamic cushion.
- To decrease input, focus more on slow, forward and backward movements that don't tip the head and over-activate the vestibular organs. This can include swinging slowly, and rocking in a linear forward and backward direction, like in a rocking chair.

- Dynamic sitting options increase input and include:

  - Use of a standing desk: Bed risers or PVC pipe can make desks tall enough to stand for work. Commercial standing desks are wonderful but expensive, so this is an excellent way to see if they will work in your setting before the financial commitment. Standing in the back and using a bookcase to write on also creates a quick, makeshift standing desk.
  - Floor desk: Lower legs can be removed from tables and desks to create a floor desk that allows kids to sit on the floor to write or work.
  - Stomach time increases neck and back extension for writing or reading.
  - Sitting on a wobble stool, a large yoga ball or wobble cushion provides subtle movement, and the cushion can also be used for floor time.
  - Rocking chairs on the floor provide back support and dynamic movement for quiet sitting time.
  - Allow the child to stand in the back or arrange seating away from distractions.

---

As a new therapist, I decided to help a dysregulated child by utilizing a movement strategy. I observed him always seeking movement so I thought a few laps out on the track would help him regulate. This was not the case! He returned to class less regulated than when we started.

When strategies don't work for some kids it is often because their nervous system won't turn off or adjust. Running put him past his threshold and he had no way to adjust. He needed help. I shifted gears and introduced heavy work strategies like pushups, carrying heavy equipment to the office, and finally, sitting with a weighted blanket to breathe. Now he was better.

If something doesn't work the first time, try something different. Don't keep pushing with something that isn't effective.

---

**Heavy Work/Proprioception:** This is probably the safest tool because these activities and strategies can alert *and* calm. When you increase the intensity and difficulty of an activity, it is alerting and sends more signals. When you focus on slower, heavier tasks, it is calming and quiets down the signals. Anything that involves working the muscles is organizing for the nervous system.

- Let them rearrange or push furniture around the room such as a chair with books for weight. They can also push on the wall to make it straighter like a wall push-up.
- Try heavy work such as erasing the board, stacking chairs, carrying lunch bags, or running errands for the teacher.
- Quiet desk time can be addressed by wrapping a TheraBand, or resistive tubing, around the legs of the desk or chair so they can push, pull, or bounce their feet as they work.

- Utilize the muscles in the mouth by providing gum, chewy snacks, or things to suck on like candies or water bottles with straws.
- Weighted lap pads are versatile options because kids can put them on their shoulders or lap, but they can also carry them down the hall, lifting them up and down to work their muscles.
- Have kids carry their backpacks with their arms instead of over their shoulders to stimulate different muscle groups and increase the amount of active exercise they get during transitions.

<u>Sensory Diet.</u> This is a term coined by Patricia Wilbarger and it refers to any kind of movement or input that can be integrated into the daily routine or schedule. Much like how we incorporate food into our daily schedule, movement-based strategies before and between activities improve

regulation and result in focused attention. You can help kids come up with any kind of movement as long as you are mindful of a few things.

1.  Make sure it is easy to implement into their day. Tools used during academic tasks might need to be subtler so they don't distract the class (such as with a chair push-up).
2.  Be aware of how a child responds. You may need a slower, heavier activity if they have trouble calming down to work.
3.  You can prep their system with heavy, hard work in the morning, and it can stay in their nervous system and improve regulation for several hours afterward. This can start their day with more success and increase their feeling of competency and independence.

\*\*see p. 277 for specific activities that can be printed and used as a tool within the sensory diet

# 7. EXECUTIVE FUNCTIONING SKILLS

Executive functions are brain-based, developmental skills that we use to manage behavior, attention, self-control, flexible thinking, and working memory. Executive skills coordinate and manage cognitive and motor functions; a child's ability to successfully "execute" depends on the maturity of these skills. If one or more of these skills are weak or underdeveloped, the execution or response will be slow or non-existent. The role these skills play in the overall assessment of behavior can affect our perspective of why behavior is occurring, which helps determine the type of intervention needed. Executive functioning is the foundation for navigating the demands of childhood, and eventually the complexities of adulthood.

Executive skills are developmental in nature so they mature in time, with practice, and exposure. Skill development is most rapid between the ages of 3 and 5. Experiences during this time are critical for skill attainment, but overall full maturity can be around the age of 25 (Arain et al. 2013). ALL children need to develop these skills for tasks like planning, goal setting and problem-solving, but some struggle more than others. Every child has a developmental timeline that determines performance; kids with attentional deficits can be up to 3 years delayed (additudemag.com). This developmental timeline can be an explanation as to why some kids don't ever seem to meet our expectations or find success.

Like anything we hope to perfect, executive skills get better with experience, so practice is a large determining factor in the realization of successful execution. Think about how a child learns to walk. They stand at the table forever. Maybe smiling, maybe fussing, but standing and standing. Maybe they rock side to side, perhaps they let go for a moment. We encourage, anticipate, and cheer on the process of walking. We would never expect a toddler to walk without first watching, standing, getting stronger, and eventually practicing.

Each time we are exposed to something new that we actively participate in and practice, more skills develop. This can be an explanation for adults with full brain maturation who lack various executive skills. There are disorganized adults who never seem to arrive on time, meet deadlines, or utilize effective organizational strategies, so developmental maturation doesn't entirely guarantee skill attainment.

Skills must be regularly addressed for effective utilization, and motivation is critical for this. Motivation supports the various experiences we seek out; motivation for practice comes in different ways that impact executive functioning. Dopamine is a neurotransmitter that motivates us; it helps determine what is "worth" doing. We have receptors in our brain that respond to dopamine and when there isn't enough, which is common with ADHD and during the teen years, it is hard to get through non-preferred tasks. When kids can play videos for hours but can't focus longer than 10 minutes at school, motivation and dopamine are involved. Play is motivating, work is not; execution requires motivation. Execution improves with active play because the act of doing is what creates endorphins and dopamine that support sustained engagement. But we can't always incorporate movement and play into academics. Since we can't prescribe medication at school to help with a potential chemical imbalance, another way to increase dopamine levels is through chunking work and providing rewards. If there is a relatively immediate reason to do something, chances are it will get done and this can serve as a great substitute until brain chemicals can take over.

Planning and the ability to adjust are just some of the critical skills that affect execution. As kids develop, and through play, they learn to adjust, which influences their performance for the next time they try something. Technology has presented options for play that unfortunately do not always translate into effective planning in the "real world". Active, sustained engagement is so critical; when things go wrong and an adult steps in to adjust the plan, the skill of planning, as well as the resultant execution, might not have a chance to develop. Like walking, if a child is always carried and never actually *walks* on their own, they won't figure it out on their own. Kids who don't practice or plan won't be good at executing or adjusting to change.

Socially, executive skills are critical because they allow us to calm inappropriate behaviors, read the room and our friends, and begin to understand a situation of non-verbal communication. If a child runs into a quiet classroom from a loud, busy recess and doesn't adjust their activity level, they will likely get into trouble. If a child is working with a peer and they don't know how to read non-verbal communication, they might not realize that their friend doesn't like having people in their bubble, or that they can't handle loud voices. When weak executive skills impair social skills, it can significantly alter a classroom's social-emotional climate, preventing learning and creating aversive reactions within the learning environment.

A lack of executive functioning can make poor behavior appear intentional; what if these behavioral challenges were actually developmental delays? If kids had the skills to do what was requested, don't you think they would? Developmental delays create dysfunction because the timeline and resultant performance are different than expected. Lagging executive skills can negatively impact self-esteem and eventually motivation. "Playing school" means a child can arrive on time, have the materials they need to learn and participate, and they can read the room or people in the room so they can behave in a way that is appropriate for the situation. Sometimes it is easy to walk into a classroom and quickly see who can "play school" and those who clearly cannot. It isn't as easy to see a child's intelligence and potential. If a child struggles and acts out, we might assume they don't *want* to be compliant. Maybe they don't have the intelligence. Maybe they are *lazy*. In the book, Lost at School, Ross W. Greene says, "Kids do well *if they can*." This is very different from the assumption, "Kids do well if they *want* to." He compares these two mindsets to demonstrate that our perspective will change how we see behavior and how we then *handle* behavior. Wouldn't all kids behave if they actually *could*?

Sometimes it is the adult who, through inappropriate expectations, sets a child up to fail. If executive functioning is related to skill *development,* that means every brain has a unique timeline of maturation and this determines success. The temporal-spatial window of development represents the time and space needed for execution once a plan is made; most plans are made in a different time and space from when and where the execution occurs. This window gets bigger with every year of life and with various experiences. Expectations come from adult assumptions of maturity and ability; a sixth-grade student should arrive to class, on time and with the required items for learning. This is because a typical child of this age *should* be able to make a plan on the way to school, arrive at their locker, get the necessary items and get to class on time. Their temporal-spatial window is certainly large enough for this sequence of events to occur and this drives the expectation. But if this ADHD student is three years developmentally delayed, there is likely *no* plan, which means there is no functional execution. A miscalculated temporal-spatial window means there is no way this student can reach the demands without help. When kids don't meet our expectations, is it because they don't want to or because sometimes they simply can't?

School discipline programs that do not address the *actual problem* but continue using the same repeated consequences with no effect on behavior cause more stress, our kids learn less, and teachers are exhausted emotionally. But why doesn't this discipline work? Are the consequences not enough to modify their behavior? Are there things we have missed in this behavior puzzle, and is this why consequences make no impression on the child? When we begin to see that a child would, if they could, suddenly the problem takes on new meaning. Educators and parents have an innate desire to help children be happy and embrace learning, yet the knowledge and tools are not always readily available. Our approach to behavior is only as good as the assumption of the problem, and for this, we must change our perspective. If we can shift our approach to include basic executive functioning deficits, suddenly we have a problem to solve instead of a "lazy" or "disrespectful" student to control.

Behavioral regulation is often related to the complex skill of "playing school." (see p. 179) IEPs and 504 plans can help level the playing field for kids with disabilities but the skill of "playing school" really applies to *all* kids. This skill will later translate to "playing work" and "playing life" so we need to prepare these kids, *all kids*, for the real world. Helping them understand why they are struggling is the first step. Successfully reaching expectations requires the basics of identifying if the skills are sufficient for the task. The finished product will look very different if one piece is missing or not fully developed. Simply put, if we ask for more than the child has regarding skills, there will be poor execution because if they could, they would.

- Try to consider the executive skills required in what you are demanding. Is it possible that a skill weakness is contributing to their response? Often a simple request involves *several* skills. If even one is underdeveloped, there is a huge potential for mishap.
- Maybe they are still processing the request. It can take 3-5 seconds to process oral instruction, especially if they are multi-stepped.
- Maybe they don't know how to start or have missed some of the steps in the instructions.
- Is there a motivator in place to supplement a dopamine deficiency?
- Is the temporal-spatial window smaller than you expected? If the developmental timeline is slower than peers, their ability may be miles from our expectations. No plan means flawed execution.

> If kids struggle with flexibility and adaptability, they can't adjust when the situation changes, so they may melt down. If they lack frustration tolerance, even little things are hard to move past or overcome. If they have weak problem-solving skills, they can't come up with an alternative to a boring situation, so instead misbehavior serves as a perfect distraction.

You may have a student who simply *cannot* behave at school, or one who can fake it for a while, but struggles when the academic world gets harder or the social piece gets more complicated. The assumption that this child is misbehaving or avoiding work by choice leaves no options for support. The level to which school and home are affected depends on a child's wiring and the gap between the demands and skills; the bigger the gap, the harder it is. Interactive learning and group work create demands that require considerable regulation and skill. Group assignments will be painful if a child struggles to read the room, focus on a goal, start a task, or take turns. It is important to know how to work with others, but for some kids, it can help to start with easier content or provide some cues to help them while they are trying to gracefully navigate the social complexities of group activities.

There are many different brain-based explanations that can change the way we engage with kids who never seem to respond to behavioral consequences. Before labeling behavior, determine what is required for the situation and whether this student has those skills. The following list provides some school-based skills that can be impacted by weak executive functioning.

### *Executive Functioning Skills* (adapted from Dawson et al. 2009)

- Response Inhibition: Do they start before instructions are given or act without all the facts? They might interrupt conversations and have trouble with behavior regulation.

- Working Memory: Can they manage and work with facts and details? If math facts are required to complete math homework, this might be why they cannot start.

- Flexibility: Does the unknown throw them? Can they shift between activities? Difficulty with flexibility when the schedule or activity changes can result in a fight, flight, or freeze response.

- Task Initiation: Can they start a task or return to work after a break? Starting a task that is not preferred (video games are very different from math) can look like they are choosing defiance.

- Emotional Control: Is performance affected by emotions? Can they control behavior or adjust behavior when things are not perfect?

- Sustained Attention: Can they focus on non-preferred activities long enough to complete them? A lack of focus will prevent follow-through with tasks like classwork.

- Planning and Prioritization: Can they plan their day and prioritize accordingly? Do they have the materials they need for class? This can also affect their test results because they might not know what to focus on when studying.

- Time Management: Do they procrastinate? Are they late? Can they estimate how long it takes to finish all the important tasks on time?

- Organization: How does their desk or binder look? Disorganized writing, messy work, and very few words on the page are common issues when kids struggle with organization.

- Metacognition: Can they evaluate their performance? Do they review work after it is completed? Are they accurate in their self-evaluation and does this impact their ability to learn from experience? Do they make the same mistakes repeatedly?

- Goal-directed Persistence: Can they follow through on longer, non-preferred tasks?

- Stress Tolerance: Do they crumble with pressure? Is change and unpredictability difficult?

"Frequent fliers" in detention can easily convince everyone that they don't care. Realizing that the consequence of detention has done nothing to change behavior might allow for more of a conversation with this child.

I met such a student who was rude to his teacher in algebra, and refused to do any work. Sitting in detention, again, he slowly revealed that his mom was in jail and his dad was just gone. He didn't know where he was sleeping, when his next meal was, or what tomorrow looked like.

Sometimes it can be hard to remember that some of these kids are simply surviving. Algebra wasn't important in this moment because finding a place to sleep was more urgent. The panic and frustration this child was feeling had resulted in poor behavior, homework not being done, and no work completion.

But no one knew this. Everyone assumed he just didn't care.

When we look at this child who truly can't find success, it is difficult to help if we don't figure out the *real* problem… in *their* world. Maybe it is something at school, or an issue with the kid sitting next to them. Perhaps they don't even realize there is a problem until it is too late. We must remember to involve the child in the process of problem-solving behavior. We might miss seeing the big picture when we don't hear their side or perspective. As adults, it is hard not to tell kids what is going wrong from *our* perspective and it is even harder to not tell them what to do. What we need is *their* perspective. We can make observations or guesses, but reminding a child that they are the expert here can be empowering and motivating. We can't care more than they do about *their* problem, and we certainly can't assume we understand more about it than they do. But perspective is something that isn't always accurate, and that is why they still need you. They need to process and often adjust, and your insight is critical to helping them see all the pieces of the puzzle to realize an accurate perception. We can guide them, even share with them, but theirs is the only perspective that will forever guide them.

Educators and lawmakers talk about our educational system and how we can keep up with the rest of the world from an educational standpoint. Children today are being challenged more than ever before and teachers are pushed to teach to the standardized tests. The "fun" is hard to create when legislation drives the curriculum to advance faster than kids' brains can manage, preventing our best teachers from using their magic to create engaging and generalizable academic lessons. Faster is not better and some kids simply can't keep up so this will influence the execution, and behavior, we see in the classroom.

Sometimes we simply need to lend our frontal lobe to a student because their skills aren't mature and nothing will change this *right now* so this may be why they aren't actively participating. There are other times when these kids don't need our entire frontal lobe but providing accommodations or modifications can be helpful. Kids on IEPs or 504s have these built into their individualized plans, but there are also ways you can adjust the expectations and demands while still teaching and addressing learning targets. Some kids miss instruction because they can't write fast enough, or they can't write and listen simultaneously. When we can simplify or adjust the challenging pieces and allow for less to *do* in the moment of a struggle, they will still benefit from the content but won't be limited due to lagging executive skills. It is a dance, helping enough but not too much, but in the end, if they aren't able to engage or participate there will be no execution or learning.

# THE PRACTICAL STUFF:
## STRATEGIES FOR EXECUTIVE FUNCTIONING

There are three main ways to address lagging executive functioning skills in addition to simply waiting for father time or loaning them our frontal lobe.

- The <u>environment</u> is a huge factor in the creation of strategies. It can be used to add, adjust, or decrease the input in the learning environment which influences regulation and a child's ability to access their executive skills. Cues that affect attention and memory can be built into the environment for increased independence and success. Sensory features in the environment can be adjusted that directly influence the signals required for regulation and skill use. Even the most engaging teachers with incredible content can utilize the benefits inherent to the environment to increase the learning and participation of students.
- Adjusting the <u>task</u> helps skills evolve and creates motivation by creating task-related strategies that present a just right challenge. Accommodations or modifications help to narrow the gap between demands and skills so success can be found.
- Tools and techniques directly affecting <u>skill development</u> can be taught or coached.

> The feeling of success and purposeful engagement releases hormones that feel good and this is exactly what kids need when they are struggling. Suddenly they have momentum which results in independence and helps to create a positive experience that might mean they don't need the help next time.

# THE ENVIRONMENT

No matter which skill is underdeveloped, there are many ways we can address the learning environment to support skill performance and combat signal issues that negatively affect regulation. Creating an environment with active, fun activities and modifying the sensory and organizational features can positively alter the influence the environment has on skill use, learning, and behavioral regulation. Playing video games or watching YouTube videos doesn't force kids to come up with ideas, make a plan, or provide input that the brain needs to fully develop, but it is FUN and this is why kids keep doing it. We know that motivation is key for participation so figuring out different, fun ways to learn the same thing can be all you need to change behavior.

## **Incorporate Play And Fun Into The Environment**

- Form letters with clay, wiki sticks, or write them in shaving cream so that more areas of the brain are used as compared to paper/pencil or typing.
- Encourage individuality by coloring outside the lines or producing a unique project to increase the creativity necessary to complete this and future projects.
- Role play scenarios and interactive social-emotional lessons that model behavior.
- Present strategies to support the kids who might not get a lot of successful social engagement due to anxiety or the fight, flight, or freeze mechanism. This can include discussing how kids in class manage their stress or "tame their dragon."
- Encourage kids to teach or demonstrate skills; learning retention increases, and so does the fun factor when actively engaging in their content.
- Incorporate movement activities with the entire class every 5-7 minutes to restore the glucose depleted in the brain and to improve sensory processing so skills can further develop; this also allows kids with slower processing to catch up.

o Play charades for vocabulary so kids have to read the body language or facial expressions of peers when coming up with a correct answer.

o Pair kids up and have them stand back to back while a problem is presented. They answer the question by holding up one finger or two to represent their answer and then quickly turn around to see if their partner got the same answer. This incorporates a movement-based strategy while "quizzing" them on the content you just went over.

o Have kids stand by their desks and quiz them on the content you just covered; make the questions true or false and they respond by jumping to the right (for true) or the left (for false). You will get a lot of laughter, smiles, flushed faces, and even content mastery.

o Chunk your delivery of content with 10-second movement breaks where a student is chosen to decide the activity for the class. Provide a list of visual options for those kids who struggle to think when they are called on (see a printable option on p. 279).

o Have them take a deep breath after moving and before resuming work. Encourage your more active students to do a deep squat while breathing because this muscle engagement will help them better adjust between movement and being still.

## Modify The Environment

Environmental modifications and adjusting the sensory features in a space can make a big difference for a child who struggles with regulation or an imbalanced threshold; it also affects skill performance. We know that signals must work or the skills won't be recruited. This list is redundant with sensory processing strategies but this reiteration presents tools that impact skills and signals. Some kids may need more input, others less, and this can be tricky to incorporate into one learning space. See if it is realistic to separate portions of the room to meet differing needs so you can do more teaching and less behavior management.

- Reduce noise distraction with headphones, white noise or music that is soothing or helpful.
- Create a clean workspace with less *visual* stimulation. Use a study carrel and eliminate clutter on the wall in areas for kids who need less input.
- Have a sensory corner with tools (not toys) that can be accessed during active listening periods. These usually involve fidget tools, resistive balls, elastic exercise bands, hand strengtheners, etc.
- Adjust lighting with fluorescent light covers or the addition of soft white, ambient lighting.
- Create a calming corner using soft, plush rugs to dampen sound, gaming chairs low to the ground that rock, and weighted items for times when a child needs to calm down.
- Utilize the senses. Oil diffusers add smell, movement and heavy work add proprioception, and fidget tools or anything oral provides touch input.
- Tape number/letter strips to the desk for quick reference.
- Use tape, carpet squares, or a hula hoop to make a visual boundary in seated learning areas.
- Have headphones with microphones or space for kids to dictate their ideas with technology versus writing. Kids can get really good at editing this material, and now all their amazing thoughts can make it to the page without forgetting what they were trying to write.
- Create preferential seating locations for kids sensitive to unexpected touch or who get easily distracted (usually near the teacher or in the back of the class).
- Provide options for different seating alternatives such as wobble stools, balls, standing space and "stomach space" where it is appropriate to lie on their stomach to listen, read, or even write. The opportunity to work at a vertical surface provides both heavy work into muscles and a large kinesthetic experience as they write on the board in large font. Give kids more control over how they use a space so their regulation needs can be met. When kids get what they need it increases motivation for focused attention and work production.

- Have an area of class with various tools such as graph paper, large-diameter pencils, larger or smaller lined paper (college ruled, etc.), post-it notes, different colored highlighters, and other items that can supplement content mastery.
- Use a whiteboard for a writing surface with easy erasing.

## Organize The Environment

Organizational strategies help create a routine and simplify an external space to increase focused attention or strengthen lagging skills.

- See-through bins/colored folders make remembering easier because they are highly visible.
- Create a TO DO/DONE folder with only *one* place to put items. One side of the folder is for items that need to go home *to do*, and the other is for items that need to be returned to school that are *done*. Items that need to be kept for later reference do not stay in this folder but can go in the TO DO side for later filing in class binders. This folder should be pulled out in every class (see www.secrettohappy.com for example).
- Accordion-type organizers allow kids to *stuff* their items in a specific slot instead of their huge backpacks. Each space is for a different subject, and kids who frequently don't bother to punch holes and open a binder can quickly put things away and still maintain a loose sense of organization.
- Hang up a schedule that shows the chunks of time and ensure the breaks and fun stuff are scheduled too! Even when kids know their schedule, this can be a point of reference to look at for improved motivation and focus. After math class, the motivator is right there, but if they lose focus and work isn't done, that free time disappears. This can help to reinforce the importance of focused attention.
- Write on sticky notes or make simple lists on the board that provide visual reinforcement or reminders for specific steps, activities, or chunks of time during their day. Schedules, checklists, or anything

that allows items to be crossed off are great ways for kids to *feel* productive and stay on task.

- Put class materials in one place of the room so that if they forget an item, they can independently get what they need instead of always asking for help.
- Create a consistent cleanup routine that helps prepare kids for transitions.
- Take a picture of the classroom or a student's space when it is clean and how you expect it to be after work. Show this image to the student or class and say, "Make your space look like this" instead of, "clean up". This way, your expectation is easily understood and everyone knows what "clean" looks like.
- Teach kids how to design an organized space with all the materials needed to complete the task at hand. This also helps them begin to plan ahead, and picture themselves *doing* the work and it prevents distractions because all the things they need are within arm's reach.

# THE TASK

Adjusting how a task is done or what is expected can be a huge relief for kids who never feel successful. We want to make sure we don't do too much, but there will be times when we simply need to adjust things. Utilizing accommodations or modifications can help us create a just right challenge designed to help kids start; initiation is hard to achieve when kids are consumed with challenges they know are too complicated. These changes and support provide critical scaffolding for skill development.

> Enabling (which is often a concern with scaffolding) is doing something for someone else without a plan for them to do it themselves. Be sure you know what this plan is so you can support their skill development without the learned helplessness that might accompany the help. Similar to the construction of big buildings, the upper floors would be impossible to solidly construct without external foundational support. This scaffold won't be up forever because it hides the beautiful building, but without it, the building would be impossible to complete. Skill building is the same. Once kids begin to find success, we can pull away some of that scaffolding, adjust our expectations and push a little harder.

- Make tasks shorter through chunking, and build in frequent breaks without the expectation that they must sit and work until the whole activity is complete.
- Allow extra time to complete something and try using a timer to track progress or demonstrate lost focus.
- Have the child repeat the instructions to you or their neighbor to ensure understanding and provide a more stimulating delivery of information.
- Create opportunities for kids to track their time to pace work which also helps them start work and plan what is next. Their planning skills improve when they can see the steps of the day or that task. When they time themselves to complete four problems, they have just increased their focused attention. Turn this into fun by having competitions to see if each student can finish more

problems than they did previously (don't have kids compete with each other because each individual has many different needs or abilities that may be out of their control and we are trying to help them find success).

- Let them dictate their answer for an easy way to start the writing process. Sometimes just getting them started by eliminating the writing process is enough to increase momentum for this activity. Dictation is a tool that is easily accessible with today's technology in our school system and dictating to you or into a device might actually improve the learning process.

- Provide cues for task initiation to signal that it is time to start. Use a bell or noise that is out of the ordinary, or one of the many focusing apps to help them self-monitor and determine how long their focused attention can last. The "Forest" app is one option that plants trees that grow with focused time. The tree will die if you leave the app before the time you designate, but the forest will grow huge and lush with additional focused time. This can be a fun, full-class visual to help kids develop work patterns.

- Use mistakes as data that shows where more practice is needed. Some of the best learning happens when kids dare to try without being concerned about their grades or making mistakes.

- Cover most of the page and only show the line(s) they should finish. This can help them start and continue until the last problem. You can also highlight the chunk they need to do.

- Supplement skill deficits with other methods of written expression or problem-solving through tools or technology, such as a calculator for math or creating a Google slide presentation versus writing a paragraph.

- Set alarms or reminders that utilize technology. Smartphone technology has made life a lot easier for people who don't get internal signals. Have kids show you how to set up alarms; they will have buy-in and will be excited to demonstrate a proficient skill especially if you aren't good at all the technology stuff.

- Provide motivators or rewards for work completed.

- Make a deal with the struggling student and only give a grade for what they complete.

- Avoid busy work! There will be times when busy work makes an hour of homework take an entire evening. Busy work is important for some kids who need repetition for mastery, but if a child shows mastery quickly, consider having them demonstrate a few problems and let them be done.
- When rewards or motivators are used and task performance remains poor, look at using different tools. Online forced-choice inventories help a child to better see what type of reward is motivating.

Some kids need to just listen during lectures and it is interesting to see how much more content some students absorb when the paper notes are provided and they can highlight or add to them during lecture. Listening, absorbing, and writing can be too much for some kids so when they can listen without the motor demand of writing everything that is said, the stress level goes down and the brain works more efficiently. If they don't have to stress over getting all the details on the page, they might digest more. These notes you provide are also legible compared to the chicken scratch they might find on their page, so this is another perk when they are trying to study for their test.

# THE SKILLS

### Coaching and Teaching Skills

Coaching is one of the greatest ways to support executive functioning; skill development improves through repeated exposure, teaching, and practice similar to how we coach athletics. The adult is the guide but the child must do the execution. You can help with the plan, goals, and accountability, but the child must *do* the actual doing. This collaborative relationship between an adult and child is also crucial to attaining social and emotional learning concepts that empower children to contribute to their community in ways that support the learning climate around them.

Coaching for executive functioning teaches kids how to improve their self-awareness to compensate for lagging executive skills.

- Realistic goals and expectations are created during coaching sessions *with* the child to address problems the child identifies. This differs from traditional meetings with students where the adult assists the child based on adult assumptions that came from observations of the child's behavior or performance.
- The child must drive the conversation and direction of goal setting or the behavior will likely not change.
- Empowerment from teaching can be very motivating and coaching sessions also allow the student to show you how they did something. Kids are talked *at* all day, so when they get to do the talking, the content usually sticks. Even a prompt like, "Show me how you got here" or "Can you help me do it your way" provides a non-threatening opportunity to figure out where they might be struggling while strengthening their communication of the process.
- Organizational strategies and tools are an essential part of supporting skill development, but remember that many of the seemingly simple things we know about organization and problem-solving are skills these kids haven't learned yet so many of them

must be taught. Never assume a child *knows* anything, even if they tell you they know, especially if they are struggling.

Coaching should consider all the factors related to discipline, expectations, processing speed, signals, and skills so a child can understand more about why they respond in a specific manner. Once the child sees that their behavior stems from something specific, it is easier to find a solution. There is an accountability piece with coaching because the adult can track the student's goals and help them adjust. This metacognition is a complex skill, but when it is realized, it creates momentum for challenging future endeavors. Unmet goals are no longer failures, they are simply a part of learning how to solve problems. When goals are met, positive acknowledgment helps with future motivation and a feeling of self-competency.

Coaching involves a quick daily check-in to review classes, homework, goals, and progress. Sometimes it can happen quickly at school if a supportive teacher, counselor, or other adult can chat with them in the last five minutes of their day. Ultimately, a coach helps the child see or create a plan. Strategies and occasional setbacks are discussed so the child can learn from the *process*. If things get negatively emotional, the tendency is to go into fight or flight and then shut down, so this process must be positive and emotionless.

Initially, prompt the child with these questions, showing them the chunk of time you are discussing:

1. What did you do in English today?
2. Do you have any homework?
3. What did you do today in Math?
4. Do you have any homework? etc.

Run through all the classes every day. They need to put themselves back in that setting to remember what was happening and if there was homework, because most kids don't effectively utilize planners. In the beginning, you can do the writing; the goal is acknowledgment of each item, not the writing. Make the beginning easy so they will talk to you and begin to understand the process. Eventually, we want them to manage their calendar or schedule on their own, but until the habits are changed, this aspect of coaching is critical. Make sure they are involved in every step of the process. Maybe you offer some ideas to start, but don't do too much or they won't feel like it is their responsibility and they won't develop their executive functioning skills.

| Monday | Tuesday | Wednesday | Thursday | Friday |
|--------|---------|-----------|----------|--------|
| Problem: | Problem: | Problem: | Problem: | Problem: |
| Goal: | Goal: | Goal: | Goal: | Goal: |
| How will I do this? | How will I do this? | How will I do this? | How will I do this? | How will I do this? |
| 1. Change environment | 1. Change environment | 1. Change environment | 1. Change environment | 1. Change environment |
| 2. Change task | 2. Change task | 2. Change task | 2. Change task | 2. Change task |
| Did I reach it? | Did I reach it? | Did I reach it? | Did I reach it? | Did I reach it? |
| What would I change? | What would I change? | What would I change? | What would I change? | What would I change? |

There are also ways you can incorporate focus-related tools into your coaching sessions. The TO DO/DONE folder is critical for this process because it further reinforces the need for this folder to be pulled out in every class. The following image shows an example of ways a child can be supported throughout their day, with each teacher and with every subject. It helps the child to get in the habit of pausing and being mindful of their awareness and the resultant plan based on their ability to focus. It is also a great way to look back at data to see if there are any trends in behavior such as less focused activity after lunch or in the afternoon; this time of the day now becomes a point of intervention. Teachers can help determine the most important missing work and reinforce the homework that should be done that night and visible in their folder. You can individualize this with parent or teacher signatures, and build in rewards for completion and use.

Weekly Plan for _____        **Please initial, circle, check box, and /or comment in the space provided**

| | Date | Date | Date | Date | Date |
|---|---|---|---|---|---|
| **Period 1** | On Task ____ Off Task<br>☐ Effective redirection<br>☐ Work completed | On Task ____ Off Task<br>☐ Effective redirection<br>☐ Work completed | On Task ____ Off Task<br>☐ Effective redirection<br>☐ Work completed | On Task ____ Off Task<br>☐ Effective redirection<br>☐ Work completed | On Task ____ Off Task<br>☐ Effective redirection<br>☐ Work completed |
| **Period 2** | On Task ____ Off Task<br>☐ Effective redirection<br>☐ Work completed | On Task ____ Off Task<br>☐ Effective redirection<br>☐ Work completed | On Task ____ Off Task<br>☐ Effective redirection<br>☐ Work completed | On Task ____ Off Task<br>☐ Effective redirection<br>☐ Work completed | On Task ____ Off Task<br>☐ Effective redirection<br>☐ Work completed |
| **Period 3** | On Task ____ Off Task<br>☐ Effective redirection<br>☐ Work completed | On Task ____ Off Task<br>☐ Effective redirection<br>☐ Work completed | On Task ____ Off Task<br>☐ Effective redirection<br>☐ Work completed | On Task ____ Off Task<br>☐ Effective redirection<br>☐ Work completed | On Task ____ Off Task<br>☐ Effective redirection<br>☐ Work completed |
| **Period 4** | On Task ____ Off Task<br>☐ Effective redirection<br>☐ Work completed | On Task ____ Off Task<br>☐ Effective redirection<br>☐ Work completed | On Task ____ Off Task<br>☐ Effective redirection<br>☐ Work completed | On Task ____ Off Task<br>☐ Effective redirection<br>☐ Work completed | On Task ____ Off Task<br>☐ Effective redirection<br>☐ Work completed |
| **Period 5** | On Task ____ Off Task<br>☐ Effective redirection<br>☐ Work completed | On Task ____ Off Task<br>☐ Effective redirection<br>☐ Work completed | On Task ____ Off Task<br>☐ Effective redirection<br>☐ Work completed | On Task ____ Off Task<br>☐ Effective redirection<br>☐ Work completed | On Task ____ Off Task<br>☐ Effective redirection<br>☐ Work completed |
| **Period 6** | On Task ____ Off Task<br>☐ Effective redirection<br>☐ Work completed | On Task ____ Off Task<br>☐ Effective redirection<br>☐ Work completed | On Task ____ Off Task<br>☐ Effective redirection<br>☐ Work completed | On Task ____ Off Task<br>☐ Effective redirection<br>☐ Work completed | On Task ____ Off Task<br>☐ Effective redirection<br>☐ Work completed |
| **Parent Signature** | | | | | |

Some suggestions that can be a part of the coaching session include:

- Electronic planners and reminder lists work well. Kids can put in chimes, reminders, and different ways of sharing information so they don't miss critical deadlines.
- Take a picture of homework on the board if it is hard to write it down quickly.
- Use the bright-colored TO DO/DONE folder. Ensure this folder goes everywhere and is pulled out during each class and coaching session. Having one consistent folder also allows them to get into the habit of using it. Some kids have pencil cases attached to these binders because they often lose their supplies. Go through this folder each day so they can file things away and you can help teach them how all of this works.
- Many kids also have computers that are required to go everywhere. Help them find a way to carry this folder with the computer so they always have a place to put those extra papers that need filing.
- Build in rewards for even the little things (especially at first). If they have a behavior chart, keep it in the TO DO/DONE

folder so they can be caught by everyone, everywhere, using it and keeping track of materials. Each coaching session can involve a plan for later, a review of today, and lots of positive attention. Ignore the things that go wrong except to briefly teach or discuss ways that prevent another of these occurrences. Try not to judge or show disappointment; these sessions are for planning and problem-solving.

- Remember that behaviors are usually rooted in skill development, not choices, so coach the behavior as if it is due to faculties that aren't quite developed. Staying positive and providing solutions instead of emotions will help these skills progress and can also help preserve your relationship with this child.

- Encourage the student to schedule some transition time into their day. This can allow additional time to process, decompress, or gear up for the next task (even if it is a mental transition because shifting is hard). It can involve movement, stretching, meditation, time with music, or any way they can recover from stress and get ready to go again. Asking the child for their ideas and contacting teachers to share the plan you come up with can be very helpful.

Coaching sessions can also involve the teaching of skills but many educators can effectively integrate strategies and alternatives into class time and instruction. There are specific issues that arise more often than others so each skill area is discussed as it relates to difficulty in class with specific techniques that support and enhance skill attainment.

## Writing Issues

*Of all the academic tasks, writing requires the most executive skills!*

Not knowing *how* to start can make a simple writing assignment an all-out battle, and each paragraph is another starting point that requires this skill. Kids' difficulty with planning, organization, and initiation will affect their ability to communicate effectively through their writing.

Think of what goes into writing.

- First, they must develop an idea, even if the subject is provided. If the topic is motivating, this step can be more straightforward, but there is a lot left to do before anyone can understand what they are trying to convey.
- Then, they need to come up with the details that must be related enough to support the topic, yet different enough to demonstrate a thorough knowledge of the subject. These different details need to be organized so that they are set apart from each other.
- Finally, they must remember all this content while the brain instructs the hand on how to form or type the many letters that will express their knowledge.

Writing is a complicated process because the various skills related to writing all reside in the frontal lobe. If this area of the brain isn't completely developed, it will throw off the entire process... even if the idea, interest, motivation, and cognition are there! When kids veer from the assigned topic and add random pieces of information, it can look like they are just trying to fill the space because there is usually a length requirement for writing assignments. They might get stuck on certain details and repeat them over and over in different ways, not because they have nothing more to say, but because they are stuck! Coming up with content may not be the problem. If they can't organize content in their head and get it on the page, the paper they write will *not* represent what they know or want to tell you.

### Use Of Pictures and Visuals

- Pictures provide a different way to organize thoughts for writing. When kids get stuck and the content they put in their organizational outline doesn't help them write, try using pictures. If a picture is drawn quickly, even one that is unrecognizable to someone else, the brain and imagination can usually come up with more content. The child who tends to copy the words straight from their outline now has a picture that represents the idea they want to talk about and it is still organized within their outline (this strategy came from Ward/Jacobsen).

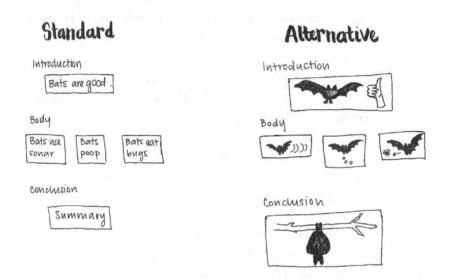

- Looking up pictures on the internet is another quick way to come up with ideas, making it easier to initiate the writing process. Have a sticky note for each section of their outline beside the computer so they can jot down ideas as they search through the pictures. Now the content from these sticky notes is more complete and can be used in a more successful writing experience. So many ideas form with images that might not happen with words, and it can be a fun way to begin the work cycle.

Pictures and visuals also help support other skills such as planning, time management, initiation, anxiety, and motivation.

- Checklists and visual schedules that show what is coming or show the steps to a task are beneficial for everyone, but kids may not know how to do this or understand why they are so useful. If the steps to skill attainment aren't easy, these kids won't try on their own. Sometimes just 4 items can feel like an insurmountable problem but when it is on paper and items can be crossed off, we tend to feel more motivated and less defeated.

- Time management and awareness of time is harder for kids to feel because everything in the world of technology is instant and immediately at our fingertips. Seeing a visual of time and the various things requiring a concept of time can help to make management of the work cycle more realistic and approachable. We can visually show kids a chunk of time to help them better manage their focused attention and energy so that the reward for work can also be achieved.

Pictures also clarify and communicate expectations. When we explain something to a child, we expect that they heard us, have a visual image like ours, and can now complete what we request. But many times they haven't heard us, or all of the instructions, and the image in their head is often quite different than ours. "Clean up around your desk" might mean to them simply pushing in their chair when really you expect that the tiny shreds of paper under their chair will make it to the trash can. Showing them a visual of what you expect and saying, "Make your space look like this" can clarify your expectation and also present a challenge with wording that is different from the "clean up" they are used to hearing.

> A third-grade student was working on an essay entitled, "My Favorite Food". This should have been easy because he LOVES food! He was trying to write ideas on the outline his teacher had provided and only managed to put down "cheeseburger". When he had to come up with the three reasons he loved cheeseburgers, he was stuck. We starting looking at pictures online of cheeseburgers and suddenly he had more ideas than paragraphs allowed. He hadn't thought of the different cheeses or the bun, and had forgotten about all the extra condiments. The pictures made him think of all this detail that could now go into his paper. He got to experience his first "A" in writing and even got to read his essay out loud to the class. His writing ability was good but it was his organization of thoughts and detailed ideas that were preventing him from showing what he could write.

## ORGANIZATION, PLANNING, AND TIME MANAGEMENT

When organization is a problem, it is seen in every aspect of a struggling student's world. You may see it in their writing, their workspace, the work cycle, and often in their behavior. Homework is usually not done or turned in and these kids can appear not to care. They can be exceptionally smart but not work to their potential because they lack the critical skills that allow for execution and work production. When organizational skills are poor there is usually a lack of planning which also affects time management. Trying to imagine the future, what the demands are, and what they will need to meet those demands involves different skill areas related to executive functioning. All of this drives the behavior behind every unsuccessful moment. Consider these scenarios and the many executive functions involved:

- A student gets to his locker but doesn't have a plan for what is next, what he will need when he gets there, and what to do now to support all this information. He will likely be late, marked tardy and probably won't have the needed materials to actively engage in class.

- A student gets to his locker, piles of stuff come tumbling to the floor and now he spends the entire passing period shoving it all back in. No way did he figure out what he needed or even find it in his "organized chaos".

- A student thinks he has enough time to run to his locker after planning the weekend with a friend, only to hear the bell ring as he works the combination.

- A student thinks she has enough time to complete an assignment, but when she realizes she forgot another activity she hadn't written down, she can't focus on this one, so she doesn't complete either assignment. Welcome to fight or flight... again.

- A student doesn't accurately monitor his time during a test so he doesn't complete it which impacts the teacher's impression of his content knowledge.

- A student who struggles to write, spends 90% of his time on the essay portion of a test only to run out of time and not answer the easy multiple-choice questions.

- A student doesn't know how to prioritize so she studies the wrong material.
- A student is reading content to add to a paper but can't pick out the important details so just writes the bare minimum.

All of these scenarios will affect our perception of work behavior. Are they lazy? Did they not listen? Do they not care about school? They are late to class again without any materials. If there are too many signals, this kid can't problem-solve through any of these scenarios to find success. If there are no signals, this kid doesn't even see that there is a problem. If the skills aren't developed for the demands of the situation, the signals become irrelevant. No appropriate response is made, and this child has failed... again. We need to strengthen the planning and time management process so that the execution can occur effectively.

## TEACH TIME and TIME MANAGEMENT

If we don't have a concept of time, it's hard to plan or execute. Today is tricky because technology has allowed us the convenience of instant everything. We don't have to watch ads on television because everything is recorded, we get instant messaging, and we can look anything up at any time with an almost immediate response. Play today is different too, so these skills aren't formed through imaginative play that requires the concept of time and waiting.

We need a concept of time for a plan to make sense. Teaching kids how time feels is yet another executive functioning skill. The concept of time is an important executive skill that can be problematic for kids to master and it also affects most academic tasks. There are many reasons time management is critical to academic success and behavioral regulation.

- Focused attention can increase, and work is better prioritized when kids know how long something will take.
- A concept of time prevents procrastination. When kids cannot visualize what time looks like, in essence, they are flying blind. Teachers are good at chunking work, but if kids do not see how these chunks fit into their schedule, they may never feel the urgency

that initiates a response. Seeing the big picture and planning where these chunks of work fit into this picture can help motivate them. When they see the fun time chunked beside the work time, they might try to push a little harder.

- Tests require a concept of time because students must gauge their pace and adjust to complete their demonstration of knowledge.

There are different ways to help kids begin to "see" time and understand how it feels.

- A calendar and some sticky notes provide great visuals for teaching time and planning; it is also a direct visual for what procrastination can look and *feel* like. This is an easy way to make a visual schedule that is flexible.

  o Go through a child's work that is due and break apart anything long enough to chunk or separate.
  o Write each step on a sticky note and have them plan with you what day they intend to work on each step; you can guide them but let them start the plan and place the notes. Each day now has notes with steps written on them.
  o When a step is completed, that note gets removed. Items that aren't completed have to be placed on a different day.

When multiple steps are neglected and the notes are pushed further down the week, suddenly the visual of what Friday looks like becomes the topic of conversation because adults know what this day will *feel* like; kids don't always have this experience or remember it from last time. Now they know why all the adults in their world keep nagging them to get things done all week long. If you can do this process with them as they plan out their week they won't miss critical deadlines and they will see how procrastination can look if they do because of the pile of sticky notes on Friday. This "what if" conversation can be enough to visually demonstrate how bad Thursday night will feel if they don't get some of those notes off the calendar.

- There is a great time tracker app called "360 Thinking" from Kristen Jacobsen and Sarah Ward, the founders of Cognitive

Connections. It gives a visual for different chunks of time to estimate how long something might take. The work cycle in their process involves the three steps of GET READY, DO, and DONE which are shown on an analog clock with color coding for each step of the work cycle: GET READY is yellow, DO is green, and DONE is red. DONE is where the motivation comes in so we can create some dopamine by talking about it first.

- Similar to the 360-thinking app, you can use an analog clock and mark on it with a dry-erase pen to show how long something should take. Estimate with students how long something will take and draw each section as a pie piece (don't forget the fun time for when they are finished). If a student's estimation of time is wrong, their fun time chunk will be affected and it is also a great opportunity to discuss how they got off track.

- The analog clock or pie concept can also be drawn on the board to show how chunks of time can be represented. Include the planning and finished stages or just show chunks of time for each of the required tasks. Even though there aren't clock arms moving through the chunks, it helps kids to see how each section of time looks compared to others. This is also a great way to introduce some dopamine because when they figure out that the "fun" time happens after the "math" time is done, it can help them initiate, focus and get work done.

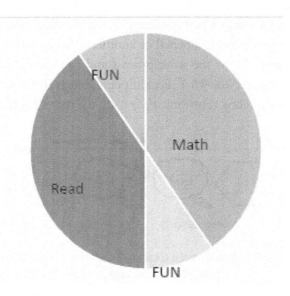

## TEACH PLANNING

The ability to see into the future and plan is not something that comes naturally, and it is often one of the last skills to develop yet one of the biggest skill deficits affecting execution. Planning will help improve processing speed, the concept of time, and always results in more effective execution.

- Imagine what "future glasses" look like with a student (another great tip from Ward/Jacobsen). Talk about what they look like doing the next activity: where are they sitting, what materials are around them, and what do they need to stay focused? All of this helps them imagine themselves in the execution state. Have them also tell you what they will be doing *after* they are done because this is the motivator that must be remembered to increase the dopamine levels in the brain.

- Discuss the work cycle and show them a visual of what the planning stages look like as compared to the actual execution stage. The end of a work cycle is discussed first during the planning stage because again, this is where motivation comes in. Presenting a picture of the completed assignment or the fun activity a child can have once finished can make starting work more manageable. Once the end of a task is discussed, the plan must include how to get ready. They must be able to plan before actually starting or they won't have the materials needed and will likely face many distractions every time they get up to get a pencil or another drink of water. When they begin to review the work process and can visualize it, planning gets better. Now what the adult envisions is the same as what the child envisions. The more they plan, the better this skill becomes.

*Fig 3. Adapted from a Concept of Cognitive Connections*
*(Sarah Ward & Kristen Jacobson)*

## SUPPORT WORKING MEMORY TO IMPROVE PLANNING

Working memory is like our brain's search engine. It allows us to hold onto and work with information temporarily so that we can use it (through the creation of a plan and then execution). Working memory is affected by anxiety, expectations, and stress; it is also often weaker in kids with ADHD. When kids understand the importance of strengthening their working memory and know there may be times they need scaffolding, it can help them better understand why they always hit the same roadblocks. There are some great tricks that can help to strengthen or at least support working memory so a plan can be created for later execution. These are things that can be included in full-class discussions (since all kids have underdeveloped brains) or during one-on-one coaching sessions.

- Say the plan out loud and encourage kids to repeat it to you or their neighbor.
- Have kids take turns listening to instructions and explaining their plan for execution.
- Help students visualize the process and the future by imagining how they will start, what it will look like and feel like, and also how they will manage difficulty. They can say out loud their plan for execution and problem-solve any pitfalls they might encounter.
- Use images and colors to help kids remember instructions or locations. Sketches, images, or colored paper/labels can help trigger memory. Put information into categories because this speeds up retrieval.
- The brain is constantly rebuilding so the more they practice certain skills, the stronger they become because repetition changes the brain. Show kids what the connections in the brain look like and help them visualize the connections increasing with each moment of focused attention. They can develop new plans or think out of the box to increase neural plasticity. This is also a great opportunity to have kids share and constructively analyze a peer's plan for execution.
- Chunking allows the brain to focus on 1 or 2 items, then move on. When they are successful, add another item for memory. This

practice will help expand their working memory for later use. Encourage them to ignore the other items until the first few are remembered. Focused attention and inhibition (stopping yourself) are both executive skills that need strengthening through practice.

- Review information after five items are taught or after a shorter amount of time. Whenever material is reviewed, the neurons fire again which helps the brain to form more synapses. Micro-learning research indicates that learning retention is optimal when content delivery is no longer than 9 minutes; this depends on age so for younger kids recommendations are every 3 minutes (Wooll 2021).
- Use visuals to support content.
- Daily mindfulness practice combats stress. Stress negatively impacts working memory. Have them focus on what they hear with their eyes shut, what their breathing feels like, or what they feel inside. This also allows kids who tend to run on high to slow down and begin learning how to focus on only one thing at the moment.
- Exercise affects the health of brain cells, improves mood, and decreases stress.
- Play fun games that involve social engagement and repetition like 3-2-1.

    o Have students write down three important ideas from the lecture.
    o Pair kids and have them choose two items from their lists.
    o Have one pair tell the class the most important item they got from the lecture.

- "Whip around" game (Goldrich 2017).

    o Tell kids how long they need to listen to content and that they will be doing something at the end of this time.
    o Have kids pair up and stand back to back after a chunk of the lecture.
    o Ask questions from the lecture and have students hold up 1, 2, or 3 fingers corresponding to an answer (i.e., true=hold up

one finger, false=hold up two fingers or have multiple choice answers for older kids that have three options).
o When they have fingers up, have them "whip around" and show their partner their answer.
o Incorrect responses are supported and discussion can follow helping to ensure all students understand the content.

# SECTION FOUR

## SPECIFIC LEARNING TYPES OR DISABILITIES

1. ADHD
2. ANXIETY
3. AUTISM OR SPECTRUM
4. TRAUMA BRAIN AND TOXIC STRESS
5. GIFTED LEARNERS
6. AUDITORY PROCESSING ISSUES
7. IRLEN SYNDROME
8. VISUAL PERCEPTUAL ISSUES
9. VISUAL SCANNING DIFFICULTY
10. SPECIFIC LEARNING DISABILITIES

    a. DYSLEXIA
    b. DYSCALCULIA
    c. DYSGRAPHIA
    d. DYSPRAXIA

11. SENSORY PROCESSING DISORDER
12. DOWN SYNDROME
13. COMMUNICATION ISSUES
14. EXTREME BEHAVIORS

    a.   Behavior or Safety Plans

# HOW ADULTS CAN SUPPORT A
# STUDENT'S IEP OR 504 PLAN

- The Gen-Ed or SPED teacher can provide a copy of a student's goals and accommodations/modifications to other adults working with a child. Everyone must know what the accommodations and modifications are when working with students on an IEP or 504 plan because these provide a safety net for success. We also want to ensure we aren't providing too much assistance and creating learned helplessness in a student.

- When paraprofessionals are taking data and documentation for IEP goals, it can be in any format and is provided by the teacher (usually the special education teacher or case manager). Make sure to always date anything you are documenting and include the time of day you are observing so that trends in behavior can be determined. When charting or taking data, keep it simple so the adult can still realistically support their student. Easy checklists with each goal, the date, time, and comments can be all that is needed with an easy 1-5 scale to circle for reporting production, behavioral responses, or independence with a task (the goal determines this and should be clearly stated on the document). If a child has an FBA (functional behavior assessment), there is usually someone from the behavior team who is supplying the data form. Data drives everything related to programming so even if it seems cumbersome, it is a critical piece of any IEP or 504 process.

- A copy of work samples or narratives summarizing work production or results are an excellent way to document progress or regression.

Accommodations and modifications are written into IEP and 504 plans to outline various adaptations the team feels are appropriate for instruction, programming, the learning environment and testing practices. They help learners actively participate, engage, and access academic programming.

- <u>Accommodations</u> are changes that affect *how* a student demonstrates learning or accesses instruction; they do not change the instructional content or level. Accommodations can be made to a student's schedule, environment, equipment, or alter how the instruction is presented.

- <u>Modifications</u> are changes that affect *what* a student is expected to learn related to academic level, content, and performance. Modifications can include decreasing the number of problems, extending the time, or allowing for alternative methods for learning or demonstration of mastery.

# ADHD

ADHD is not a problem with attention. It is a
problem with *regulating* attention.

This is one of the most important sections of the book because attentional regulation is critical for school. We know that all kids have underdeveloped executive skills and the reality is that ADHD is, by definition, a regulation issue affecting these skills. ADHD is the most studied and one of the most common neurodevelopmental disorders diagnosed in childhood and it directly impacts the brain's self-management system ("Attention-Deficit/Hyperactivity Disorder (ADHD)"). There are structural and chemical differences that prevent activation of the brain, which affects not only attention but also emotional and behavioral regulation (Brown, 2021). Recent indications suggest that approximately 10% of U.S. kids are diagnosed with ADHD. It is the second most impactful condition affecting childhood health in the U.S., up 30% from previous reports (BlueCross BlueShield, 2019). Research published in *The American Journal of Psychiatry* revealed that 90% of kids diagnosed with ADHD will have it into adulthood so tools and awareness can have a lifelong effect for individuals and families of people with ADHD (Sibley MH et al. 2021). Russell Barkley, Ph.D., and pioneer of ADHD research reported, "the heritability of ADHD averages approximately 80%", meaning individuals with ADHD have a very strong chance of having a relative with ADHD (Barkley 2011). The environmental and hereditary factors often mean that parents may struggle to support their child because they have similar skill weaknesses and this is where educators can make a big impact (Sherman, 2022).

In 1980 clinicians were diagnosing ADD and ADHD, but in 1987 the term ADHD came to describe all of these cases with the designation of three different types to help with more accurate identification (Anderson, 2023).

- Inattentive (previously ADD):

  o Difficulty organizing or finishing a task and sustaining attention
  o Trouble paying attention to details, following instructions or conversations, making careless mistakes, being easily distracted, or forgetting details of daily routines
  o Moving slowly or not caring to keep up with the pace of others
  o Procrastination, resisting, or avoiding tasks that aren't preferred
  o Losing items or not being prepared for class
  o Shy and perfectionistic (especially in girls)

- Hyperactive-Impulsive Presentation:

  o Fidgeting, talking, making noises, humming
  o Very active: running, jumping, climbing, restlessness, difficulty sitting still
  o Impulsivity, acting before thinking, interrupting, blurting, getting hurt because of the activities they keep engaging in, difficulty waiting their turn, listening to others, or waiting for instructions

- Combined: symptoms of the above two types are equally present

ADHD can mean traditional learning and academic programming often isn't effective. The behavioral implications of ADHD can make these students appear to be purposefully failing, lazy, not listening, not motivated, or not trying. ADHD manifests as a roadblock between potential and performance so teachers are often the first to notice symptoms because many academic tasks that are not preferred will be more challenging; parents may see behavioral signs related to chores or homework.

When a child isn't doing what they need to, it is often because they *can't*, not because they *won't*. If they don't have the skills, the neurotransmitters, or when task demands don't align with a child's ability, maladaptive behavior is often the result and many children don't have control over the elements required to recover and find success.

- When they are moving around the room or fidgeting and not looking at the board or teacher, does this mean they aren't listening? The reality is that they are probably getting more of the content because this movement is improving their regulation and attention.
- When they don't turn in their homework, is this because they are lazy? Many students with ADHD have lagging executive functioning skills and planning is one of the big ones determining if homework is done or turned in.
- When they aren't responding, is it because they don't care? Attentional deficits mean that regulating attention is poor so maybe they missed the instructions because their brain is busy with other things which will impact processing speed and how or when they respond.
- When they are misbehaving, is it because they are defiant? When the gap between demands or expectations and skills or regulation is too big, kids often respond with maladaptive behaviors because they are either trying to distract people from knowing they don't know how to do something or responding to potential failure and the following frustration.

ADHD has typically been considered a "male disorder" because symptoms in girls tend to fly under the radar. Behaviors commonly seen in girls include perfectionism (continuing to work on a test long after everyone is done), looking out the window, or quietly drifting. Girls might be thought to be talkative or moody and often behavior issues in girls result in emotionally-based diagnoses such as anxiety, depression, or mood disorders. Boys who display hyperactivity or inattention are more likely to receive help or medical intervention because these behaviors have been identified as impacting functional performance. Girls tend to "suffer in silence," so they may be harder to identify and referrals are less likely to occur which means undertreatment and more significant issues with emotional health because there is no accurate explanation for the behavior. Girls also tend to internalize and blame themselves, while boys might be more inclined to blame the "stupid test" (Jacobson, 2023).

Despite the research findings related to gender and ADHD, all kids feel the shame, struggle, and exhaustion that come from being unable to do what is expected.

> "It is estimated that those with ADHD receive 20,000 corrective or negative messages by age 10. They view themselves as fundamentally different and flawed" (Dodson, 2022).

ADHD rarely travels alone, so while we may think ADHD is the primary contributor to behavior, many other things could be more relevant to behavioral regulation issues. According to MentalHelp.net, comorbidity with other mental health disorders ranges from 60% to 80%. Mood or anxiety disorders are present in 1 of 4 cases, including oppositional defiance (ODD), depression, anxiety, bipolar, conduct disorders, sensory integration, learning disorders, or speech and communication problems. One-third of autistic individuals and those with learning disabilities have a 20% higher chance of having ADHD. The issues can worsen with age because of the increased expectations and responsibilities.

There are actual physical and physiological differences seen in the brains of individuals diagnosed with ADHD. Structural differences include a smaller prefrontal cortex and basal ganglia; these structural differences impact focused attention and regulation (Silver, 2022). The ADHD brain has impaired activity in four different brain regions according to ADDitude:

- The <u>frontal cortex</u> controls attention and executive functions. Delays in executive functioning can impair planning, organization, metacognition, and many other skills necessary for learning and active engagement in learning.
- The <u>reticular activating system</u> has a gate that relays information within the brain; when this system is under-developed, we see problems with impulsivity, hyperactivity, and attention.
- The <u>basal ganglia</u> deficiency can cause a malfunction in communication within the brain, resulting in information that isn't effectively producing a signal for a response. This may cause attention issues, impulsivity, emotional dysregulation, and sometimes slower processing speed.
- The <u>limbic system</u> regulates our emotions, so impairment here can result in difficulty with emotional and behavioral control.

Neurotransmitter levels are also lower, directly impacting the neural network within the brain and affecting the performance of brain functions. Lower levels of norepinephrine impact dopamine, meaning persistence to complete non-preferred activities is poor. These brain and neurotransmitter differences support the need for creating a different learning approach.

Individuals with ADHD may be as much as 30% delayed in their executive functioning skills (Goldrich, Cindy, 2013). Kids with attentional deficits will likely struggle with these executive functioning skills more intensely; many try harder than neurotypical peers because of the many symptoms associated with this brain type. But all kids have underdeveloped executive skills. Some will find success and meet expectations, but we often see maladaptive behaviors in those who do not. The adult perspective, strategies, and tools utilized for individuals with ADHD are also effective for challenging childhood behavior in general because if a child *could* they *would*. Whether a child is diagnosed with ADHD or not, benefits are often seen when programming and expectations are adjusted. Executive functioning covers a broad array of skills so when any child is struggling, addressing the skills is never a bad idea.

The skills that develop within these affected brain areas will make it easier to play school and find success. It is important to understand the behavioral implications often associated with ADHD and the present executive functioning weaknesses.

1. Performance

- Difficulty with inhibition means they struggle to stop- blurting, jumping to conclusions, and seeking out distractions. This means they might miss instructions, struggle with peer or group interactions, and behavior can be disruptive.
- Organization, planning, and prioritization deficits affect writing, management of materials, knowing what to study or prioritizing tasks. This impacts when and if they show up for class, and sometimes even how they do on tests (despite their knowledge) because they didn't know what to study.
- Time management and focus affect how kids do on tests because they may struggle to monitor time and problems so they run out of time before demonstrating their knowledge. It also influences task initiation because they can't conceptualize the chunk of time needed for work completion; many kids miss out on the fun after work because they couldn't effectively manage their on-task performance.
- Working memory is the ability to hold information in the brain while working or talking. Weakness here may be the reason for the blurting or interrupting because they don't want to forget what they want to say. It can also be why thoughts don't get on the page or math is never started because they struggle with the details and facts that should be automatic. Working memory issues also impact planning because the steps required for execution are difficult to hold onto long enough for an effective response.
- Task initiation is a common skill that makes it hard to start anything perceived as boring, difficult, or unimportant.

2. Language

- They may have trouble slowing down or organizing their thoughts which affects verbal and written communication.
- Noises, involuntary verbal tics, humming, blurting, or excessive verbal processing can be distracting in a classroom full of kids. Still, for kids with ADHD, these sensory anchors feed the nervous system to improve focused attention. When socially inappropriate means are utilized to manage threshold needs, intervention should focus on replacement behaviors instead of simply telling them to "stop" or "be quiet."
- Impulsivity can mean blurting or saying inappropriate or off-topic things, making it appear like they don't understand the content or are not following instructions.

3. Social and Emotional Regulation

- Flexibility can be impaired, causing problems when switching between tasks or transitioning. Meltdowns or rigid behaviors that appear volitional or defiant can sometimes occur without warning.
- Excess frustration, trouble calming down, or difficulty regulating emotions (i.e., going from 0 to 100 in no time) can be related to weak skills.
- Self-restraint and emotional control can affect relationships with peers and classmates, especially during recess or unstructured times.
- Social skills require multiple executive skills, so delays will impair their ability to read the room or read peers' emotions or non-verbal communication. They may have trouble making or keeping friends. They may feel defensive and unsettled about working in a group because they don't know how to navigate the necessary requirements for this level of social complexity. Many times kids don't know "how" to play so while this seems like it should be automatic, many kids need to learn this skill to successfully engage with peers.

4. Motor

- Fine motor skills are almost always impaired so handwriting can be sloppy, there may be careless mistakes, and disorganized or illegible work is common. Remember that this is due to under-developed skills so they just might need the expectations adjusted and a little patience and scaffolding of skills so they can perform at their *developmental level*.
- Many bright kids with ADHD can also have terrible handwriting because their brain moves too fast for their hand, and working memory is required to hold onto the ideas long enough to get them on the page.
- Gross motor skills can be affected so this can be seen with overall coordination or safety issues on the playground. Kids who have trouble sitting still on the carpet may be struggling with postural control because of lagging developmental skills. Impulsivity means potential safety issues on playground equipment.

# THE PRACTICAL STUFF:
# ADHD

Research indicates that kids with ADHD can be up to three years developmentally delayed, so aside from the behavioral symptoms we might see related to brain and neurotransmitter differences, we may simply see that executive skills are slower to mature. This affects everything required for academic performance and social engagement so supporting a child based on the difficulties they are experiencing may involve significant "scaffolding" until these skills have matured. When nothing is working, it is often necessary to temporarily loan our frontal lobe to these kids so they can still benefit from the academic material even though they can't independently find success or meet the situational demands. There are many ways to adjust the work, demands, and expectations to create that ever-important just right challenge. When kids never seem to find success, learning becomes aversive and behavior gets worse. Strategies and tools are critical for success, but even more important for their mental health is helping these kids see that their brain (and how it works) is truly amazing, but it is different. And differences are hard when school isn't designed to meet them.

> "If someone has Attention Deficit Hyperactivity Disorder (ADHD), they have executive dysfunction. However, if someone has executive dysfunction, that doesn't mean they have ADHD."
>
> — BILLY ROBERTS, LISW-S

## Points to Consider and things you can share with your student:

(Adapted from the "HOW TO ADHD" which is a website and YouTube channel I highly recommend looking at and sharing with your students and/or families!)

- The more you put something off, the bigger it feels in your head.
- A plan is critical for execution but sometimes kids need help to create even a simple plan.
- We need to chunk things to meet attainable goals.

- Define what *done* looks like with a set time (using a visual timer) and a clear representation of the expectation or finished product.
- Respect transition or response time and acknowledge that it may need to be longer than a peer might need.
- Reflect on how things went and why. This can help to adjust the plan for next time.
- USE VISUALS to represent goals, plans, and roadblocks.
- Forgiveness, understanding, and non-judgmental relationships help these kids not to lose hope.

## ADHD brain types typically need:

1. New, ever-changing, interesting, urgent, and FUN tasks.
2. Organization, A PLAN, structure, routine, and verbal or visual cues.
3. Encouragement to embrace their creativity, sensitivity, and thoughtfulness.
4. Acknowledgement of the effort they are putting in despite how the outcome might look.

## Learning Retention Activities:
(adapted from class by Cindy Goldrich, 2013)

Chunking your teaching content can be done using fun, movement-based, interactive activities. These give those kids who need a little extra processing time an opportunity to pause while still engaging in the material. Consider some of these ideas that could easily be incorporated into your daily lessons with chunks of content that are no longer than 10 minutes long.

- Pass the Paper: Pause after instruction and have each student write their name on a piece of paper. Have them write what they thought was most important about what you just discussed or have them write an answer to a question you pose about the content you just presented. Then they pass this paper to the student on their right. Continue your lecture and when you stop, have the students write on this new paper just like before (by answering a question or writing a key concept). Then they pass this page to their right. Keep doing this until it is time to get their paper back. Give students time to look over what is on their page and review some of the comments they might not have thought of themselves.

- Whip Around: After each chunk of content, have students stand back to back with another student. Ask a question about the content you just taught with multiple choice or true/false responses that can be indicated by holding up one, two, or three fingers to correspond to their answer. Have them whip around and see if their partner had a similar response. If not, discuss.

- Toss the Ball: Tell students you will be asking questions about the content in _____minutes (insert what you believe is appropriate, but less than 10 minutes). When you stop, have a large, beach ball or balloon that you toss to a student. That student can answer or toss to a friend for an answer. This gives an "out" for the kids who can't think on their feet but also increases the movement, spontaneity, and focus for applying this newly acquired content.

- Jump the Line: Again, after a set amount of time teaching content, have students stand to answer questions about what you just discussed. True answers mean they jump to the right, and false means they jump to the left. Do about five questions before having them sit to listen to more content. You can mix this up and have them lunge, step, or turn to the right/left, etc.

- Stretch and Tell: After your chunk of content, have students stand, stretch and when you ask a question about the material, they answer a question while stretching. You can mix this up with whisper responses, yelling, singing, or acting out answers... get creative to make it fun.

## Growth Mindset or Fixed Mindset?

Before kids can learn anything, they have to believe they have the ability. Carol Dweck (2007) coined the terms growth mindset and fixed mindset to describe the motivational patterns related to failure and intelligence.

She researched thousands of students and found that those who believed they could get smarter, put in more effort and time resulting in higher achievement (growth mindset). This differed from those who held the mindset that intelligence is an inborn cognitive ability you either have or don't have (fixed mindset).

This is why many don't try the hard stuff. What is the voice in their head saying? There are a few things you can share with students that will help them better understand this amazing brain they have and it begins with determining if they have a growth mindset or a fixed mindset. Teaching kids the difference and how to change their mindset for growth is one of the most valuable life lessons you can share.

| **Growth Mindset** (Positive self-talk) | **Fixed Mindset** (Negative self-talk) |
|---|---|
| My attitude and effort make me successful | Performance is unchangeable (all or nothing) |
| I can learn anything | My ability determines what I learn |
| Failure means learning | Failure means I'm no good |
| I am not afraid of a challenge | I don't like to be challenged |
| I am inspired by others' success | I am threatened by others' success |

Another aspect of mindset involves the adult. What is *your* mindset or belief in this child's abilities? Does this influence your expectations or demands? Praising effort and focusing on *trying the task* versus the *results of the task* frequently results in perseverance. A fear of failure can result when we praise intelligence (a fixed trait) versus attitude and effort. Research shows that performance worsens and kids are more likely to give up when the result, not the process, is all that is deemed important (Dweck, Carol. 2007).

> Many teachers inadvertently create a climate of fear in the way grades are given; when mistakes result in an unchangeable poor grade, kids are less likely to try and learning is stifled.

# STRATEGIES FOR ADHD-TYPE BRAINS

***See strategies for executive functioning since ADHD
and skill weaknesses are closely correlated.

- All strategies must occur at the POINT OF PERFORMANCE. This means in the moment of execution so it can directly influence functioning (Barkley, 2012).
- Mix up your teaching methods and use various media to increase interest that meets the needs of all learning types in your class. This can include the use of audio, visuals, pictures, videos, and interactive activities.
- Remember the importance of a connection with students. Use their name, learn something about them, and show them you are invested in who they are.
- Always teach *how* because even extremely bright kids struggle with the process of planning and execution so the *how* is often missed.
- Have a consistent routine with a visual schedule showing breaks that are visually chunked.
- Show the assignments for the week, not just the day, so kids can begin to see the big picture. You can use this visual to help them begin to plan for the week, prevent procrastination, and even build in rewards for the chunks completed.
- Have the necessary tools visible so they are visual reminders for use (but not distractions).
- Acknowledge when a child does their best work. Some do better earlier in the day, some later, so this can be individualized for specific needs but often there is a time of day that is more functional.
- When struggling, avoid group work because of the various social skills required.
- Make tasks interesting: if the goal is writing, have *them* choose the topic. If the topic is set, have them decide how to demonstrate their knowledge (i.e. Google Slides vs. written paper, etc.)
- Make them accountable with a deadline and review how to complete each chunked portion. Peer check-ins involve pairing kids

up and having them show each other work toward an end product; this can be more effective than teacher check-ins sometimes.

- Utilize coaching to help teach ways to improve initiation, organization, and work-cycle completion.
- Provide an *immediate* payoff for work or good behavior with a reward or motivator that has been determined to be effective for *this* child. This can be confirmed using a forced-choice inventory (which can be found online in various places).
- Address the skill deficits and focus specifically on planning, initiation, and use visuals to show what work feels like when it is done.
- Daily mindfulness forces kids to be in the moment to assess their attention span (or metacognition) and to avoid "squirrel moments." Take moments out of your day to encourage planning, visualizing the future and coming up with ways they can master challenging tasks.
- Incorporate movement and exercise throughout the day because it improves the health of brain cells, increases mood, and decreases stress.
- Create replacement strategies for blurting or interrupting through the use of a "thought page" they can write on during discussion so they don't forget what they want to say at the moment.
- Focus on the goal of each activity; if it is science try dictation or the creation of a slideshow versus writing a paper.
- Handwriting is a critical developmental skill so see if they are better with cursive or a combination of manuscript and cursive. Younger kids may need an OT consultation, but older kids might simply need alternatives or methods for adapting how writing assignments look when they are struggling to get legible content on the page.
- Teach them how to organize their thoughts better and more effectively plan out the process of their writing through the use of visuals or colored Post-it notes/highlighting for different topics.
- Dysregulation during times when kids sit on the floor can be due to postural issues related to developmental ability and control. Try them in a different position or have them stand in the back,

behind the group for this instruction. Create a space they can move within so they aren't distracting peers but have a space for movement during listening.

- Create a plan for recess to help younger kids begin to develop the necessary skills for engagement during unstructured times.

- Support transitions by putting them visibly on the schedule or warning at specific timed intervals ("In 10 minutes we will be doing math and putting away our computers. In 5 minutes we will be…, etc."). This allows time to process the change and gear up for the next task. Timed warnings for transitions are effective because they grab the attention of those who might be drifting. Transitions can include simply changing subjects, going from computers to writing, or larger, more movement-based changes such as going to different classes, etc.

- Adult assistance is good, but too much can result in overstimulation, opposition, or learned helplessness.

  o Having an adult who is always helping and *doing* the execution can create learned helplessness and prevent the development of executive functioning skills.
  o When the adult makes a request and there is a poor response, don't engage any further. Provide a quick visual (on a post-it note or with a cue card) and walk away. This gives the student time to process without interruptions or an active audience.

- Procrastination can be a subconscious behavioral response to dysregulation. When things are put off and the deadline is *now,* a shot of cortisol is released that helps with motivation and execution in the brain. This is not a functionally sustainable strategy so creating check-ins and other ways to create this sense of urgency can be a good way to stay on track.

  o Trick the brain with challenges such as timing themselves and racing, or providing a reward for effort (and if the student perceives them as fun, this will increase their motivation even more).

o Chunk work and create deadlines that help the student to gradually get work done with healthy levels of cortisol. If there is a way to introduce rewards for work done immediately, this will increase the dopamine that supports continued focus and motivation.

o Pair students and encourage peer check-ins so kids can show each other progress toward an end goal or project.

- Poor work production or not starting work can be due to shutdown.

o Looking at a visually busy page can be enough to create so much stress that fight/flight kicks in and nothing happens. Try copying only a few problems and give the student *only* this page.

o Reward and notice their effort, not the amount of completed work at first. Challenge them to do one more problem than last time. Make sure they are only challenged to improve upon *their own* previous successes, never that of peers.

- Processing time is critical when making assumptions about behavior.

o Neurotypical kids can need 3-5 seconds to respond after a request.

o Many kids with special needs (including ADHD) can need 7-10 seconds before they can do what you are asking. Moving away and allowing this wait time can be the difference between regulation and meltdown.

- Sensory-based breaks are critical and often best when prompted with a visual cue that is predetermined and created with the child's help.

o Often kids with ADHD need to work for 10 minutes with a 3-minute break to get the neurotransmitters built up again for attention and endurance.

- ○ Glucose is depleted in the brain with learning so movement-based tools can help increase the thinking power during longer academic chunks. Movement is one of the most effective strategies for ADHD brains.
- ○ Let the student decide when they are ready for a break. If the adult can see they need one (because the student isn't sensing it internally), present a visual of two or three (pre-determined) options and walk away, telling them they can decide which they will do.

- Images are powerful reminders or prompts that can be subtly used during instruction. This can be a printed image of a snack, water break, or movement strategy such as a chair pushup or standing to work. Kids love to be involved in the conception of the many tools available for use and are able to come up with brilliant ways to address their attentional needs when they are in a regulated state. The added social and emotional bonus is that this type of activity also shows them that you care enough to ask for their expertise in creating this classroom tool. Many of these kids have never had an adult willing to support and encourage their out-of-the-box tricks that help their brains work better during difficult non-preferred activities.

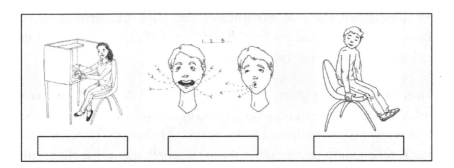

# ANXIETY

In 2022, research results from a 2016-2020 study concluded that 9.2% of kids (birth to age 17) were diagnosed with anxiety and 4% with depression (Lebrun-Harris et al. 2022). ADAA cites that anxiety disorders affect 1 in 8 kids and are comorbid issues commonly seen with ADHD, depression, and eating disorders. While many such mental health issues are treatable, 80% of kids diagnosed with anxiety are not treated (Child Mind Institute, 2018).

This means that many of our students deal with fear, shyness, social isolation, avoidance, and potential behavioral challenges that prevent us (and others) from seeing their inner greatness.

When kids are in a heightened nervous system state there are many ways it manifests physically and emotionally; all of this influences behavior and impacts learning. Sometimes our assumption of behavior is completely off so it is important to understand some of the implications that align with anxiety disorders.

- Emotional changes are seen such as appearing on edge, restless, or acting out.
- Aggression with both self-injury and bullying can be common.

- Social isolation can occur especially after age 13, with fewer successful peer interactions and difficulties with unstructured time.
- Physical changes or symptoms can include headaches, dizziness, nausea, or sweating and many of these kids are frequent fliers in the nurse's office. Panic attacks can be scary physiological responses that are difficult for kids to understand.
- Sleep disturbances are devastating for behavioral regulation, social engagement, and learning. Kids between the ages of 13 and 18 need 8- 10 hours of sleep per night; many don't get even close to this.
- Poor school performance can include frequent missing assignments, feeling overwhelmed, or procrastination.
- School refusal, elopement, and tardies occur because avoidance seems easier than engagement. Even when kids begin to come back to school or participate, many are so far behind that this further exacerbates their ability to find success or feel like they are a part of their current learning environment and community.
- Tantrums and severe behavioral responses can be due to overstimulation and the fight, flight, or freeze mechanism hijacking their system.
- Obsession with perfection can prevent work completion because they know they won't do things right so they give up before even trying

# TOXIC STRESS AND "TRAUMA BRAIN"

Toxic stress is a response that occurs when a child experiences intense, recurrent, or prolonged adversity without adequate adult support (Franke, 2014). Physical or emotional abuse, chronic neglect, exposure to violence, caregiver mental illness or substance abuse, and extended family hardship have all been shown to affect the brain in ways that can have long-term repercussions. When we get cortisol that's released all the time from constant stress there are many dangerous side effects and research shows how hard this is on the system. The Ph level of the gut is affected and we know that many neurotransmitters important for behavior, mood, and motivation are formed in the gut. Stress affects digestion and the absorption of B12 which affects energy, mood, and even vision; all of these are critical for school. Long-term health issues and decreased immune function are linked to increased inflammation, heart disease, diabetes, depression, and brain structure changes (Koch et al., 2017).

"Trauma brain" is a condition where the brain's protection mechanism is stuck in emergency mode due to stressors. Emotional trauma is different from the physical trauma of a traumatic brain injury. Rigid pathways form in the brain with prolonged stress that are resistant to change so the emotional network now only over or under-responds- regulation and balance are non-existent. A 2006 study by NIH found that recurrent trauma causes the amygdala to go into overdrive, responding to stress as though it were experiencing trauma for the first time so protection becomes *the* priority at any cost (Bremner, 2006). The prefrontal cortex or thinking brain doesn't work during extreme stress so there is no way to utilize logic to prevent behavioral responses from becoming purely reactive. Changes in memory and decreased activity in the hippocampus make it difficult for the brain to distinguish *actual* trauma from the *memory* of trauma so this child is in a constant state of emotional over-reactivity (Mickley Steinmetz et al. 2012). The parts of the brain required for school, experiencing joy, recognizing personal strengths, or interpersonal bonding are not working because scanning for danger is the most pressing matter. This susceptibility is not so different from our typical fight, flight, or freeze responses except that the duration is different; protective responses generally don't extinguish easily and can be triggered by minuscule and often overlooked demands. Research indicates that a positive relationship between a child and a teacher can help increase resiliency which may minimize stress responses (Franke).

Students who experience toxic stress will struggle with learning retention and social skills, and we often see extreme degrees of emotional dysregulation. Our priority must be recovery because no learning or control over behavior occurs when the brain is hijacked. Kids often don't express their discomfort, so their behavior can be erratic and intense with little warning or prevalence of a clear antecedent.

# THE PRACTICAL STUFF:
# WORRIERS AND ANXIETY

Neural plasticity is the ability of the brain to rewire depending on how we use it. Techniques for anxiety are designed to expose the nervous system to input. Avoidance and escape worsen anxiety, so kids need to understand why techniques that increase exposure and experiences are so important for their future responses and emotional well-being. Sometimes just expecting this child to be present for class discussion is the most appropriate starting point. Every time kids meet our expectations, their nervous system adjusts and their perspective of self-actualization improves, leading to more opportunity and exposure. Creating a just right challenge is critical when dealing with anxiety because shutdown and recovery from our protective mechanism of fight, flight, or freeze can be very difficult. Don't forget to include concepts of self-monitoring so they know what they are feeling and can identify when a tool effectively decreases physical symptoms. It is critical to respect preferences and cues to ensure that something else isn't going on that should be addressed before trying out new tools or strategies.

- When we are worried we often don't remember that we have had previous successes, so remind kids of this and help them see the good and catch them doing good.
- Take physical steps toward success. Motivation comes from *doing* first, so even small steps are critical to reward. A study found that 34% of motivation comes from thoughts and 66% from actions (Gottfried et al., 2008). This means just "doing" is progress; effort, not results, should be the focus.
- Document success in a journal or on Post-it notes so they are reminded of the positives.
- Add breathing, movement, and self-regulation strategies during exposure to something they are trying to avoid or during times they are triggered. Present these tools in picture format, such as when managing fight, flight, or freeze behaviors.
- Avoidance feeds anxiety so help kids experience as much as they can. Even if you or a peer give them more support initially,

mere exposure should be considered a success. When positive emotions are experienced during this exposure they are more likely to try again. This is often best done with the support of counselors, social workers, or staff trained to support mental health.

- o Make an exposure hierarchy with steps to expose them slowly (imagine being there, watch a video of being there, see it from afar, try it with no expectation for engagement or participation, try it out with knowledge of what is expected and what might happen).

- Remember to allow time for processing. Sometimes you have to walk away so they can come up with ideas or make decisions about how they will manage a situation or specific environment.
- Catch them using coping skills or exposing themselves to stimuli even if they are slight.
- We don't want to (and often can't) eliminate problems but we can *provide space* between the challenge and the reaction. Encourage them to experience a small amount of stress and then practice strategies like breathing, shutting their eyes for a moment, or getting some movement before they form an opinion about how that stress felt to them.
- Name and address the feeling. Talk or write about what they see, feel, or think about a stressful event.
- BREATHE. 4-7-8 breathing is done by putting your tongue behind your teeth, breathing in for 4 seconds, holding for 7 seconds, and exhaling for 8 seconds, keeping your tongue in place.
- Practice facing what is hard and staying exposed longer and longer (which makes the emotional muscles stronger for next time). Challenge them and try to make it fun or at least less scary. Someone trained in mental health can support this process.
- Don't focus on the worry all the time. Create a worry time, a worry box, or a worry journal that can be used at one specific time so the worries have a place to go and don't constantly nag or

distract. Dawn Huebner authored the book, "What to Do When You Worry Too Much" and talks about worries similar to tomato plants that get bigger with more attention. This is a great resource to share with your entire class (Huebner 2005).

- Remind kids that WORRIES LIE…or Dragons lie…however you want to explain that sometimes signals are deceptive, so don't let them trick you! When kids can take control of the dragon or the signals in the nervous system, they tend to become helpful instead of hurtful.

- Preparation is critical: pre-teach, practice, and role-play how to deal with stress through the use of warm-up exercises. Tell a student that you plan to call on them and give them the problem they will be answering so they can be prepared and succeed when they answer in front of the entire class. Remember that answering aloud is not always appropriate for kids who are experiencing severe anxiety. If your goal is for them to be present and learn the material, the social aspect of answering aloud may not be the best idea right now for this student.

- Quiet breaks with dim lighting can help them reset before more exposure.

- Firm, deep touch is organizing but always ask if they are ok with being touched. Light touch generally increases signals so unless they ask for it, always err on the side of firm input.

- Use calming sensory tools such as lavender, chamomile, and sandalwood aromatherapy.

- Change the features of their environment. Simplify a space, use fewer words, reduce visual clutter, allow kids to move to a different space, use quiet music, and build structure through visuals and forecasted activities.

- Be in the moment to really listen and allow space, time, and quiet for their thoughts.

- Worry rocks, worry jewelry, worry books, and fidgets are great tools for worriers.

- Ask about their signals as long as they aren't in the elevated state of fight, flight, or freeze. "Is your dragon being reasonable now? Are you in true danger? Did your dragon forget we already solved this problem?.....Silly Dragon, maybe he needs a time-out!" Dragon talk de-escalates behavior quickly because you are helping to solve a dragon problem, not "their problem," so it serves as a great distraction that usually ends up with a solution they can use.

- Visual schedules, checklists, and emotional charts that show various emotions and tools can be powerful. Often kids can't find words or tell you what is next so when it is concrete and in front of them, stress decreases and communication increases.

- Create a worry/stress tree for the entire class to prevent holding onto emotions. Have kids write one of their stressors or worries on a green Post-it note and put it on the worry tree (similar to leaves). Group discussions can address some of the anonymous worries. When solutions are found, they are written on a different colored paper to replace the worry that has now been solved. Worries that are solved fall off the tree like old leaves and the new leaves show a beautiful new color of tree that reminds everyone about the importance of creating a positive climate of support among your learning community. Everyone has worries (even the teacher) and solutions are always out there.

- Remind kids that discomfort doesn't always mean danger through responses like, "I hear you; that sounds hard and uncomfortable but not dangerous."

- Ask, "What is the worst part of this?" and help kids figure out how to fix this one aspect so the bad can actually end up good.

- Question thought patterns. Similar to fixed and growth mindsets, negative thoughts distort the severity of a situation. Continue to find positive ways to dissect a situation or emotional encounter and reframe what is happening or how things feel. Try to find words that are similar but more positive. Is fear really excitement? Fear is physiologically close to stress and can feel the same, so help them see this different viewpoint.

- Use a visual scale of 1 to 10 with images of examples to help kids better determine how bad or stressful a situation *actually* is. Maybe it isn't actually a 10 so a solution might be possible. Work with the child and have them come up with three images relevant to their world (ie. 1=broken pencil, 2=flat tire on a bike, 3=house burning down).

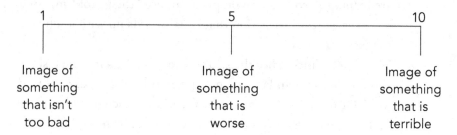

# AUTISM OR ASD

ASD, or Autism Spectrum Disorder, is a developmental disability characterized by distinct brain differences that can lead to communication, behavior, and learning challenges. Each person with ASD is unique, and their abilities can vary significantly. As a result, different treatment approaches are often required to address the diverse strengths and challenges individuals with autism may experience. While symptoms may improve over time, it is important to note that, similar to the brain differences seen in ADHD, people with ASD can exhibit varying learning and social interaction needs. High-functioning individuals with ASD may appear similar to their neurotypical peers and can exhibit high intelligence. It is crucial to gain a better understanding of the various symptoms of ASD to avoid making assumptions about behavior and to provide appropriate support and accommodations for individuals with autism. With increased awareness and support, individuals with ASD can lead fulfilling and meaningful lives.

Behavioral challenges are often exacerbated by comorbid factors commonly associated with autism. Sensory processing disorder often means sensory overload. Individuals who must constantly manage unique and intense sensory signals frequently miss opportunities for appropriate engagement and contend with problems related to behavioral regulation.

Other comorbid issues further compound difficulties in managing school, expectations, social interactions, and equanimity. Research indicates that 50-70% of autistic individuals also have ADHD ("What is Autism Spectrum Disorder? | CDC"). For this reason, strategies similar to those used with anxiety, fight, flight, or freeze and ADHD are generally helpful.

The medical model defines autism as a disability within the person; a problem with the brain and how it processes input. This is similar to what we have seen with ADHD, anxiety, and traumatic stress. Programming can be designed to address these brain differences, but there is also a movement suggesting an alternative way of thinking about autism that might more effectively help autistic individuals. The Neurodiversity Paradigm is a "new and different way of looking at Autism and other human neurocognitive variations. This paradigm frames diversity as being similar to gender or ethnic diversity" (Zur Institute). This paradigm shift does not view autism as a disorder and suggests a different approach to supporting autistic individuals. Jac den Houting discusses, "Why everything you know about autism is wrong" in her 2019 TEDx talk. When autism is described as an explanation of behavior in *certain settings* with *certain tasks,* she suggests that the setting and task are the primary influences on behavior, rather than a defect within the individual. The Social Model of Disability further proposes that disability happens when the environment or task doesn't cater to the individual brain and wiring needs. This suggests that the disability is being done *to someone* by what is around them (Houting, 2019). This unique frame of reference creates many opportunities to support autistic students. When we shift our focus to address sensory and environmental needs, we find that a different direction for strategies, tools, and perspectives becomes possible.

## Common Issues Seen with Autism:

- Difficulty recognizing how to engage socially or relate with others, their interests, or feelings.
- Trouble reading body language or facial expressions. They may struggle to notice changes in speech or fluctuations in tone, so sarcasm and other speech variations may be misconstrued or not understood.
- They may be unaware when people talk to them or become distracted with certain sounds so they may prefer odd noises or music which pulls them away from social interactions.
- Processing sounds, words or cues can take much longer and they may not know to look when someone points to an object.
- They may experience intense sensory issues or overstimulation that prevents behavioral regulation. You may notice that they want to be alone, have poor eye contact, have anxiety with any type of change, or have avoidance that prevents further learning and engagement.
- Difficulty with verbal communication can make it difficult for others to estimate their ability or level of interest in a situation, topic, or social interaction. They may have difficulty communicating their feelings or needs so helping them find solutions can be challenging.
- Background noise can mean missing words or entire parts of speech.
- Oppositional defiance behaviors may be seen because of the many regulation deficits related to sensory integration, anxiety, and brain differences.
- Aggression and self-injury can be due to sensory processing deficits where they may not be experiencing input in the same way neurotypical peers do. Many need to feel more because what they experience is not effective enough to make them feel good inside. Others may feel too much and respond to this with self-harm to block the stimulation they don't know how to manage. Aggression can simply be a fight, flight, or freeze response to overstimulation.

- Stimming behaviors can be repetitive motor movements or verbal responses that create distractions in class. It can appear that these students are seeking attention, but many times with keen observations, you can determine that these behaviors actually help with regulation. Many kids will make noises or motor movements with absolutely no awareness that people are watching them. Stimming is an attempt to regulate and, if managed, can effectively increase focused attention, managing anxiety or overstimulation/understimulation.
- Aversion to maintaining eye contact.
- Literal thinking might also be seen in their writing or oral responses.

# THE PRACTICAL STUFF:
# AUTISM OR ASD

- Increase the schedule, routine, and consistency to increase awareness of what is coming.
- Provide frequent rewards and tie interest into activities and interactions.
- Practice social interactions starting with highly motivating topics and/or provide reinforcement as they continue to engage appropriately.
- Try to provide eight positives to one criticism or negative and set up an opportunity to give those eight positives more easily at first so they have buy-in for the activity.
- Create a safety zone with special attention to the sensory aspects of the environment.
- Remember the importance of break time and recovery for de-escalation.
- Try to find the why behind the behavior. This might require reading non-verbal cues since their ability to communicate can be challenging or inconsistent.
- Provide choices to help with ideation for what to do, which will also improve initiation and knowing how to start. Don't present too many options for choices (no more than three depending on age) as this can create more stress and overload.
- Try to identify triggers, times of difficulty, and times of no difficulty to determine expectations and needed reinforcers.
- Visuals are incredibly effective for everything, even things you know they understand. The use of PECS (picture exchange communication system) for multiple steps or the day's schedule has been repeatedly studied with positive results. Real-life pictures are even better for preparing individuals for an activity or new environment, and often school technology allows for pictures to be taken at the moment with an iPad or Chromebook. Many apps also allow these images to be quickly and easily put into a "first/then" format or visual schedule that can be individualized

or manipulated for specific situations (Choiceworks or Pictello are two I commonly use).

- Use videos and pictures in addition to live instruction so the social intensity of one-on-one interactions doesn't limit understanding of the material.

- Use visuals to support various areas of life: label items in the room and use colors and real objects to show what items are used for.

- Social stories are excellent ways to teach concepts because they narrate the steps of a successful experience. They can be personalized to address specific problems utilizing a child's strengths and highlight tools that can compensate for weaknesses. These can be printed and laminated or integrated into assistive technology.

- Comic strip conversation strips (Graycenters.org) are wonderful ways to show emotions and non-verbal communication through fun and interactive conversation strips. It also shows different elements of a conversation that might be too abstract for linear thinkers and can give you insight into their perspective or what they are dealing with. It has a visual representation for interrupting, hearing everyone talk at once, listening or thinking; colors can even be added to show emotions or exclamatory phrases. This is a highly effective tool for high-functioning individuals who don't seem to understand social nuances. You can do this with a student drawing stick figures of peers and possible social situations they may have recently encountered. Ask them what they could have said or done at that moment and have them add or erase pieces of the images you are drawing together (this works great on a whiteboard). This can also become a full class activity with students who can come up to the board and change the scenario by drawing in something else. Discussing personal space can be represented by drawing a circle around the stick figure; everyone has a different-sized "bubble" and this can be clearly represented with an image that kids can manipulate. This process allows for active engagement, role-playing, and social-emotional learning that is visual.

- Increase engagement using the child's interests and create purposeful jobs, with a visual of the steps that increase the interactions with adults or peers.
- Rehearse situations before they occur. Scaffold with pictures first, practice with a familiar person, and finally try it out in the real world.
- Be aware of the various comorbidities that travel with autism or ASD as they might be the primary influence on behavior. If strategies typically successful for ASD aren't working, consider utilizing tools for ADHD, sensory overstimulation, or any other diagnoses a child might have.
- Reading the social aspects of a space can easily over-stimulate. If regulation is poor in specific spaces with dynamic social situations, teaching them about reading emotions and non-verbal communication should not occur until they demonstrate regulation with their behavioral responses. We want everyone to be exposed to the unpredictability of social engagement, but learning how to read behavior and adjust is very complicated.

# GIFTED LEARNERS

Many times we assume that when kids are bright, they must be competent and high-performing. But gifted brains are wired very differently, and similar to ADHD brains, some skills don't develop when we expect them to. Just because kids are smart doesn't mean executive functioning is fully intact compared to their peers. Executive functioning skills *will* affect success with school, grades, study habits, and social demands. Work production and focused attention are common issues that impact success due to skill development and motivation; if they figured out how to do the problem twenty minutes ago, they likely aren't still focused on math. They need to see the worth in what is requested, so motivation is a huge factor in success with gifted kids.

One of the hallmarks of giftedness is asynchronous development; the more gifted the child, the more asynchronous their abilities are believed to be. This asynchrony is so relevant that some believe this trait to be a more defining characteristic of giftedness than ability or potential (Webb et al., 2008). This means that many executive functioning skills will develop at *very* different times from peers; some skills may be excellent while others may be frighteningly non-existent or lagging. This lagging of executive skills seen with giftedness is very similar to traits seen with ADHD; one diagnosis is considered a disability, and the other a gift. Both will likely benefit from similar strategies for regulation. Vast differences between intellectual, physical, social, and emotional development are seen with this asynchronous development and many say that gifted kids seem like they are different ages all at one time; they have the intelligence of an adult but the social skills of a young child. This is especially true from the ages of 3 to 9 because their cognitive functioning cannot override the nervous system response and skill deficits as easily (Houskamp, 2021). This can make teaching, counseling, and supporting their complex needs very challenging.

An additional primary characteristic of giftedness is overexcitability; this is inborn and affects how a child responds to input (Lind, 2011). This heightened sensitivity in the nervous system affects the intensity, sensitivity, and awareness of sensory input that can influence behavior in a different way than it might for peers. The higher the level of giftedness, the more likely they experience increased responsivity to pain, touch, and input from other sensory systems. This is similar to what we see with individuals who struggle with sensory processing disorder. In a study by the STAR Institute, 35% of gifted kids exhibited issues with sensory processing compared to 5% of the general population (SPD Foundation, 2007). This does not mean all gifted kids need occupational therapy to address sensory processing disorder but this high occurrence of comorbid sensory issues can certainly drive the explanation behind possible maladaptive behavior and tools needed to address behavioral regulation.

Common Overexcitabilities include (Neville, 2021):

- Intellectual- Incredibly active minds, intense curiosity, keen observers, and moral thinkers.
- Psychomotor- Active, energetic, verbal processors, enthusiastic, impulsive, compulsive, competitive, and misbehavior can be due to a misunderstood surplus of energy.
- Imaginational- Inventors, dreamers, and distracted by thoughts.

- Emotional- Strong emotional attachments, compassionate, sometimes intense behaviors or beliefs, and somatic symptoms (like stomach ache or headache).
- Sensual- Altered processing of sensory input (especially visual, touch, smell, and hearing), interest in aesthetics, music, language, and art.

The problem with traditional academic programming is that it is often not designed for the needs of this brain type. It is hard to remember that gifted kids fall in the ninety-eighth percentile, which is as far from the norm as those students who fall in the second percentile and need significant intervention or alternative programming. There is a designation called 2e or "twice exceptional" where gifted students can fall on both ends of the curve with other diagnoses such as LD (learning disabilities or differences), ADHD (attention deficits), ODD (oppositional defiance), OCD (obsessive-compulsive), anxiety, or other mental health issues. This can make school even more challenging because strategies must now address more than one area of need.

- Social interactions and the ability to form friendships can be affected by rigid or narrow interests with a preoccupation on specific things that can influence social reciprocity and conversations or engagement with others.
- Behavioral regulation can be demanding when other issues are at play; attentional deficits, executive functioning weaknesses, and sensory processing disorder all impact regulation and arousal levels foundational to success in school and with relationships.

Expectations can be one of the biggest hurdles for these kids because a high IQ comes with a higher expectation for potential. It is often assumed that these kids should be motivated, focused, and able to finish work quickly. Intelligent kids are held to high expectations because their teachers see the cognitive potential. However, we don't know *which* skills aren't quite mature yet and how this might hinder performance. When these kids struggle, it is usually because they have yet to fully develop certain executive skills, so they can't meet expectations successfully. Grades are designed to report the level of content mastery but when there are executive skill deficits, the grade may reflect the lack of work completion more than the actual content knowledge. They may not demonstrate their knowledge through writing because the ideas come into their head so quickly that they forget them before being able to get them on the page. The *why* is still just as important to figure out if you are trying to understand why a bright child struggles in school or has no friends.

# THE PRACTICAL STUFF:
# GIFTED STUDENTS

Change how information is accessed or knowledge is demonstrated to create a just right challenge.

- Response format:

  o Oral versus written
  o Cursive versus manuscript
  o Type versus write, or dictate versus type
  o Multiple choice versus essay
  o Google slides versus typed paper
  o Sketch pictures in organizer versus written words or sentences

- Environmental Changes:

  o Experiment with preferential seating (separate desk space) or partitions to prevent visual distractions or overstimulation.
  o Address over and under-stimulation with strategies designed for sensory processing deficits.

- Change the work:

  o Shortened work (5 problems v. 30 when mastery is demonstrated). Offer the most difficult problems first so they can quickly show mastery.
  o Have extension activities ready to allow fast learners to take concepts to the next level independently in class or for homework.
  o Have more complex math or reading available for students to choose from.
  o Allow students to take a test before doing all the homework. If they get higher than 90%, excuse them from this homework or practice work.
  o Provide alternatives to work that allow students to generalize or apply their knowledge to real-world problems or situations.

- Extend time if a student shows overexcitabilities that affect their ability to focus or regulate.
- Scheduling:

  o Consider morning versus afternoon for academic work, depending on their regulation.
  o Create a schedule for kids of similar ability, not age, to work together on academic content.

# CENTRAL AUDITORY PROCESSING DISORDER

This child often says, "What?" While you might suspect a signal or regulation issue, a central auditory processing disorder is different because it affects *how* the brain processes sound or language. Auditory processing disorders (APD) affect how concepts and thoughts are retained, so repeating instruction isn't as helpful as saying something differently. A student's hearing may be fine, but living with an auditory processing disorder makes life and communication seem "garbled." According to Martin Kutscher, "The brain processes these electrical impulses into sounds, then into words, and then into meaningful sentences and ideas" (Kutscher, 2008). For most, this happens automatically, but when there is difficulty converting the electrical impulses, we see confusion and frustration. Some of the behavioral symptoms may appear like ADHD, receptive language issues, or motor planning deficits, but if you utilize strategies to address these with no success, this disorder is important to be aware of and might require consultation with an audiologist. Some of the typical symptoms include:

- Trouble paying attention and remembering things presented orally
- Strengths in math but difficulty with language arts

- Poor listening skills, needing the volume very high despite no hearing deficits
- Getting lost around the school
- Trouble with reading, comprehension, vocabulary, or spelling
- The need for additional processing time
- Problems with multiple-stepped instructions
- Potential learning and behavior issues

# IRLEN SYNDROME

This is a problem with the brain's processing of visual information that includes light sensitivity, problems with reading, learning, headaches, or migraines. The brain gets overstimulated when reading black print on white paper, so symptoms can include blurry vision, words that move on the page, or seeing a halo around words. Most kids will struggle with reading and even math problems on a page. You can try different colored paper, colored overlays, or lines to help with visual tracking. Visit Irlen. com for more information.

# VISUAL PERCEPTION

These skills will affect everything we do visually and can affect a child's ability to read fluidly, comprehend what they are reading, perceive equations in math, or quickly process information that is read. Visual perception allows us to better understand the information that goes from our eyes to our brain for processing. There are many different skill areas related to proficient reading, and visual perception is one of the first foundational skills required. If a child is always frustrated when reading, struggles with sight words, can't see the patterns of letters in forming words, reverses or confuses letters (like b and d after the age of 7), or struggles with a visually busy page, they may be dealing with visual perception deficits. These skills can affect reading, writing, spelling, and math. Similar to executive functioning skills, different skills impact ability for various reasons, but there are things that can be done in the classroom to help develop these skills. If you suspect a child has a visual processing disorder, the following activities or ideas can be easily implemented in class to help strengthen different skill sets and improve the neurological pathways that connect the eyes and the brain.

Visual Figure Ground: This skill requires finding an image hidden among visual details (like *Where's Waldo?* or finding an item in a cluttered drawer). When this skill is intact, students can focus on the words they are reading without getting distracted by other visual details. Issues with figure-ground affect reading fluency and speed. It can also make it hard for students to see chunks or trends within a word (such as vowels that commonly go together). Below are a few classroom activities that can be integrated to enhance this skill, along with suggestions for adapting assignments until students' proficiency improves.

- Find images hidden among visual detail or word searches.
- Modify the page they are reading by limiting the amount of text on a page to decrease distractions.
- Use a different color paper, font, or font size.

Visual Closure: This is the ability to recognize what something looks like even when parts are missing or not visible. When this skill is intact, the brain can quickly comprehend without going through the laborious process of seeing all the details because the brain fills in the missing parts (knowing that THA* probably means "that"). This affects reading speed and decoding. Here are some activities to try in the classroom to help strengthen this skill.

- Write words and leave important parts out to see if the child knows what it is. This is a fun way to reinforce vocabulary words to the entire class.
- Show portions of figures and see if they can guess what the object is.
- Provide jigsaw puzzles.
- Supply patterning and sequencing activities for them to complete.

Visual Memory: Visual memory is remembering the visual detail you see. It is foundational to reading because it allows for quick recall of sight words since letters and combinations of letters are easily remembered. It helps with copying from the board because more can be held in the working memory, so students don't need to look up to the board for reference constantly. Here are some activities to try to strengthen this skill.

- Use games that involve remembering silly things or silly words.
- Help kids turn random, visual detail into something logical and easier to remember.

Visual Discrimination: This is the ability to see the differences and similarities related to visual detail. It is critical for reading, writing, letter formation, spelling, editing, math equations, and it helps with processing speed because everything gets faster when you see differences or similarities quickly. Seeing differences helps a child understand and notice the difference between a 5 and S, b and d, or - and ÷. Here are some games to try in the classroom.

- Memory games or "Can you find the difference" activities
- Sorting games looking for colors, shapes, patterns, or purpose
- Matching games that involve similar images or words

Form Constancy: This is what helps a child to understand that a T is still a T even when the font, size, color, orientation or case is different. It is a situation of "the same but different," which also aligns with the ability to recognize categories for cognitive and organizational skills. Try these ideas:

- Play "I Spy" having kids find all the different letters of "T" in various environments around the school.
- Find various versions of a word on a busy page from a magazine or newspaper ad and identify the different fonts, sizes, spaces, colors, etc.
- Change the font for various passages to help introduce different angles or appearances (y or y, a or a, g or g).

Spatial Orientation: This is the ability to recognize similarities despite their orientation on the page. We read left to right for not only words but time and numbers. If a child has trouble understanding spatial relationships, this can lead to much confusion with any of these different concepts. The spacing around a word and our perceptual ability to recognize this space determines how quickly a word might be identified. Appropriate spacing between words is critical for writing and legibility. These will help strengthen this skill:

- Provide graphing games with left, right, up, and down instructions.
- Show images in various positions and have the student pick the one that matches the stimulus.

225

# VISUAL SCANNING

The visual system plays a critical role in approximately eighty percent of school activities. There are many developmental skills and milestones that go into *when* this system will mature. Reading can be significantly impacted when there are difficulties in how the brain communicates with the eyes. Visual scanning issues are particularly noteworthy, as they often cause children to skip words or lines, losing their place in the text. Fortunately, tools such as pointing to each word or using a tracker can help address these challenges but by understanding and addressing these visual hurdles, we can support children's reading development more effectively.

- For a child to visually navigate their academic surroundings, there must be postural control that supports the head because this is the platform that supports the receptors for vision.
- Only when there is a stable base for the eyes to anchor from will visual scanning be possible. If the eyes aren't fluidly scanning from left to right, words will be missed and comprehension will be poor.
- Endurance of the visual motor system is required for repetitive tracking and the ability to sequence design concepts.
- If the brain has to tell the eyes *how* to scan across the page, scanning will be slow and reading will be exhausting.

There are many developmental skills, aside from postural stability and mobility, that relate to the visual system and impact reading. Fusion of vision is the skill of having both eyes working together, but for reading, we must have fusion of vision *with* motion at near-point (from the chest to the end of a child's outstretched arm). On average, this does not developmentally occur until age 8. This can explain reading difficulty before that age. Developmental timelines differ between kids, so what one child can do at age eight might look very different among your students. Dissociation of the head from the eyes is another indication of developmental maturity and the stable base of the head on the body is important for this to occur. When a child moves their entire head while scanning (after age 6), this can indicate that their developmental timeline is delayed. Kids with ADHD and developmental delays will struggle with reading expectations. Delays simply mean these kids may need more time and strategies to improve reading because the foundational systems are still maturing. There are strategies, ways to modify work and even exercises that can help visual scanning to develop.

Eye exercises to Help with Reading

- Bounce and catch ball games. Do these either with a partner or alone to help improve visual tracking and hand-eye coordination.
- Scanning exercises. Have the student lie on their stomach or sit with their head resting on the desk. Have them start by looking to one side (right). Have their (right) hand slide up and down in front of their face while their eyes track that hand. Do this 5 times up and down. Switch sides.
- Throw at target. Crumple paper and have them throw it at a target. This addresses visual motor skills and fine motor skills needed for writing and copying from the board.
- "Lazy eight" scanning exercises. Stand facing the board with a pen or simply do the motions in space (like pantomime). Start with the right hand at chest level, move it up as far as it will go to the left while moving the eyes (not the head) to follow the hand. Follow the design of an infinity symbol or "lazy eight," making

sure the movements are as big as they can reach (Dennison and Dennison, 1986).

### <u>Reading Strategies or Modifications that allow</u> <u>Foundational Skills to Mature</u> (adapted from Chronologically Controlled Developmental Therapy program)

- Use a projector to make print very large or copy a page with larger print.
- Read at a distance (at or beyond the length of the child's outstretched arm).
- Use flashcards for fast retrieval of sight words or math facts. The goal of this activity is to assign meaning to a set of symbols for fast retrieval that is automatic and doesn't require analysis or calculation each time they see the stimulus (like C A T is understood to be the furry, purring animal rather than having to sound out each letter). Here is an alternative way to do flashcards for sight words or math problems (CCDT):

  o Make a card or paper 4 x 11 inches, or half a letter-sized page of paper in landscape position.
  o Using a thick black marker, write a sight word or math problem (without the answer showing) as large as possible on this page.
  o Hold the card 8 feet away and slightly above eye level (I love having a child lie on their stomach and look up to see the cards).
  o Present the card quickly; the brain can process certain input in 13 milliseconds (Pradhan).

o Flip only three cards at first and say the word or math answer (not the problem) each time with the child as they look at the problem or the word.

o When the child can say the word loud and fast, no longer say the answer with them but let them continue on their own as you present the card. When these three are mastered, add in more, one at a time.

# SPECIFIC LEARNING DISABILITIES

**Dyslexia-** Many undiagnosed cases of dyslexia can be subtle and affect reading, writing, spelling, and speaking. When kids struggle to read despite having the intellect to be much better readers, dyslexia may be the issue. Dyslexia is a learning disorder that involves confusion of letter order, difficulty identifying speech sounds, and trouble understanding how those sounds are used in speech. Students may have poor comprehension, struggle with sight words, or have difficulty sounding out words. Dyslexia affects areas of the brain that process language. A comprehensive assessment for dyslexia will examine academic achievement, intellectual ability, and language skills such as receptive and expressive language, phonological skills, phonemic awareness, and rapid naming of letters and numbers. Results from these tests provide areas of intervention that should be addressed through an individualized intervention plan or 504 plan. School psychologists, speech pathologists, or neuropsychologists are often the clinicians who would test for dyslexia.

**Dyscalculia-** This is a learning difference in which kids have trouble with numbers and understanding concepts related to more or less than. They struggle with recalling math facts and seeing how numbers fit together. Counting, calculating, and telling left from right can all be common trouble areas. They may have confusion with math symbols, not understand the place value of numbers, or have trouble with everyday tasks such as managing money and understanding correct change. These kids might simply be "bad at math," but if identified, there are many ways adults can help them improve. This isn't a condition of poor intelligence but rather a specific learning disability that affects success with numbers, time, and money. Ways to support these kids can include technology with calculators and math applications, and using number lines or manipulatives such as blocks to help them visualize how to solve math and number problems. Many kids benefit from the accommodation of extra time for any problems involving numbers.

**Dysgraphia**- Dysgraphia is a neurological condition that affects transcription skills, such as handwriting, typing, and spelling. Legibility can be poor because of inconsistent spacing between words or letters. The amount of effort and thought that goes into letter formation, spelling, or mere transcription can mean slower writing production and often avoidance of tasks involving writing. Dysgraphia can be due to different motor issues; the child must be able to utilize a motor plan to create the letters. The execution of this plan is dependent on good gross motor skills for foundational stability to support the fine motor skills required by the hand and smaller muscles that hold and control the pencil.

- Finding a balance between understanding the student's problem and holding them accountable for the best work they can produce is vital for a positive learning environment. It is easy to label a child "lazy" when they have handwriting issues, but there may be many reasons that can be addressed with tools or strategies.
- Gifted students or kids with advanced verbal and thinking skills can struggle with handwriting because their brains work too fast for their hands. This does not mean they have dysgraphia, but providing alternatives, such as dictation for getting thoughts on the page, can help them remember everything they want to say.

# HOW TO MANAGE HANDWRITING ISSUES IN SCHOOL

There are two main ways to manage dysgraphia: remediation that supports writing, and accommodations or modification that can be utilized during work.

## Remediation

Instruction and assistance with handwriting and activities that can make writing easier fall into the remediation category. Strengthening hand muscles and addressing the core muscles of the body that affect posture and provide stability during writing are basic foundational needs if the hands are going to work. Ideas that can be utilized in the classroom setting or at home should be incorporated into a fun daily routine and can include:

- **Varied positions for writing tasks.** Options can include lying on their stomach, standing to write at the board, utilizing dynamic sitting options such as a wobble stool, large yoga ball, cushion, or allowing them to stand during writing.
- **Allow EITHER cursive or manuscript.** Don't force them to remember two different ways a letter is formed when they are already struggling with just one. If they have trouble with printing, consider teaching them cursive but don't demand it. Some kids will do much better with cursive because they don't have to pick their pencil up as frequently so make sure these kids are exposed to both writing styles to see which works better.
- **Feel the letters.** Have them close their eyes while you trace a letter on their palm. Then see if they can reproduce that letter on their hand or, harder yet, on a piece of paper.
- **Write big.** Kids with dysgraphia forget how to form letters correctly, so using big body movements increases the kinesthetic awareness of the letters by stimulating the proprioceptive receptors in the muscles and joints. Information also goes in different channels and parts of the brain for improved memory and processing.
- **Use other materials.** Roll clay into ropes and practice making letters; this also builds hand strength and reinforces letter shapes.

Use shaving cream, damp sand, finger painting, or a smooth layer of clay on a cookie sheet to etch letters into the surface with a pencil.

- **Practice pinching.** Strengthen fingers using clothespins to hang items, crumple paper and toss at a target trash can, or pick up items with tweezers, tongs, or chopsticks.
- **Build strength and stability.** Sitting properly and controlling the pen and paper require muscle strength and stability in the shoulders and core muscles, so any exercises that strengthen these muscles will further support writing *and regulation too!* Try planks, push-ups, wheelbarrow walking, crab walking, shooting baskets, hanging from monkey bars, and rope climbing. Reading while lying tummy-down on the floor builds strength in the shoulders and upper extremities.
- **Cross-body training.** Both sides of the body must work together to write, so incorporate activities that coordinate movement. This can include two-handed games and cross-body coordination like jumping jacks and touching alternate toes before sitting down to write.
- **Speak it first.** Kids may have many ideas, but getting them on the page can be hard. Dictation or drawing pictures to organize these thoughts is a great way to start.

## Modifications or Accommodations Appropriate for Kids with Symptoms of Dysgraphia

The overall goal of an academic activity should always be considered when attempting to modify work or methods for work completion. When a child can handle the academic content but struggles to get their knowledge on the page, it might be time to look at ways to modify the assignments.

- Reduce the amount of work that needs to be rewritten. Choose questions that should be answered in full sentences, then allow for the remainder to be simple answers in phrases.
- Shorten work or written requirements when mastery is demonstrated.

- Grade assignments based on what is being evaluated: spelling errors should not be handwriting errors, etc.
- Grade assignments on the individual elements within the writing process. Make one assignment focus on grammar, the next on spelling, then sentence structure (especially during the draft writing phase, this can be a great way to chunk work and get a student to turn it in before the final product is due). This allows for focus on phases of writing without affecting the different elements that go into a final grade.
- Allow additional time for note-taking, copying, and tests.
- Provide teacher notes, note-takers, or outlines that can be easily filled in or highlighted.
- Have them dictate longer pieces so they can focus on the content and editing.
- Try different types of paper with varying line widths or raised lines that can be felt while writing.
- Utilize graph paper or turn lined paper on its side for math to help line up columns.
- Give positive feedback for trying or writing more than was expected or assigned.
- Provide 2 grades on a page: one for content and one for legibility or neatness.

*** Remember that we want to provide a just right challenge for writing when it is hard. Some days more help is needed than others. If we jump in too quickly with assistance or accommodations, we can create learned helplessness that will prevent students from believing they *can* write. It is a dance, so ensure they are encouraged to do as much on their own first because the ultimate goal is independence.

**DYSPRAXIA (also referred to as a Sensory Processing Disorder-SPD (see p. 242)** This is a developmental coordination disorder that affects the planning (or idea) and processing of motor function. Seemingly simple, multi-stepped tasks can be challenging, and often the complexity of these various steps is overlooked.

- Consider the "simple" task of cutting: one hand holds the page and turns it while the other opens and closes the scissors to follow a line. The number of steps embedded in this activity might be the reason this child can't find success during a class project; it may not be the content that is challenging for this student.
- A child with dyspraxia might have behavioral issues on the playground because their body doesn't know how to actively engage in the equipment their friend wants them to play on.
- They can appear clumsy or non-compliant when following through on longer, more involved instructions.

Dyspraxia can be a significant explanation for the *why* of behavior and work production, especially when kids are elementary age.

## Strategies to Support Dyspraxia

- Give simple step-by-step directions and consider writing these down for a child for reference during an activity.
- Use a consistent approach to instruction for novel or multi-stepped tasks and present the directions that align with their learning style: auditory, visual, or multi-sensory.
- Allow for practice and repetition when challenging tasks are new.
- Extra time can be critical for assignments, tests, and transitions.
- Create brainstorming sessions to help students formulate ideas they can later execute.
- Help a student plan the steps of an activity or their day. "What materials do you need?" or "What do you need to do first?" are great ways to begin chunking the many steps involved in various tasks.
- Play games like Simon Says or create obstacle courses with various fun activities that require planning and execution.
- Watch for bullying, as these kids can struggle in ways that make them easy targets.
- Support skills to help this child initiate conversations and interactions with peers.

- Watch your rate of speech when engaging. Processing time will be an issue, so talk slower with exaggerated pauses and intonation as needed for understanding.
- Consider placement for seating and lockers so they can easily and quickly access their space.
- Provide notes that can be highlighted versus written and utilize any tools that support the writing process because there are many steps involved in writing and this will be a similar area of difficulty if a child struggles with dyspraxia.

# SENSORY PROCESSING DISORDER (SPD)

SPD is an invisible neurological disorder, and understanding how it impacts function is critical when assumptions of behavior are being determined. Many of the issues related to sensory processing disorders also impact neurotypical kids. The difference between children who exhibit preferences or sensitivities to sensory input and those experiencing a sensory processing disorder is determined by symptoms' severity and subsequent responses. Kids with SPD are stuck to the point of not being able to manage anything on their own at this moment. You can utilize accommodations or modifications, practice repeatedly, try strategies, and dissect the very nature of signals and how they affect behavior, but these kids stay stuck.

- This may mean that a child reacts unexpectedly to the simple request of going to art or PE because the sensory components inherent to these classes are too much for their system to process and manage.
- A child's lack of response can be due to a lack of processing.
- Play and social interactions (like a high-five) can be too rough, leading to discipline issues when really, this child doesn't know where their body is in space or how hard they are "playing."

- A student may always be getting up, moving around, distracting others, or finding reasons to be out of their desk because they are not processing enough input to allow for regulation so they seek it out in any way possible.
- Difficulty with bathroom accidents can be due to poor communication within the body so this child doesn't have an accurate sense of urgency.
- A child who cannot sit on the carpet square might display maladaptive behavior during circle time because of postural control deficits.
- When a child strictly adheres to rules despite negative social interactions.
- Kids might also create distractions when asked to do something they don't know how to do; distracting everyone and the consequences of creating a scene might be preferred over having friends know they can't do something.

Understanding the legitimacy of sensory processing and how it affects functional ability and independence is critical in addressing these kids' behavioral responses.

---

"The hallmark of children with Sensory Processing Disorder is that their sensory difficulties are chronic and disrupt their everyday life. Children with SPD get stuck."

-Lucy Miller

---

Many other conditions travel with sensory processing disorders that further complicate behavior and regulation. Individuals with SPD have four times the risk of developing emotional problems such as anxiety, and three times the risk of behavioral regulation issues such as conduct disorders and aggression. SPD is often present with hearing loss, and while it may not be identified as the *primary* deficit, it can significantly impact behavioral responses and alter the effectiveness of strategies and tools. The following comorbidity rates correlate with sensory processing disorders as summarized in a research journal article (Galiana-Simal et al. 2020).

- 80-90% of people identified as autistic or with autism spectrum disorder (ASD) have sensory processing disorder
- 60% with ADHD have comorbid sensory issues
- 35% of kids identified as gifted and talented
- 40-85% with developmental delays have sensory issues
- 25% with asthma
- 49% in Down Syndrome
- 44% with urinary incontinence
- 49% with epilepsy

The *why* behind the behavior you see is critical because it *will* affect how you address various and often extreme behavioral issues. Understanding that a sensory processing disorder can be present with other conditions can help you better identify the *primary factor* behind a behavioral response, and this will influence the tools or strategies chosen for support. A child might be developmentally delayed but if sensory processing deficits are not completely understood, it might be difficult to find tools to meet the sensory needs behind the struggle because we continue to pay attention to only the delays inherent to this child's current diagnosis.

More than ever, looking at this child through a different lens is critical. They need our patience and kindness. When sensory processing issues are present, a child's behavior may appear volitional when really it is their nervous system trying to achieve balance. You may be looking at a child who is just trying to survive in a world that is not designed for how they are wired. We all have bad days, but if there are more bad days than good, there is likely an underlying issue that hasn't been identified. Awareness is the first step, and three main areas of sensory processing disorders manifest in different behaviors. The following briefly summarizes the various aspects of Sensory Processing Disorders (SPD) as defined by the Sensory Therapies and Research Center (STAR) founded by Lucy Miller.

## SENSORY MODULATION DISORDER

This will affect <u>*how*</u> the child responds to input or signals. They might over-respond or do nothing, affecting behavior because of *how* the system responds to input. When signals come in, the nervous system might send out a big, fast, urgent response even when it isn't needed. This can mean behavior is loud, fast, forceful, and usually inappropriate for their setting or what they are trying to do. Other times there will be a significant delay or no reaction because the nervous system doesn't know it needs to do more. This child doesn't answer questions or they forget to do what they are asked.

There are three ways that signals affect behavior:

- <u>Over-responders</u> have a sensitive system that reacts too quickly or dramatically to *everything*.
- <u>Under-responders</u> don't get enough of a reaction so they tend to miss what is going on around them.
- <u>Sensory cravers</u> need *extreme* input and often don't calm down even after they get it.

## SENSORY DISCRIMINATION DISORDER

This is primarily a *signal issue.* Like a bad game of telephone, there is a signal, but details aren't coming through accurately, so the thinking brain has to do its best with what it is given. When the signal doesn't communicate the *details* that affect the response, we get behavior that isn't regulated or different than expected. This can occur with *all* eight senses:

- Visual: They might not catch visual detail or might misjudge the depth of something.
- Auditory: They might not hear certain parts of the instruction or sounds.
- Tactile/touch: They might not accurately feel the item affecting motor skills and knowing where their body is in space.

- Gustatory/taste: They might not differentiate food from glue.
- Olfactory/smell: They might over- or under-respond to certain smells.
- Proprioception: Sensors in muscles and joints tell where the body is and how much force is needed for a demand, so they might appear clumsy, stomp their feet or miss a chair as they go to sit.
- Vestibular: Sensors in the head and ears tell us where we are, if our head is tipping, or if we are moving. Difficulty processing vestibular input can make a child fear basic movement activities, or input might need to be so intense that it gets in the way of functional behavior and prevents regulation.
- Interoception: Sensors in our organs report how things are functioning inside which might mean not sensing a need to use the bathroom or overreacting due to hunger.

---

If someone is confined to a wheelchair, we would never expect them to run across the field because we know that their body and nervous system won't sustain this activity. SPD is the same, but it isn't as easy to *see*.

- If a child experiences extreme pain with light touch, we won't see this as easily as we might see the wheelchair. We might even have the response of "toughen up" or "get over it". We might view this child as weak or sensitive when really their nervous system is sending so many signals it feels like a razor just cut their arm.

- If a child doesn't know how their body moves through space, they might break everything in their path. They can appear clumsy or even become the class clown because their behavior was once funny and this child desperately needs a friend. Little did anyone know they just didn't know where their body was so they missed the chair when they went to sit; pretending to do this on purpose is better than the embarrassment of missing the chair.

## SENSORY-BASED MOTOR DISORDER

This disorder has two primary categories: dyspraxia and postural disorder.

**Dyspraxia-** This is a problem of, "How do I do that?" These kids have trouble coming up with a plan and carrying out movement patterns. Coordinated motor responses require an idea and sometimes doing simple things takes a lot of planning. When seemingly simple tasks are really hard, kids often create behaviors that distract anyone from figuring out that they don't know how to do something.

- We might see this child play only a particular game, or always need the rules to stay the same because change means they need a new plan.
- Some kids make up their own rules that get them out of part of the game they can't do; now the obstacle course only has three things instead of six according to these new rules. A child might be viewed as a poor sport when actually, they can't manage the many different, changing rules or steps required to play.
- Rigid behavior and difficulty with change or multiple-stepped tasks can be commonplace for this child.
- A child may know where a piece goes in a puzzle but can't figure out how to rotate it to fit.
- A child might have trouble independently completing tasks like cutting out a shape and pasting it to the page or a seemingly simple activity that requires sequencing steps.
- Coordination and balance may be tricky so this child thinks of himself as clumsy.

**Postural Disorder-** This is a problem often associated with "oops". These kids battle with control of their bodies for the demands of the activity. This isn't always recognized as a disorder, so many kids are considered clumsy or absent-minded. They lack adequate signals and some way to get rid of the traffic jam along the pathway between the brain and the body so information can come in faster and more accurately. Often the issue lies in the vestibular and proprioceptive senses, so the body isn't getting

242

accurate information about movement or from the limbs to know where it is in space.

- They might not know where they are, so when they sit down, they miss the chair.
- Their behavior might appear silly because then no one knows they messed up.
- They might have poor balance, strength, and posture or have trouble using both hands together.
- They may have trouble sitting on the floor because they don't have the postural control to be still *and* listen. Their disruption may be related to focus, but it might be worth seeing if regulation improves when they sit supported in a chair or stand in the back.

# DOWN SYNDROME

You may have students in your class with Down Syndrome and there are features that are consistent among these individuals that can affect programming and expectations. All individuals with Down syndrome have an extra copy of chromosome 21 (which is why this is referred to as Trisomy 21). This affects how the baby's brain and body develop, which can cause both mental and physical challenges. Common physical features include:

- Shortened neck with instability so somersaults and extreme range of motion activities should be avoided.
- Small ears and hearing loss are common.
- Resting tongue position is often out of the mouth affecting speech intelligibility and feeding.
- Small hands with a single line across the palmar crease, and small pinky fingers that may curve toward the thumb can create issues with writing, dexterity, and tool use.
- Poor muscle tone or loose joints should be acknowledged and always be a consideration in physical education requirements.

## Strategies for Teaching Students with Down Syndrome
(NCSE: National Council for Special Education)

- Students with Down syndrome are often visual learners so encourage the use of pictures and illustrations and try to integrate visual demonstrations as much as possible.
- The teaching of phonics and phonological awareness should not be neglected.
- Use manipulatives and activity-based learning for math and number concepts.
- Encourage social activities as much as possible during learning activities if the student is motivated by peers, as social skills are generally a strength. Structure learning and teaching opportunities to enable the student to engage in tasks with other students who can also act as appropriate role models.
- Tactile or hands-on activities often appeal to many students with Down syndrome.
- Speak directly to the student using clear language, short sentences, and appropriate, unambiguous facial expressions.
- Allow adequate time for the student to process language and respond.
- Encourage independence and be aware that a student may become unnecessarily dependent on the availability of excessive one-to-one support.

# COMMUNICATION ISSUES

Many maladaptive behaviors can stem from an inability to have needs met so when kids are non-verbal or can't find words when they are stressed, make sure they have some way to communicate. Pictures, communication boards, and non-verbal responses are all viable methods for communication but students may need help with a prompt or suggestion. Be aware that your interpretation of non-verbal communication can greatly influence your reaction to behaviors. If you are stressed or over-react, this can startle the child and result in fight, flight, or freeze. Especially when kids are non-verbal, there are many indicators that might be an attempt to communicate.

Indicators or Behavior that might be an attempt to communicate:

- Looking around
- Verbalization that is loud, urgent, or alarming when really it might be excitement
- Agitation
- Self-Injury
- Disruption
- Crying or screaming
- Moving their body next to people and things they are interested in

- Turning their body away from people and things they aren't interested in
- Using gestures and facial expressions
- Reaching with an open hand for things they want or grabbing items or people
- Taking your hand to get you to do things for them or to lead you somewhere
- Pointing to things they want and then at you for assistance
- Using pictures
- Making noises

How to expand on speech in the classroom when you aren't a speech pathologist:

- Observe vocalizations and mimic or expand on the noises a child makes to you.
- Utilize and encourage the use of a communication device everywhere throughout the school and with any activity.
- Remember that only 7% of communication is verbal, so watch for non-verbal.
- Respect wait time (often up to 10 seconds) so the child has an opportunity to process and respond.
- Build off what a child initiates and target preferred activities or items for conversation.
- Model communication aloud with attention to the speed and intensity of your speech.

# EXTREME BEHAVIORS

Sensory processing issues and executive functioning weakness can be challenging for kids because when adults don't consider brain-based explanations for behavior they can assume this behavior is a controllable choice. Maladaptive behavioral responses can be similar in nature to a child who doesn't participate in PE because they have a broken leg; they aren't refusing because they are lazy or unmotivated, they have a broken leg that won't support their weight to run. Behavior issues can occur for many reasons but many behavior-related issues stem from lagging developmental skills that affect performance and make it hard to control behavior. Behavioral regulation will be very tough when kids don't have the right skills for the given situation. This occurs whether we are talking about a six-year-old or a sixteen-year-old. Brain development is responsible for skill development, and if the skills aren't there, this child will struggle to find fun or success because executive skills are always a huge part of the puzzle. Since behavior is an intuitive way to better understand a child's world, we may form assumptions based on the behavior we see. When kids know they aren't good at something, they can easily create a distraction to prevent people from figuring this out. This can occur in an academic or social situation.

o   If they are working with others but don't understand the assignment, being silly is a great way to make friends and avoid what they might not be able to do successfully.

o   If they are out on the playground but don't know how to join in with peers, their behavior might prevent friendships.

Neuroscience has come a long way, and there are many studies and scans that support the correlation between brain development and behavior (Amen Clinic). Schools often employ discipline programs focusing on fear-based motivation through detention or suspension. This works for some students, but for those who are frequent fliers in detention or who never seem to respond to consequences, it might be time to try something else. Similarly, when school discipline programs try to manage behavior using rewards and positive reinforcement, there are still some kids who simply can not earn the reward. Discipline approaches are only effective if they *affect* behavior. If a child could, they would. This concept is very important to remember. Why are they not finding success? If discipline is attempting to address the motivation and nothing is changing, it is time to look at the child's ability or adjust the expectations.

No amount of motivation can help if the signals are not communicating or the skills are not intact. Despite positive or negative consequences, repetitive behavior stems from an unsolved problem that prevents the adjustment of a behavioral response. When an imbalance prevents regulation, the difference between a child's ability and potential can be huge. When the expectations or demands are so much higher than the signals or skills of the child, we generally see maladaptive behavior because the gap is too big to overcome, and there is no just right challenge to be found anywhere.

## HOW ADULTS CAN SUPPORT BEHAVIORAL REGULATION

How an adult interacts with a child can be half the battle. If you can help a child better understand how their system works and then how to begin using tools that meet the demands of that situation, you will be dealing with an entirely different set of behaviors. When kids can't adjust, adults need to. When kids can't regulate, adults need to be regulated. Adults affect the regulation of a child almost immediately because children feed off the emotions, anxiety, and intensity of the adult that is supposed to provide the emotional foundation that allows them to try new things, persevere, and safely push limits. Aside from managing your own energy, there are many ways that an adult can affect a situation or influence behavioral responses by altering the adult perspective of the *why* behind behavior and engaging in a different manner to present a new approach to struggling students. When kids can't communicate effectively, they depend on you to help them regulate and this requires reading their behavior. This applies to kids who have actual special education needs that affect communication as well as those kids who shut down when they are stressed.

- Help adapt their work or the situational demands and create a more appropriate challenge for their needs or level of arousal. This just right challenge requires identifying the demands of the situation (pace, noise, intensity, or task requirements that are too easy or hard) and helping them find tools to counteract them such as chunking work, using noise-canceling headphones, requiring less work or allowing for extended time.
- Provide emotional support and input for regulation through movement strategies, the use of recovery areas, or techniques and self-monitoring strategies that give words to strong emotions, such as dragon talk or identifying the Zone of Regulation that needs to change.
- Some kids need the stimulation another person provides to improve focus; these kids can work with an adult sitting beside them but struggle to complete work when they are on their own.
- They might not know they need a break, food, or the bathroom.
- You can affect the physical environment by helping them figure out what isn't working for them. Are others too close? Are too many people involved? Are the people making demands too intense? How stimulating is the space they are in?
- Anticipation helps with anxiety. Do they know how to do the steps required for success? Do they know what is coming next in their schedule?
- Have they had adequate time to process information or instructions?

- Use very few words, be specific with instructions, use a firm voice and be consistent. Creating boundaries for kids can help them feel more in control because they need to know there is a limit and what or where it is. Make sure all adults are using the same terminology and approach.

I work with lots of kids who have behavior charts. These are working documents because change happens, rewards differ week to week, and tools might need to be adjusted. Here are some ways to create a simple behavior plan that doesn't take forever to change.

This behavior plan should live in a folder that is bright in color and has two pockets (one for things "to do" and the other for things that are "done" or ready to be turned in).

Have the behavior plan on a piece of paper that can be copied each week instead of a laminated version that takes time to make and preserve.

Focus on a maximum of four specific goals, with bullets of the specific behaviors we expect.

Have the rewards or motivators clearly shown on the page to remind the student of *why* they are working so hard.

Have a list or pictures of appropriate tools below the goals to remind the student of successful options to improve regulation (or to help adults cue the student).

Provide space for teachers or parents to initial when behavior is appropriate; sometimes the more initials, the faster the reward.

# BEHAVIOR OR SAFETY PLANS

<u>Behavior or safety plans</u> are best utilized when they outline goals and specify rewards with visual reinforcement for each moment of success. These can be motivating for many reasons because they are unique to *this* child and their challenges, so the goals are achievable and this document is tangible proof that they have succeeded. This important document often goes home for parents to admire too, so even more positive energy is being paid for good behavior. Whether these plans are a formal piece of an IEP (Individualized Education Program) or simply something a teacher or administrator designs to help a child track their good choices, some important things should be included in each of these plans.

- For kids with extreme behaviors and short attention spans, try using small chunks of time to earn a minute at a time toward a reward. If a behavior program takes things away, many kids just give up because they have already lost the reward. Instead of losing time for poor behavior, they simply don't earn it.

- For the kids who don't respond well to the concept of having to *earn* reward time, have them start with a given reward with the understanding that their behavioral choices will either allow them to keep this reward, or lose portions of it (for example, they lose 1 minute of the 15, etc.).

- When kids struggle to regulate behavior when a reward plan is in place, consider that the requirements for earning the reward might be too difficult. Adjust the chunks of time to provide more frequent rewards until they can achieve small steps toward their goal behavior. This is important at first so they have buy-in for the plan and how it benefits them.

- Be specific about the goal or desired behavior and use positive wording that is specific in the plan (for example, "I will use my strategies when I am frustrated" instead of "I won't blow up").

- List examples of goal behavior so people unfamiliar with this student can still follow the content and catch them being successful. For example, a goal for responsible behavior means having materials ready, not disturbing others' learning, and utilizing appropriate learning tools. Have the goal with the specifics easy to read so everyone has the same expectation and knows when something has been achieved.

- Only focus on a few goal items so it is more achievable for the child and easier for adults to support and reinforce. Remember that the brain doesn't work during stress so specific bullet items that describe the goal and what that behavior should look like can also serve as a reminder and visual cue for the child.
- If parents are involved and supportive, include a home goal. This will encourage active communication between home and school and remind everyone that we are all in this together to help this child. Parents can celebrate school goals and teachers can celebrate completed home chores. The more positive the better!
- Have the child decide what the reward or motivator might be. Some kids would rather have lunch with a special teacher while others might want a tangible item. The rewards likely start as extrinsic (snack or toy) but hopefully become more intrinsic (pride in doing well) but they must be designed *with* the child. When adults decide the goals and rewards, they can miss what might really matter to *this* child. There are *Forced-Choice Reinforcement Menus* available to print off the internet that can help determine what is motivating.
- Have this behavior plan or data collection on a regular sheet of paper so it can be carried everywhere during the day, and even taken home at night so parents can see successes or add goals being addressed at home. If they can carry this paper in their TO DO/ DONE folder this will also increase the motivation for using this very important organizational tool and maybe this will become a habit. (see www.secrettohappy.com).
- Have adults put their initials on the chart instead of a checkmark. At the end of the day, this child can see all the different people who caught them finding success and this can be a great reminder for them when those negative thoughts start to bubble up.
- Make sure the back of the page shows the tools they need to use for success and include visuals to help support this tool use. This allows other adults to see that this child might need a snack or

movement and it can also help the child when their brain starts to go into fight, flight, or freeze because the tools are listed clearly for all to see.

- For kids who have really struggled, start easy. Give initials and kudos quickly and readily. When the momentum of success begins, you can always back off a little or increase the demands, but one of the fastest ways to sabotage a behavior plan is through expectations that are too high or chunks of time that are too long.
- Don't forget to integrate movement-based strategies into breaks with clear options that adults can see are appropriate for this child's needs.

# THE PRACTICAL STUFF:
# STRATEGIES THAT ADDRESS OR
# *PREVENT* EXTREME BEHAVIORS

### Aggression or Self-Injurious Behavior

Often aggression or self-injury is a sign that a child needs more or heavier input to feel better. Sometimes there is an inaccurate perception of what is happening in the body so intense input is sought out because they just need to feel *something*. Pain or intense behavior is usually the most intense sensation that can be felt. The goal of managing self-injury is to replace the input they are getting in a safer, more sustainable manner. The goal with aggression is safety through recovery. Self-injury and aggression can be treated similarly, and the following ideas might help in the recovery process.

- The very first thing to do when a child is engaging in extreme aggression or self-injury is to secure the immediate surroundings to prevent additional harm to them or others (such as with heavy, sharp objects or anything else that can be used as a weapon).
- Recovery is critical so decreasing the environmental input is the safest, most hands-off way to help a child calm down. Turn down the lights and decrease the noise (often by moving them to a different space or removing others from their space depending on the intensity of the situation). Do not engage, provide solutions, or introduce more input unless you have had experience with this student in this type of situation before.
- If you have worked with a student who frequently self-harms or doesn't aversively respond to you during aggressive episodes, one way to help them stop is to provide deep pressure down into the shoulders from behind. This should be performed by a trusted adult known to the student, ensuring minimal conversation or interaction. Sometimes the deep pressure is more appropriate through the use of a heavy lap pad or weighted blanket.
- Distraction toward movement or heavy work activity is a good tool after recovery. Encouraging a job where they get a change in

environment and carry something (preferably heavy) to a different place can sometimes replace the input they are getting from the self-injury.

- Replace maladaptive behaviors. If they are biting, give them something oral. If they hit their head, give heavy input into their shoulders. Try to determine what and where they need the input and provide a safer alternative. Use visuals to show them what you can do to help them before touching them or applying deep pressure.
- Encourage them to spend some time in a different space, especially if it involves different sensory aspects (such as a dark corner with different textures to explore). The use of a visual (versus talking) to suggest this change in environment can prevent further escalation.
- Provide fidgets that require the use of the hand muscles such as hard squeezing.
- Provide heavy work opportunities that make them use their muscles such as errands carrying heavy things, pushing heavy furniture, or any type of activity that they might enjoy but also allows them to lift, push, pull, or move.

## Times of frustration, Outbursts, and Meltdowns

- Recovery may need to focus more on regulation than engagement or participation for *now*.
- Refrain from talking the student through the moment; let them *just BE*.
- Allow for a break or change in scenery before problem-solving or engaging.
- Picture prompts and simple "first/then" commands are effective ways to cue a child to utilize previously discussed tools or strategies that help them feel better when they are stressed.
- Consider the sensory aspects of the space; try a different environment that is clutter-free, with dim lighting and calming or quiet music.
- Allow extra time to process or respond.

- Present visuals that show deep breathing or techniques they already know how to do that have proven helpful in the past.
- Ensure that your expectations or the demands are within the zone of a just right challenge and adjust this so that they can meet manageable demands once they have recovered.
- Take turns doing some of the work until they find consistent success.
- Use modifications such as additional technology to aid in work.
- Break up activities that are difficult or multi-stepped with frequent rewards.
- Catch them finding success; even little moments can give them momentum for bigger ones.
- Remember communication needs. Do you know what they want or need? Have they expressed their needs?
- Consider the number of steps and how you are instructing them in the task.
- Build control for the child. Let them decide which problem to start on, which tool to use (out of 3 maximum options), or which space they need to move to.

## Difficulty with Change

Kids who depend on structure and predictability for self-regulation can have difficulty managing behavior when they are on their own or have an inaccurate perception of what is coming next. They may not know how it will feel or what they will have to do and this can result in a meltdown.

- Prepare kids *beforehand* with pictures or a visual schedule, then WAIT or walk away so they can process independently.
- Distract them during times of transition (such as during a walk, have them find various sight words, play a silent game of "I Spy" or count all the yellow things they walk past, etc.).
- Incorporate heavy work into transitions (carry heavy objects, walk in a lunge pattern that requires the big muscles of the legs to work hard, etc.).

- Try using a timer to help kids see how long they have until their next transition.
- Assemblies and sporadic special events at school may not be appropriate for them to participate in (especially if it hasn't gone well in the past).
- Allow the child to have some control (choice board).
- Utilize social stories that show different tools to help with transitions, or provide various ideas for strategies to help with the feelings that come with change.

## Ideation- Tell them what TO DO vs. what NOT TO DO

This gives them the idea of what we want them to do and creates a clear expectation. Providing positive ideas for behavior means kids won't get stuck on the behavior we don't want to see.

- o "Gentle hands" instead of "Don't hit."
- o "First book, then computer" instead of "No computer."

## Critical Things to Remember

- Only engage with a child if no one else is. Observe the situation before engaging so that only one adult is actively dealing with the child. During intense behavioral situations, another adult is important for support but they are only backup.
- Avoid power struggles and build in control any chance you can.
- Allow for and consider processing time.
- Ensure that there is a method of communication for non-verbal students no matter where the child is or where they are headed in the building. Verbal *and* non-verbal students can benefit from visuals that show options for recovery (see the "cycle of recovery" tool on p. 262).
- Pay attention to *your* regulation. The adult is usually the most critical factor in a child's regulation and responses.

## Create a *Cycle of Recovery* © (Murray-Robison)

A Cycle of Recovery is an effective visual representation of a cyclical, tiered system of support. It shows that they can always recover no matter how extreme a situation might become. The child must be familiar with how it works before they experience stress and they are involved in the creation of tools or strategies to help them recover.

- The goal of the Cycle of Recovery is to help a student recover, begin to regulate, and return to class with tools and the feeling of empowerment that comes with recovery.
- If the behavior does not improve, this means the sensory-based strategy they chose is not the appropriate tool for the needs of this moment.
- A request for use of the recovery tools must be honored.
- This space or time is designed for de-escalation so do not engage with a child during this time. Ignoring noises and behaviors is appropriate. The adult should allow the child to recover on their own unless they specifically request assistance or are beginning to challenge the safety of themselves or those around them.
- The adult is nearby for safety reasons but the child needs to utilize tools to recover and these should be presented in picture format (see p. 264).
- Self-monitoring can be challenging when a child escalates, so use the Cycle of Recovery visual to cue the child that they are escalating toward dysregulation.
- The back side of the Cycle of Recovery visual should show three or four options for tools to use that the child has identified to be effective for how they are wired.
- All of this "plan" should be familiar to the child because it was discussed during a time when they were regulated.

It is really important to understand that when kids sit on a ball or a wobble stool they are supposed to be bouncing or wiggling because it is the movement that is helping them regulate.

If it is hard for *your* wiring to have kids bouncing on a ball or spinning back and forth, you might need to move that "movement station" to a place in the room that you can handle. Kids should be bouncing and spinning side to side because it is that input that is feeding the focused attention.

Expectations are critical when using tools; we need to expect that it will look different but the end result is what we are going for. Obviously, safety is a key consideration as well as the learning of others so if a child's movement is negatively impacting those around them, adjustments must be made.

## Specific Information for Use with the Cycle of Recovery and Tools or Strategies to Utilize

- Fidgets are designed to be boring and not draw attention away from a task or learning opportunity. When they are needed, the student will show improved behavior and attention. If they are distracting or draw attention from the task, they are not the appropriate tool for this moment.
- Keep in mind that a child does not need to be looking at you to be "listening." If a child is looking at the item while fidgeting, confirm that they are listening to determine if this tool improves focused attention.
- Movement or dynamic sitting options include pacing or moving in the back of the class while listening. Sitting on a wobble stool or using a yoga ball should result in improved focus, not disruption. If behavior worsens, this is not the time to use movement.
- The child can actively participate in the creation and tools of choice in the Cycle of Recovery process. This increases buy-in for the process and can also provide an opportunity to role-play how it can be used during moments of escalation.

- Private verbal praise for *effort* and successful recovery or regulation can be more effective than focusing on the performance of a task once a child has attempted to rejoin an activity.
- Ignoring and walking away from disruptive behavior is very effective, especially if the goal is to receive attention (whether from peers or adults).
- Visuals with few words are better for times of struggle but make sure these "cue cards" or visuals are familiar to the child before use. The goal is to be able to set the image in front of the child and walk away. It serves as a visual cue for regulation with options and tools they have used successfully to recover. It is also a good idea to have it laminated so it can't be ripped up in a moment of frustration.
- Stimming is repetitive or unusual movements or noises that are sometimes seen with autism and observable during times of high stress. Stimming can help individuals manage emotions and cope with overwhelming situations or sensations but sometimes it is difficult to determine if behavior is related to stimming or merely attention seeking. If the child looks around for a response from others, this behavior is likely for attention. If they are in their own space and rocking, flapping hands, flicking or snapping fingers, bouncing, jumping, or twirling, pacing or walking on tiptoes, or repeating words or phrases these are typical stimming behaviors that can indicate the system is getting overwhelmed or attempting to regulate. An appropriate course of action might include:

1. Ignore
2. If behavior escalates or is disruptive this can indicate the need for a break

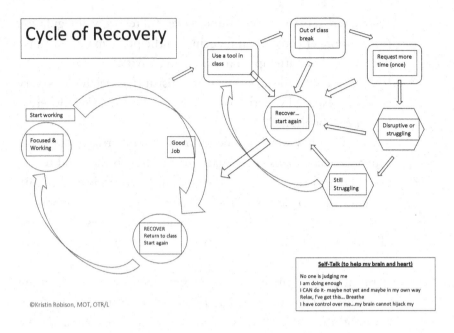

**Cycle of Recovery**

Out of class break

Use a tool in class

Request more time (once)

Start working

Focused & Working

Good Job

Recover... start again

Disruptive or struggling

Still Struggling

RECOVER Return to class Start again

<u>Self-Talk (to help my brain and heart)</u>
No one is judging me
I am doing enough
I CAN do it- maybe not yet and maybe in my own way
Relax, I've got this... Breathe
I have control over me...my brain cannot hijack my

©Kristin Robison, MOT, OTR/L

## Create an *Integrative Regulation Tool-Box* © (Murray-Robison)

This tool is a wonderful way to show adults and students how to visually navigate the process of regulation. It draws on the colored zones (Zones of Regulation) and provides strategies, scripting, and tools that encompass behavioral and sensory approaches. There is a more detailed version for the adult and a simpler version for the student (especially for younger students you would have more visuals and fewer words). This tool is a nice way to ensure everyone is on the same page in the determination of where this child is (red, yellow, green or blue) based on observable behavior so that even if adults aren't familiar with a student, they can still identify the area of need and what to do because consistency is critical.

## Adult Version

- The first column shows the behavior or verbiage a child might exhibit in each colored zone for easy identification and a potential conversation starter regarding self-monitoring.
- The second column shows possible staff responses to behavior and reminders for adults to consider in each zone; red and yellow zones may have very different sensory-based responses or more simplistic language. This allows for specific jargon or strategies for the student to use with the help of the adult.
- The third column is a list but can include images for younger kids or for kids who go into fight, flight or freeze and can't handle the busy lists of words. This section also serves to remind the adult what strategies work for this student.
- The back of the page shows very simple images that provide tools that can be used both in and out of class. Motivators can be shown as well as accommodations/modifications that are part of a student's 504 or IEP. The details on the back page are highly individualized and will vary according to the ability and developmental level of the student.

| What STUDENT SAYS/DOES | Staff Response to Behavior | STRATEGIES FOR THE STUDENT TO USE |
|---|---|---|
| **RED ZONE**<br>-Slamming/throwing materials/objects<br>-Screaming, crying<br>-Scratching, hitting, kicking<br>-Lying on floor<br>-Shallow Breathing<br>-Resists assistance or effort to calm | -USE VISUALS & VERY FEW WORDS<br>-Position yourself to block aggressive attempts toward students/self<br>-Position self to prevent elopement<br>-Use calm, monotone voice<br>-Move her away from others<br>-Point to the zone you observe her in and/or possible (visual) strategies | \*\*\*REFER TO IMAGES ON BACK\*\*\*<br>-Ice pack for neck, face or independent student use<br>-Move to a quiet, visually boring space away from others<br>-Trumpet breathing or timed, assisted breathing |
| **APPROACHING RED: Agitation/Anxiety**<br>-Refuses help/support/calm<br>-Escapes/avoids work<br>-looks around<br>-Plays with objects unrelated to task<br>-Crying, Whimper→Screaming | -Limit language, refer to pictures or demonstrate<br>-Use calm, monotone, firm voice<br>-Give 5-7 seconds for processing, "when you're ready..."<br>-When calm give redirection; if behavior starts again, ignore <u>If problem behavior is for seeking attention</u>: Ignore, attend to something else, continue with your instruction <u>If behavior is due to not getting preferred activity/item</u>: Provide simple redirection, don't give item until calm or asks appropriately, | \*\*Refer to images on back\*\*\*<br>-Offer ice pack<br>-Adjust the task to ensure quick success<br>-Adjust the environment: away from others, different lighting or intensity of space, different sitting options (standing, sitting on ball/cushion)<br>- |
| **I FEEL AWESOME**<br>-Sits at desk/instructional area<br>-follows instructions<br>-Has only one stuffie<br>-Looks at peers/teacher for cues<br>-Follows simple directions | -Provide choice reward/motivator<br>-Give verbal praise paired with visual supports/positive cues (smile, pat on back, thumbs-up, thank you for having your pencil out/cleaning up/trying to do your work, you're sitting in your chair, your eyes are on me)<br>-Reinforce expectations by demonstrating appropriate behavior/response | YOU'RE DOING IT!!<br>KEEP DOING IT!!<br>\*\*REFER TO BACK FOR REWARDS\*\*\* |
| **BLUE ZONE: Bored, Tired, Content too hard, demand too high**<br>-Not engaged in activity/discussion<br>-Disruptive<br>-Getting up, seeking input<br>-Making noises<br>-Doing something besides what is requested (distracting you from the task at hand) | -Remind her about work first, then reward (show image of reward first, then circle what she should do before getting that reward; if computer activity point and use very few words)<br>-Encourage standing, lying to work, use of a different pencil, anything new will increase motivation<br>-Create a game for work completion or compliance (time yours vs. hers, do a silly motor movement after one task)<br>-Chunk work/task with positive attention for each part | Image of strategy to increase response     Image of strategy to increase response |

(back page)

IN CLASS TOOLS

MOTIVATORS/REWARDS

- Gum
- 5-minute free time
- ???

(need images here vs. words)

OUT-OF-CLASS TOOLS

 How long? _____

(add image of where student can go out of class)

(add image of where student can go out of class)

Accommodations:

- Headphones
- Extra time
- Shortened work
- Dictation

<u>Student Version</u>: The student should have a more visually simple option that is similar to the adult version but without extra detail. Both the student and adult will have the same back page that shows visuals for in-the-moment support.

| What STUDENT SAYS/DOES | STRATEGIES FOR THE STUDENT TO USE |
|---|---|
| **RED ZONE**<br>-Slamming/throwing materials/objects<br>-Screaming, crying<br>-Scratching, hitting, kicking<br>-Lying on floor<br>-Shallow Breathing<br>-Resists assistance or effort to calm | ***REFER TO IMAGES ON BACK***<br>-Ice pack for neck, face or independent student use<br>-Move to a quiet, visually boring space away from others<br>-Trumpet breathing or timed, assisted breathing |
| **APPROACHING RED: Agitation/Anxiety**<br>-Refuses help/support/calm<br>-Escapes/avoids work<br>-looks around<br>-Plays with objects unrelated to task<br>-Crying, Whimper→Screaming | **Refer to images on back***<br>-Offer ice pack<br>-Adjust the task to ensure quick success<br>-Adjust the environment: away from others, different lighting or intensity of space, different sitting options (standing, sitting on ball/cushion)<br>- |
| **I FEEL AWESOME**<br>-Sits at desk/instructional area<br>-follows instructions<br>-Has only one stuffie<br>-Looks at peers/teacher for cues<br>-Follows simple directions | YOU'RE DOING IT!!<br>KEEP DOING IT!!<br>**REFER TO BACK FOR REWARDS*** |
| **BLUE ZONE: Bored, Tired, Content too hard, demand too high**<br>-Not engaged in activity/discussion<br>-Disruptive<br>-Getting up, seeking input<br>-Making noises<br>-Doing something besides what is requested (distracting you from the task at hand) | Image of strategy to increase response / Image of strategy to increase response |

<u>(back page)</u>

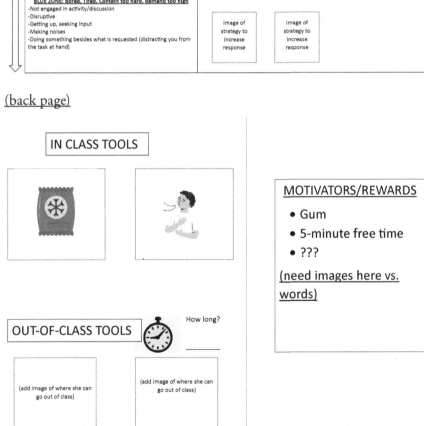

**IN CLASS TOOLS**

**MOTIVATORS/REWARDS**
- Gum
- 5-minute free time
- ???

<u>(need images here vs. words)</u>

**OUT-OF-CLASS TOOLS** How long?

(add image of where she can go out of class) (add image of where she can go out of class)

265

# SECTION FIVE

## RESOURCES, PRINTABLES AND EVERYTHING ELSE

### SELF-ESTEEM AND FOCUS ON THE POSITIVE

Humans are social beings; we depend on each other for survival and we desire acceptance from others. When behavior is negative, disruptive, rude, disrespectful, or mean, it can be very hard to see the good in this social human. When people rarely experience acceptance, they have no motivation to behave, help someone else, or be kind. They survive on their own, depending on no one, and tend to react instead of connect. Helping children develop self-belief and self-esteem involves self-talk, but it's also critical to watch what you and others say. Negative labels such as clumsy, hyper, lazy, or stubborn can become self-fulfilling prophecies. When kids are reminded that behavior is often a result of wiring or coping mechanisms, they can begin to understand that they have control over their responses. Hyper can be enthusiastic or energetic. Aggressive can be assertive. Unpredictable can be flexible.

Ask a child to think of something positive and something they *can* do. Just shifting how we think can make a huge difference. I have had clients start a Book of Positives. This can be done at home, but if they are struggling at school, this could easily be something the teacher can help them with too. Make sure the things in this book focus on specifics, like, "I chose a desk away from my friend and finished my math," because there is *specific* input about a *specific* task that might have been challenging. When they begin the self-doubt that often bubbles up, you can look back at this journal as proof that their dragon *can* be trained, and maybe the messages this student is getting right now are wrong. Perhaps the issue is temporary because there is proof that poor behavior doesn't *always* happen.

Often noticing just one simple positive thing can make a smile appear; modeling this is powerful too. Make comments in front of them that show them how to embrace positivity. This doesn't have to be mind-blowing, just positive and realistic.

- Celebrate even the little successes.
- Share *your* successes and excitement.
- Practice scenarios where negativity might take over, and then present different ways people deal with them to find the positive.
- In every negative, challenge kids to figure out a positive. It can be really hard and even get pretty silly, but it is a great way to shift the habit of a negative mindset.

> IF WE FOCUS ON THE POSITIVE, WE WILL
> GET MORE POSITIVE BEHAVIOR

Counteracting negativity is challenging for many reasons and research-based explanations reveal why positivity can be so much harder to achieve when relating with others.

- Studies with couples conducted by Gottman and Levenson determined that five positives were required to counteract the effects of one negative (Gottman and Levenson 1992).
- In the paper, *Bad Is Stronger Than Good*, the authors state, "Bad emotions, bad parents, and bad feedback have more impact than good ones, and bad information is processed more thoroughly

than good. Bad impressions and bad stereotypes are quicker to form and more resistant to disconfirmation than good ones." (Baumeister et al. 2001).

- Brickman, Coates, and Janoff-Bulman concluded in a 1978 study that "...gradually, even the most positive events will cease to have impact as they themselves are absorbed into the new baseline against which further events are judged." (Brickman et al. 1978).

Despite the often human tendency to default to negativity and the amount of energy required to focus on positivity, there are many reasons that this tendency must be overcome. Positivity doesn't just feel good, it actually does good. What if we could change patterns of behavior to include more positivity? Imagine how much healthier we would be, how much better we would feel every day, and how much more learning would occur. Hormones and neurotransmitters flood our system when we are happy, benefiting our mental and physical health in many ways.

- Dopamine is critical for motivation but it also improves blood flow, digestion, memory, focus, mood, emotions, and motor skills. It helps in sleep, stress, reward seeking, pain processing, and is a key factor in executive functioning. We get a flood of dopamine when we are praised or rewarded (Cristol 2021).
- Oxytocin is called the love hormone because of how it works in the brain to improve arousal, trust, and bonding; all of this is critical for learning and mental health (Schneiderman et al. 2012).
- Serotonin is boosted by exercise and it has been shown to improve brain and nervous system communication, help with digestion, mood stabilization, sleep, anxiety and depression (Lin and Kuo 2013).
- Endorphins decrease discomfort and pain so we can continue even when uncomfortable, which historically was critical for survival. Endorphins also support social relationships and increase with movement or exercise (Davidson 2021).
- Adrenaline increases heart rate, blood pressure, and the air in our lungs. It enlarges the pupil in the eye and regulates glucose levels in the brain to help stabilize blood sugar. Sprinting, splashing cold

water on your face, or trying something new can all increase the adrenaline in your system (Spinasanta, 2021).

When a child focuses on the negatives or what they *can't* do, it also prevents them from embracing their self-worth. Sometimes we need to help them see how amazing they are. Everyone has traits that are unique and incredible, but sometimes these traits make it hard for us to find success in *all* situations. Even if you don't say it aloud, having a positive mindset can alter how you engage with a child. There are many ways to support the process of positivity to help a child and this will help you to feel better too.

We all remember moments of success when we made someone happy or proud; kids really need this. Shifting our perspective to the positive allows us to provide tools instead of criticism. Dopamine drives the brain's reward system, and it controls motivation and the feeling of well-being that allows for learning to happen. Constant monitoring of the negative stuff can result in fight or flight, which makes learning impossible. Dopamine can increase through setting *realistic* goals and achieving them… kids need help with this process. When we get the behavior we want and attention is given to that behavior, it is remembered and we will see it again. If they *could* behave, they *would*. We are dealing with brain chemicals and must find the best way to address behavior.

> When a child has reached the just right challenge and we point this out to *other* people, the impact is huge! When I know a child is in ear shot and I brag about them to someone else, this helps instill a sense of pride because what they did was good enough to share, and now others know how awesome they are. Even for those kids who have very little good coming from their behavior, just the notice of one small, specific thing can change the momentum for future behavioral regulation.

# TABLE OF AWARENESS

One way to see a child's true inner greatness is through the Table of Awareness. This tool is easy to use and the process becomes more automatic the more it is utilized.

- First, identify any wiring that contributes to behavior and any strengths that can be built upon for success.
- Next, think of a goal related to where the child is struggling. It should be specific and should include input from the child since they are the one who feels the struggle, and we need their buy-in to reach this goal.

The following is an example of how this table can look for a child.

| BEHAVIORS/WIRING | POSSIBLE STRENGTHS | GOALS |
|---|---|---|
| Impulsive and not catching all the instructions because they start before they know fully what to do | Eager to start, enjoys being independent | Listen to all steps of the instructions or demonstrate the use of a strategy to remember steps and complete them on their own (make a rhyme or story out of steps, etc.) |
| Excitement and zest that disrupts group discussions | Positive, creative, excited with new activities | Find strategies that help decrease interrupting when someone talks, like counting to 3 before talking |
| They don't look like they are listening, they are doodling, and not watching the teacher | They might be trying very hard to do what we are asking but they need more input. They may need to doodle to attend or perhaps they can't watch the teacher and write. If they are wriggling, they might be trying really hard to pay attention | Work production! Use tools to increase follow-through with work, and utilize strategies that allow them to move and get more signals so their focus will improve |
| Difficulty reading peers and adjusting to their non-verbal cues. Often engaged in peer arguments and frequently getting into trouble | Enjoys peers and likes to make others laugh. Doesn't seek extra attention, but enjoys it | Learn to wait, observe, plan, and then execute. They may need help with any of these steps |

## <u>Consequences are Still Vital</u>

Kids will be kids. This means that while you might try really hard to find an explanation for their behavior, sometimes there just isn't one. Kids need boundaries, structure, and discipline to mold behavior; natural consequences are a perfect way to do this. However, it is vital first to understand and consider all the factors that affect behavior. If you are missing something significant, your reaction to a child might be the one thing that completely shuts them down; it is hard to mold behavior when a child doesn't care anymore. Try to think through the various things you know about the *why* of behavior.

- First, rule out possible signal issues. Are there too many? Not enough? What about sensory needs that should be addressed, like sleep, hunger, and pain? Their environment will affect their behavior based on their wiring and threshold. Is there too much going on? Not enough? Is there something about an activity that creates too many signals and puts them into fight, flight, or freeze?
- Next, think of the skills and the demands of the situation. How big is that gap between the skills and demands or expectations? Are they able to do what you are asking? Have you given them enough time to respond? Do they understand the directions?
- Finally, revisit what you know about *who* this child is. How they are wired, how they communicate, their strengths, and their self-confidence will *all* affect how they can respond. Maybe they have a motor issue, like not knowing how hard they are pushing on something, so that is why the high-five was so hard. If there is a learning issue, they might not remember what they read, so the list of twenty questions is impossible for them to answer. Are they always in fight or flight at the thought of new things?

Knowing the rules and having consequences when they are broken is how we create boundaries and structure. Even if a child has signal or skill issues, natural consequences help them learn the process and significance of their behavior. We are preparing these kids for the real world so they need to *feel* the natural consequences in our safe, controlled environment. They likely still need our guidance to determine if their system prevented them from making good choices, and they often need our support to recognize the importance of recovery. At some point, all kids will manipulate, and *all* kids will show frustration and misbehave… we all do.

This journey of helping children is a dance and one of the biggest ways to prevent a child from finding success in life is through learned helplessness. If you do too much to solve their problems or make life too easy and buffer them from feeling the natural consequences of their actions, they will continue to blame you when things go wrong. They need to make the connection that their behavior resulted in what they are feeling right now. You can still support them and empathize with their struggle, but as hard as it is for *you* to experience, *they* must feel the struggle or behavior will never change.

# THINGS TO REMEMBER

- Teach kids that fair doesn't always mean the same or equal. We all get what we *need*, which sometimes looks different for each person. Teaching the value of differences allows for empathy, tolerance, and ultimately happiness.

- If you are implementing consequences repeatedly and nothing changes, you are probably not dealing with the true problem affecting their behavior. Remember, if we don't hear the problem from the child's perspective, we may not be addressing the primary root of their behavior. Helping a child understand why they see things in a certain way and then advocating for their needs is a tremendous life skill that will help them everywhere. Guiding this process can be lengthy and exhausting but well worth it in the end.

- Examine the situation. Misbehavior usually means something is off. Is this child feeling out of control? Is there something in their world that is just too much? Are our expectations more than they can handle? Have we really listened to them... taken the time, without distractions or interruptions, to *really* listen? Sometimes that is all they need... *our time and attention.*

- Behavior evolves over time, and it is dependent upon what came before. Teaching kids is one of the hardest jobs out there, and we don't always have the necessary tools in our toolbox. Consider getting more strategies for your arsenal or trying to adjust your perspective. It is okay to admit you were wrong or made a poor choice. Children need to see that adults make mistakes too, but they also need to see that how we respond to those mistakes is what really matters. Be honest about your struggles and how you got through them.

- Time is our most precious gift. Try to take a breath before reacting. Remember that each child needs time to respond and every child has a different timer. Demonstrating patience and responding calmly during chaotic situations can be one of the most valuable lessons you can teach a child.

- Allow time to reset and recover. When the nervous system goes into fight or flight, it doesn't often bounce back easily or quickly.

Allowing for time and even a different setting can help with this transition back to a regulated state. Many kids need 5-7 seconds to process what we say; this is a long time! Behavior can appear defiant if we don't wait long enough.

- We are all in this together, and *everyone* needs help sometimes. Talk to this child, talk to your co-workers or partner, talk to your friends, talk to your dog. Let people into your world and ask for help.
- Try to catch kids being good. Even a wink or verbal praise can do the trick. Be specific about the praise so they know what they are doing right.
- Replace behaviors. When we see inappropriate behaviors or potential safety risks, we must remember that this behavior serves a purpose. Instead of asking them to stop, try to figure out why they are doing it, and find a more appropriate strategy for them to try. Kids often need assistance with socially appropriate options, and this assistance should be one-on-one and when they are not in fight, flight, or freeze.
- Deep pressure can be very organizing and help the nervous system recover after stress.

  - Bear hugs: face the child away from you if you are in a school setting or if they don't like face-to-face contact.
  - Self-hugs: little kids who miss their parents while at school can squeeze themselves hard for a self-hug and blow a kiss home that will stick until they can do it for real.
  - Weighted lap pads, blankets, or pressure down into the shoulders provide organizing input for regulation.

- Ignore behaviors that you can and give your energy to the kids doing what you want. We all want attention and so many times kids behave in disruptive ways just to be seen because this is how they have learned they can get adult attention. If the behavior is not harmful, it's important to take a moment to acknowledge and appreciate a child who is following your instructions and is within hearing distance. Ignoring poor behavior and praising appropriate choices can help a child who is seeking attention.

- Respect preferences. Many kids will show us exactly what they can handle through their behavior. Forcing a "get used to it" approach sets off the nervous system and takes them away from the logical part of their world.

- Take a moment and breathe. With some deep breathing and mindfulness, just slowing the world down for a moment can go a long way in recovery and regulation. Have a child close their eyes and focus on what they can hear, smell, taste, and how they are breathing.

- Create a Picture Schedule. Use a picture to prepare kids for what is coming. Images are fast to process and don't leave anything unknown because it is right in front of them. You can show them the sequence of an activity, what the day looks like, or what the finished product should be.

# ADDITIONAL OUTSIDE RESOURCES

## Lives in the Balance and Dr. Greene's approach to CPS (Collaborative Problem Solving)

Dr. Greene says, "Kids do well if they can." This paradigm shift addresses our most vulnerable kids and helps teachers and caregivers see them through a different lens so our engagement is more effective. This program provides evidence-based strategies that help kids find success because their behavior is no longer seen as a choice but rather as a skill deficit. If you are constantly trying to help an intense child and having no luck, there are free resources, podcasts of the CPS model, training, and countless ideas through the website. Dr. Greene has also published books that are wonderful resources to utilize in your classroom or school.

- The Explosive Child: A New Approach for Understanding and Parenting Easily Frustrated, Chronically Inflexible Children
- Lost at School: Why Our Kids with Behavioral Challenges are Falling Through the Cracks and How We Can Help Them
- Lost & Found: Helping Behaviorally Challenging Students

## The Nurtured Heart and Dr. Glasser's Approach

This is a social-emotional program that focuses on helping students become intrinsically motivated by recognizing positive reinforcement through specific strategies that are perfect for the classroom. The goal is to simply reframe poor behavior as inner greatness that has yet to be realized. We don't want to change the child, just help them manage their behavior. Rather than continuously focusing on a child's poor behavior, give your attention to the child who is making a good choice. This helps to reframe and celebrate good behavior. This approach is very effective for intense children and those with oppositional defiance and attentional deficits. Howard Glasser has many resources but these are three books I have found especially helpful.

- Transforming the Difficult Child: The Nurtured Heart Approach
- Transforming the Intense Child Workbook
- The Inner Wealth Initiative: The Nurtured Heart Approach for Education

I have been in many situations where a student's difficult behavior was unintentionally supported. When a child is disruptive or not working and we continue to prompt them or publicly reprimand them, we are giving them our energy. Some kids need attention and it doesn't matter if it is negative. If poor behavior isn't urgent or hurting anyone, ignoring it to focus on a student who is doing what we have asked, helps to solve the attention problem. Anytime we can publicly celebrate behavior we want to see, the kids who are in the habit of getting our attention from poor behavior now have a reason to change.

# PRINTABLE VISUALS FOR
# THE CLASSROOM

There are many reasons visuals are effective. They provide ideas for strategies that don't involve a conversation and can prove effective even when the adult is feeling stressed. When you are dealing with a disability that prevents a child from responding in a way that you are used to teaching, these tools can be simple ways to prompt a child and also provide options for tools that they may not be able to come up with on their own at that moment.

- Kids are "sensory sponges". They soak up our energy. They gauge the safety of their world by the adults who are interacting with them and sometimes it is really hard to have our emotions in check when we have to help them manage regulation needs and strategies. Adults who are stressed often escalate behavior. Having a visual can provide a tool for an adult to utilize with minimal engagement until their energy is back in check and supportive of the regulation needs of this child.
- Kids with autism need visuals because their brain responds better to this type of input and it removes the social interaction piece that can be too intense to benefit their regulation.

- Kids with ADHD benefit from visuals because they provide a quick reference when attentional drifts have prevented them from catching all the information.
- Kids with anxiety spend a lot of time in fight, flight, or freeze and this means the thinking brain doesn't work as well. Visuals or lists can support their needs because a familiar and concrete item can be referred to at any time.
- Visuals allow the adult to give their attention to the behaviors they want to see instead of always attending to maladaptive behavior. If a page can be set down in front of a child when they are beginning to escalate, this adult has now, in essence, 'loaned' their brain to the child. This visual can serve as a cue that this child is displaying behaviors indicating trouble (because maybe their self-monitoring ability is still a work in progress). It also provides options for tools that can help with recovery or regulation without an adult talking to them or attempting to problem-solve in a moment of stress. The adult can also show the child the visual and walk away for them to process in their own time independently.
- Problem-solving ideas for images should always be discussed with a child *before* they are stressed so they are familiar with the content, know what it means, and how to use it. Tools are only effective if they help to solve problems. The child must be involved in the problem-solving and 'what now' aspect of this process when the frontal lobe is working. When the brain hijacks the system, it can be very empowering for a child to feel they know how to regain balance.

# SIGNAL STRATEGIES IN PICTURES

Carry heavy Objects Breaths

Deep

Give a hug

Chair pushup

Push hands together

Helper Squishes

Rocking

Find a Quiet

Space

©Kristin Robison, MOT, OTR/L

# WHAT TO DO WITH FIRE DRAGONS

---

## Slow Rocking

## Chair Push-up

## Helper Squishes

©Kristin Robison, MOT, OTR/L

## Deep Breathing

## Heavy Job

## Stand up or Move

## Quiet Work Place

# WHAT TO DO WITH SLEEPY DRAGONS

## Push Hands Together

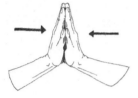

## Chair Push-up

## Drink of Water or Snack

## Wall Pushup

## Heavy Job

## Stand up or Sit on a Cushion

## Big Hug

©Kristin Robison, MOT, OTR/L

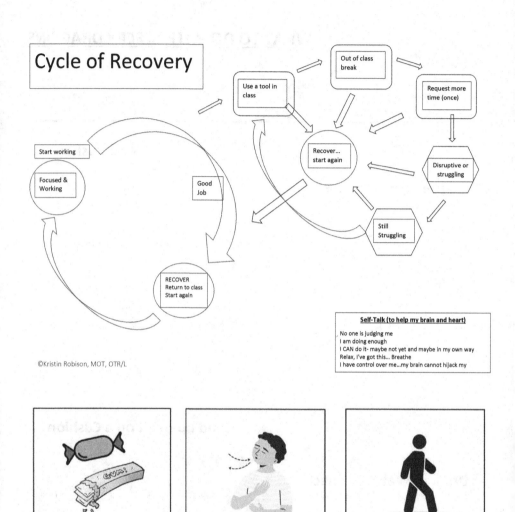

# Cycle of Recovery

Out of class break

Use a tool in class

Request more time (once)

Start working

Focused & Working

Good Job

Recover... start again

Disruptive or struggling

RECOVER Return to class Start again

Still Struggling

**Self-Talk (to help my brain and heart)**

No one is judging me
I am doing enough
I CAN do it- maybe not yet and maybe in my own way
Relax, I've got this... Breathe
I have control over me...my brain cannot hijack my

©Kristin Robison, MOT, OTR/L

| **Get a Snack** | **Take Deep Breaths** | **Take a Walk** |

©Kristin Robison, MOT, OTR/L

## Size of my Problem

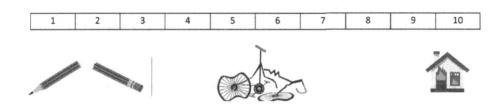

## Images for Self-Monitoring

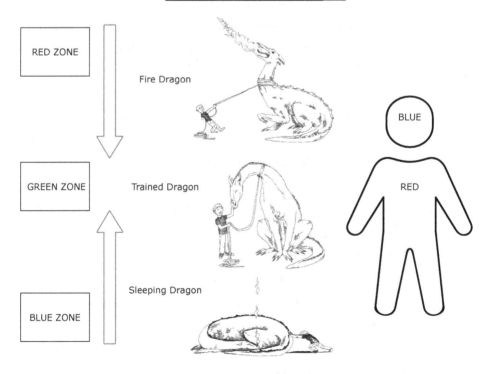

# Refocus, Reset, & Re-Enter Form
# From Office/Refocus Room to Teacher

Student Name _____ Grade_____

Sent to the Office/Refocus Room by _____

Reason _____

### *Notes from Administration/Refocus Team conversation with child:*

- What happened or is happening?

  _____

- What emotions do you feel inside because of it (angry, sad, embarrassed, afraid, etc.)?

  _____

- Allow these emotions and thoughts to settle in your body. Where do you feel something *physically* in your body (tightened chest, stomach pain, etc.)?

  _____

- Is this something you have experienced before?

  _____

- What were you thinking of at the time of the incident, or what are you thinking about now?

  _____

- What is the worst part of all of this?

  _____

- Who has been affected by what you have done?

  _____

- In what way?

  _____

- How does this make you feel?

  _____

- What do you think you need to do to make things right? What are your next steps?

  _____

  _____

Recommendations/Consequences - Administrative Notes - Refocus Team Notes...

_____

_____

_____

Adapted from a form created by Hoppe & Rankin

Additional questions to consider-

- What do you think is the root cause of the situation?
- What is going on in the child's life?
- Can we pinpoint what's really going on?
- What can we do next to help this student?

  o New seating
  o New SEL strategies (Zones, Dragon Phenomenon, MTSS/PBIS)
  o Rewards (utilize a forced choice inventory)

Mindful Techniques:

- Breathing exercises
- Additional brain breaks
- Put positive notes on the student's desk
- Meet with the student 1:1
- Conference with the student's parents

Adapted from a form created by Hoppe & Rankin

# SUMMARY OF VARIOUS TOOLS WE CAN USE

**Dynamic sitting options:** Cushions, big therapy balls, and standing to work are great ways to help kids get the input they need to increase signals. When we have to put effort into our postural muscles, it keeps us alert. The cushions give a feeling similar to a big ball without the trouble of transporting it around, and work well for kids who might not be coordinated enough to sit on a ball safely. Remember that kids are supposed to be moving when they are using these tools; they should be bouncing on the ball or possibly spinning side to side on a wobble stool because movement helps them regulate. As long as they aren't a safety risk or bothering others, *and* as long as they are doing what they need to, let them move.

- **Creating Unique Sitting Options:** Many teachers are raising the height (or using bed risers) of their tables to provide alternative heights. You can also take the lower legs off of tables to provide for sitting on the floor while at the table. Making various "centers" in your room with different seating options will let all students benefit from movement-based input for work time.
- **Rocking or Spin Chair:** Rocking chairs can be calming; spinning chairs are alerting and kids can wiggle without banging into their neighbor. If they spin, do no more than ten revolutions each way even if they think they want more.
- **Thera-Band on Chair:** Tie a stretchy band around the legs of a chair so the child can push/pull and work leg muscles to feed the nervous system.
- **Chair Push-up:** Sitting in a chair, put hands under your legs or hips and push, so legs and buns are up off the seat and hold as long as possible.
- **Extension of the Body:** When we lie on our stomach, we get extension of the neck which is alerting and will create more signals.

There is also important input into the arms and shoulders which helps support fine motor and writing foundational skills.

- **Vestibular Input**: Anything that involves tipping the head is vestibular. Vestibular input helps with auditory processing, so have them try rolling on their stomach over a ball to put their head down, swinging, stretching, or sitting in a rocking chair.

**External Reminders or Alarms:** These can be reminders on smartphones, checklists in obvious places, or even a schedule or a list written on a Post-it note on the desk. Helping kids with the details of their world can lead to improved work habits.

**Chunking:** Whenever you can break up work or projects, it helps make the task more manageable and less overwhelming. If the page is visually busy you can cover some of it up so they only have to focus on the part they should work on. Providing rewards after these chunks introduces dopamine into the system for motivation.

- **Motivators:** Providing quick breaks or rewards after chunks of work are complete can give the motivation to push through stuff that isn't fun and improve feelings of independence and success.

**Deep Pressure:** Anything that makes the muscles work, such as carrying books, stacking chairs, or games like wheelbarrow will provide heavy input into the nervous system. Have the child hug themselves tight, push hands together and hold, or shrug shoulders and relax. Use firm, deep pressure versus light touch whenever you touch the child.

- **Weighted Pad or Vest:** Weight can be on the lap, shoulders, or worn. Ideally, it's 10 minutes on, then take a break, but usually the child will know when they want it off. If you keep it on all day, the nervous system gets used to it and it doesn't have the same effect.
- **Compression Shirt:** Some kids need the pressure of these tight-fitting shirts to feel good in their own skin. These are usually put on in the morning and taken off before leaving school or when the child requests.

- **Play-Doh/Thera-putty:** Squishing, smashing between fingers, and rolling can all improve fine motor skills and provide heavy input for regulation.
- **Joint Compression:** Teach the child to gently push and pull their fingers at all joints or push their hands together firmly.
- **Vibration:** Hand-held massager on hands, arms, legs, or lap pads that vibrate can work.
- **Weighted Medicine Ball:** This activity is good before seat time or for transitions.

**Oral Input:** This can be a critical tool that has many options.

- **Water Bottle:** It's important to encourage children to stay hydrated by sipping on water while they work or move around..
- **Gum:** Pending approval from administration and if used as a tool and not a toy, gum can be one of the best tools we have.
- **Chewy or Crunchy Snacks:** Bagels, licorice, jerky, taffy, carrots, or pretzels will work.
- **Chewelry or Pencil Toppers:** Necklaces, bracelets, even fidgets or pencil toppers made for chewing can help; keep in mind there will be slobber with this one, so determine if this is something appropriate for your setting.
- **Chewy Sippy Cup:** These provide water and a more socially appropriate way to chew without the drool potential. They look like sippy cups but have a chewy mouthpiece designed for chewing.
- **Heavy Oral Work:** Try sucking applesauce, pudding, or yogurt through a straw.
- **Change Breathing:** Hold your breath and bear down for 5 seconds. Trumpet breathing is putting your thumb in your mouth as if blowing into an instrument. Changing breathing patterns and speed is also a great way to focus on how breath affects regulation and energy level.

- **Eat or Drink Something:** Foods like bagels or gum provide a strong workout for the jaw muscles and can contribute to regulating the nervous system. Chewable items or jewelry are often used with autism, very young children or kids with sensory processing issues. Sips of water, especially cold, can also create enough input to affect focused attention. *Getting up* to get the drink gives even more input.

**Auditory Input:**

- **Quiet Corner:** Providing a quiet workspace for times when focus is difficult can be critical. Some teachers set up a study carrel with headphones/earplugs, or place a beanbag behind a screen. Sometimes a tent or enclosure of some sort can be all the child needs to still hear what is going on while getting the break they need.
- **Noise Canceling Headphones:** These allow for participation while dulling the noise often associated with classroom time. These are not to be used all day, but more periodically.
- **Deep Breathing:** Breathe in to the count of 3 ("smell the flower") and blow out counting to 5 ("blow out the candles").
- **Personal Bubble:** Picturing a bubble can help kids understand that sometimes people have bigger bubbles than others and this can help them be aware of personal boundaries. Many kids needing movement or seeking touch are always in personal bubbles and this is tough, especially for the kids who don't do well with touch. Allowing kids to stand in the back during circle time or have a space that allows for a bigger bubble can keep them participating while not setting off their sensory system.
- **Foster Calmness with your Speech:** Speak with a low volume and pace.
- **Touch to get Attention:** When input doesn't register, sometimes simply touching their shoulder can help gain their attention instead of using more words.

- **Bell for Initiation:** A different sound to indicate "go" can sometimes make more of an impression than simply saying "begin".
- **Music:** Calming music in class or in headphones can help kids struggling with loud times. When kids are always telling others to be quiet it can be a way to manage auditory input that is too much.

**Movement:** Remember, every time we move our bodies, we get a shot of endorphins that help wake us up. This is effective especially in the morning because it can last for hours in the nervous system. Studies indicate significant benefits of movement, even 20-40 minutes three times per week, can positively affect the mind and body and improve anxiety or depression symptoms (Mayoclinic.org "Depression and anxiety: Exercise eases symptoms").

- **Play and Move Bodies before Work:** Many people think movement and what they might consider "play" is for *after* work, but most people need to move their bodies before working. Similarly, if a child must earn the yoga ball by working, they may never meet that demand because they need movement to regulate and work.
- **Sports, Exercise, Jobs, and Chores:** Movement and heavy work into muscles feed the nervous system with effects that can last 2-6 hours. Incorporate this input into their daily routine. If you need to impose a  consequence, try an exercise break instead of recess; kids still move but losing free time is the consequence.
- **Sensory Diet:** This is any activity we integrate into a child's schedule to help them regulate. For example, before transitions, do deep breathing and put chairs on the desk, or do ten wall or chair push-ups after recess before sitting to work (Wilbarger, 2002).

- **Perform Jobs for the Teacher:** Running errands, even made-up ones (especially if it involves carrying something heavy), not only feeds the nervous system but allows for a change in the environment and can help the student reset when you notice they are struggling.
- **Stretching or Yoga:** This is usually an entire class activity done when the teacher notices that most kids aren't regulated or attending. It can be 30 seconds and done right at their seat, so it is easy to transition back to work.
- **Breaks for Movement:** This doesn't have to be huge, even a walk to the drinking fountain will work.
- **Hand or Pencil Fidgets:** Provide squeeze balls, pencil toppers that twist or move, or anything to fidget with during listening time.
- **Heavy Walking:** Have the child do deep lunges on each step so they can use the big muscles of their legs, and walk on tiptoes or their heels with toes up.

**Wait Time:** Ensure you have given enough time for processing AND responding. This can range from 3-10 seconds depending on the child and how much they are facing.

**Visuals and Visual Input:** This will provide a quick, easy clue that doesn't require the brain to work, which will help to simplify what we are asking their brain to do. It also gives them a reference for later in case they missed some of the instructions.

- **Structure in Pictures:** If a child knows the general sequence of the events in their day, they can better anticipate and prepare for it.
- **Visual or Picture cues:** Letting the student see what is expected, what the end result is, or what the motivator is can help with starting work. It also fills in gaps and allows them to determine what they might have missed in verbal instruction. Using a break card as a picture or visual tool can also help kids who are embarrassed or can't find the words for times when they need help.
- **Picture Schedule:** Pictures are processed differently than words, so simply utilizing them in a schedule can help a child begin to

process what is coming. They can see the sequence of events for a day or for a multiple-stepped task. Modern technology puts this capability at our fingertips with a smartphone; snap a picture of something a child needs to do and then show the motivator. Present the picture and say, "First this" then show them the motivator and say, "Then this." Fewer words make it easier to understand and leave little room for negotiation. You can also have pictures showing what the day will look like; this is a great way to talk about the hard things for this child. Now you can review strategies *before* they struggle. Come up with a plan, and then a backup plan. This is especially important if their typical schedule is going to be different, like when there will be a substitute teacher or an assembly.

- **Reinforce with Written Instructions:** Kids that shut down may miss verbal instruction so written lists allow them to have something for reference later.

- **Lamps vs. Fluorescent Lighting:** The bright lights of a classroom can feel like razor blades to some students. Providing alternative lighting options even for just certain times, or covering fluorescent lights with shades (commercially available) can help these kids focus and continue learning.

- **Decrease Visual Clutter:** Cover busy bookcases, or create spaces in the room with less stimulation (nothing on the walls or hanging overhead).

- **Hoodies:** Blocking out the visual world can be as simple as allowing for a hoodie or hat in certain environments.

**Respect Anxiety, Preferences, and Fear:** These are real and usually based within the nervous system and they may not be under the child's control.

**Get creative:** The goal is to feed the nervous system by utilizing the sensory system and providing for movement, force or pressure, heavy work, or by stimulating the senses.

**Control:** When behavior problems occur, children are usually feeling out of control. When you allow them to control something, their behavior usually gets better. It can be as simple as making a deal with a child during work time. Maybe they choose the next break activity when they work through a certain number of problems. Make sure the choices you give them are all acceptable to you so they will be successful no matter their choice.

**Timer:** When kids have trouble attending or beginning an activity it can be related to motivation. Seeing how much time they have before a break (even a 30-second stretching break) can help them muster the energy to begin.

**Velcro on Desk:** Attach Velcro to the underside of a desk so the child can rub their fingers along this texture while listening.

**Line Placement and Tools:** Kids who need to move or need input often struggle when standing or walking in line. Putting them in the back or giving them something to carry while in line can distract them or give them the input they need to be successful. When kids are in the front or back of the line it decreases the chance of unexpected touch.

- **Line Buddy:** A student who respects and understands personal bubbles could be paired with one who struggles with standing/ walking in line.

# SUMMARY

When I talk with teachers, many feel alone trying to help tough kids. Administrators who continue to implement their school discipline program with little success frequently express frustration because they are often the last step in addressing behavior problems and when every viable technique has failed, they have no idea what to do next. The most important thing to remember here is reframing. These are not bad kids. We are dealing with a very real issue that can make it hard for them to find success. Strategies, tools, and knowledge are important, but *how* we engage with kids is the framework around everything we do. Sometimes we need tools and other times we need to try things that might be more out of the box.

Keep in mind that tools are just that; they aren't the be-all or end-all, and they certainly aren't a magic pill that cures all. Some work, some don't. The important thing to remember is that if they aren't working, they aren't tools. If a child doesn't want to try one, don't push it. If a child isn't benefiting from one, don't use it. If you see they are misusing it, it's a toy, not a tool, so it's time to try something else. Not every strategy will work for everyone; it is important that kids know they are the experts but that sometimes they need a guide.

I have met many incredible administrators, teachers, caregivers, and kids on my journey as a therapist and a mom. I have always said it truly takes a village to raise a child and YOU are a very important part of this village. Sometimes all it takes is a different way to look at a situation to make everyone realize that this too shall pass. Maybe it doesn't matter if they can't finish the entire page of math if they are still trying and learning. Adapting and modifying can create a just right challenge very quickly.

Step back and refocus. What matters is the connections we have with each other. These connections come from acceptance and learning, and most importantly, understanding. As a therapist, I have one big goal for any child... happiness. Happiness is dependent on the journey and all that is discovered along the way. If we can send kids home after a long day of learning, adventure, and challenges and they come back the next day ready for more, we have done it right. We have guided them to a place where they are safe, can refine their skills, find success, and hopefully feel like someone in their world understands and cares about them.

Sometimes when we are wrapped up in our emotions from the day, it is hard to remember what really matters. In twenty years, this child might be a completely different human because of what you saw in them. You may be that one person who believed they could do anything, so they did. You might be a ray of sunshine in a really dark place... and this is what matters! They won't remember how hard the math was, but they will remember the smiles, the laughter, and the lessons that each of us must learn during this incredible journey. Even a wink or smile will increase the effect an adult can have on a child because they might feel for a moment that they have been seen for *who* they are and not what they do. It will let a child know they are valued, no matter what kind of wiring they have.

We have an opportunity, especially when kids are young, to help them embrace who they are, be proud of it, and then maybe problem-solve how to make their wiring work in the real world. It can be hard, and life may be hard. So much can happen when just one special person sees the good this child can bring to the world.

Your perspective and positivity will have a ripple effect that our children will see and feel. Thank you for your commitment to our children; they are our biggest asset for the future!

For more information, consultation, or for training purposes, please contact me at

Kristin Robison, MOT, OTR/L
Secrettohappy.com
secrettohappy@gmail.com

# ACKNOWLEDGMENTS

This book was written in response to all the amazing administrators, teachers, and paraprofessionals I get to work with every day. My book for parents was the beginning, but the people who teach and guide children are so incredibly vital in the journey of a child. There are similarities between my parent book and this one for educators because the message is the same: we are all here to better understand each other so we can support, teach and better enjoy the journey of working with these amazing kids.

I wish to thank the people in my village who helped me become the therapist and educator I am today. I would love to personally thank each child I have worked with because each one has taught me something along the way. My mom, Betty Christianson Martinsen, read every single word again to make sure it was correct. My husband Drew, and kids Jens and Annika, have been so supportive in helping me realize the completion of this book. To Joyce Cook, for being my "Mary Poppins" and sharing her joy and happiness with my kids so I could work. Thank you to Deb Oliver for more of her vision, business management, and opportunity. I so appreciate the "Think Tank" of Miya Mackenzie, Peggy Borgeman, Molly Dahl, and Deb Oliver. Trisha Sagare designed my cover, again, and still knew how to push me in the right direction. Bekah Rosas did all my illustrations so perfectly in both books and I even got my daughter to do some of the artwork! To Kyra Fields, thank you for all your incredible wordsmithing and brilliance with writing for my cover and introduction. To my sister Julie Broxson who is one of the most amazing marriage and family therapists, thank you for sharing your insight and ideas. My sister, Janel Ulrich, helped with edits and shared her ideas to help me meet the needs of "gifted" kids from her very unique perspective. To Carrie Ayarbe Fields, Joanna Kaiser, Christi Lenox, Gail Murray, Marvalee Clayworth, Chelise Crookshanks, Amy Robinson, Sarah Santos, and Kristin Sharp Lang, thank you for your constant and professional positive energy that helped me to complete this project. And to the entire Carson City School District, its administrators, teachers, paraprofessionals, and students, thank you for the exposure, support, and enthusiasm.

To my amazing village of friends, I thank you from the bottom of my heart. And a special thanks to you, the reader, for investing in our kids and making our future that much brighter.

I am thankful for all the positive energy and people in my world who are kind, giving, and just trying to make a better life for their families and those around them. We must always remember that we are in this together and the road is much more fun with people beside you.

# REFERENCES

*ADHD Comorbidity.* (n.d.). MentalHelp.net. Retrieved February 27, 2023, from https://www.mentalhelp.net/adhd/and-comorbidity/

Alber, D. (2020, July 24). *Bubble Bounce! Mindfulness for Children (Mindful Looking).* YouTube. Retrieved April 15, 2023, from https://www.youtube.com/watch?v=UEuFi9PxKuo

Amen, D. (n.d.). *Child Psychiatry Treatment | Mental Health Therapy.* Amen Clinics. Retrieved March 25, 2023, from https://www.amenclinics.com/conditions/child-psychiatry/

Anderson, D. (2023, January 25). *What is the difference between ADD and ADHD?* Child Mind Institute. Retrieved February 27, 2023, from https://childmind.org/article/what-is-the-difference-between-add-and-adhd/

Arain, M., Haque, M., Johal, L., Mathur, P., Nel, W., Rais, A., Sandhu, R., & Sharma, S. (2013). Maturation of the adolescent brain. *Neuropsychiatric Disease and Treatment, 9*(April 3), 449-461. NCBI. https://www.ncbi.nlm.nih.gov/pmc/articles/PMC3621648/

*Attention-Deficit/Hyperactivity Disorder (ADHD).* (2023, February 22). Cleveland Clinic. Retrieved July 11, 2023, from https://my.clevelandclinic.org/health/diseases/4784-attention-deficithyperactivity-disorder-adhd

*Autism and the Neurodiversity Paradigm – Zur Institute.* (n.d.). Zur Institute. Retrieved February 27, 2023, from https://www.zurinstitute.com/clinical-updates/autism-and-the-neurodiversity-paradigm/

Barber, A., & Phang, K. (2017, July 13). *Toxic Stress: How the Body's Response Can Harm a Child's Development*. Nationwide Children's. Retrieved April 12, 2023, from https://www.nationwidechildrens.org/family-resources-education/700childrens/2017/07/toxic-stress-how-the-bodys-response-can-harm-a-childs-development

Barkley, R. (2011, January 24). *Fact Sheet: Attention Deficit Hyperactivity Disorder (ADHD) Topics*.

Barkley, R. A. (2012). *Executive Functions: What They Are, How They Work, and Why They Evolved*. Guilford Publications.

Barry, K. (2011, January 23). *Notes on Teaching and Learning* [Wait-Time: The Role of Silence in Increasing In-class Interaction]. University of Notre Dame. https://sites.nd.edu/kaneb/2011/01/23/wait-time-the-role-of-silence-in-active-participation/

Baumeister, R. F., Bratslavsky, E., Finkenauer, C., & Vohs, K.D. (2001). Bad is Stronger than Good. *Review of General Psychology, 5*(4), 323-370. https://psycnet.apa.org/record/2018-70020-001

Baxter, S. (2021, March 7). *Vagus Nerve Massage For Stress And Anxiety Relief*. YouTube. Retrieved January 15, 2023, from https://www.youtube.com/watch?v=LnV3Q2xIb1U

Bonaz, B., Sinniger, V., & Pellissier, S. (2018, February 1). *Vagus Nerve as Modulator of the Brain–Gut Axis in Psychiatric and Inflammatory Disorders*. Frontiers. Retrieved January 15, 2023, from https://doi.org/10.3389/fpsyt.2018.00044

Bremner, J. D. (2006). Traumatic stress: effects on the brain. *Dialogues Clin Neuroscience, 8*(4), 445-461. https://www.ncbi.nlm.nih.gov/pmc/articles/PMC3181836/

Brickman, P., Coates, D., & Janoff-Bulman, R. (1978). Lottery Winners and Accident Victims: Is Happiness Relative? *Journal of Personality and Social Psychology, 36*(8), 917-927. Research Gate.

Brown, T. E. (2021, August 25). *How Does ADHD Affect the Brain? Executive Functions and More.* ADDitude. Retrieved January 15, 2023, from https://www.additudemag.com/inside-the-add-mind/

*CCDTherapy Ed Snapp C.C.D.T. Chronologically Controlled Developmental Therapy Ed Snapp Therapy Snapp Therapy is a Snapp CCDE.* (n.d.). Snapp Therapeutics. Retrieved February 28, 2023, from http://www.snapptherapy.com/ccdtherapy/understandingccdt.html

Cristol, H. (2021, June 14). *Dopamine: What It Is & What It Does.* WebMD. Retrieved February 21, 2023, from https://www.webmd.com/mental-health/what-is-dopamine

Davidson, K. (221). *Why Do We Need Endorphins?* Healthline. https://www.healthline.com/health/endorphins

Dawson, P., & Guare, R. (2009). *Smart but Scattered: The Revolutionary "Executive Skills" Approach to Helping Kids Reach Their Potential* (1ˢᵗ ed.). Guilford Press.

den Heijer, A. (2018). *Nothing You Don't Already Know: Remarkable Reminders about Meaning, Purpose, and Self-Realization* (J. Willard, Ed.). CreateSpace Independent Publishing Platform.

Dennison, P. E., & Dennison, G. E. (1986). *Brain Gym: Simple Activities for Whole Brain Learning.* Edu-Kinesthetics, Incorporated.

*Depression and anxiety: Exercise eases symptoms.* (n.d.). Mayo Clinic. Retrieved May 12, 2023, from https://www.mayoclinic.org/diseases-conditions/depression/in-depth/depression-and-exercise/art-20046495

Dodson, W. (2022, August 24). *ADHD and the Epidemic of Shame.* ADDitude. https://www.additude.mag.com

Dündar-Coecke, S., Tolmie, A., & Schlottmann, A. (2020). The role of spatial and spatial-temporal analysis in children's causal cognition of continuous processes. *PLOS One, 15(7)*(July 30, 2020). https://doi.org/10.1371/journal.pone.0235884

Dunn, W. (1999). *Sensory Profile Users Manual*. NCS Pearson.

Dunn, W. (2007). Supporting Children to Participate Successfully in Everyday Life by Using Sensory Processing Knowledge. *Infants & Young Children, 20*(2), 84-101. https://journals.lww.com/iycjournal/fulltext/2007/04000/supporting_children_to_participate_successfully_in.2.aspx

Dweck, C. (2007). *Carol Dweck: Praising Intelligence: Costs to Children's Self-Esteem and Motivation*. Stanford School of Humanities and Sciences Bing Nursery School. https://bingschool.stanford.edu/news/carol-dweck-praising-intelligence-costs-childrens-self-esteem-and-motivation

*5 Ways To Stimulate Your Vagus Nerve – Cleveland Clinic*. (2022, March 10). Cleveland Clinic Health Essentials. Retrieved April 10, 2023, from https://health.clevelandclinic.org/vagus-nerve-stimulation/

Franke, H. A. (2014). Toxic Stress: Effects, Prevention and Treatment. *Children, 1(3)*(10.3390), 390-402. https://pubmed.ncbi.nlm.nih.gov/27417486/

Galiana-Simal, A., Vela-Romero, M., Romero-Vela, V. M., Oliver-Tercero, N., Garcia-Olmo, V., Benito-Castellanos, P. J., Munoz-Martinez, V., Beato-Fernandez, L., & Schumacher, U. (2020). Sensory Processing Disorder: Key points of a frequent alteration in neurodevelopmental disorders. *Cogent Medicine, 7*(1). https://www.tandfonline.com/action/showCitFormats?doi=10.1080%2F2331205X.2020.1736829

Gibbs, V. (2017). *Self-Regulation and Mindfulness: Over 82 Exercises & Worksheets for Sensory Processing Disorder, ADHD, & Autism Spectrum Disorder*. PESI, Incorporated.

Goldrich, C. (2013). *PTS Coaching*. PTS Coaching: ADHD Services for Parents & Professionals. Retrieved January 26, 2023, from http://www.ptscoaching.com

Goldrich, C. (2015). *8 Keys to Parenting Children with ADHD*. WW Norton.

Gottman, J. M., & Levenson, R. W. (1992). Marital Processes Predictive of Later Dissolution: Behavior, Physiology, and Health. *Journal of Personality and Social Psychology, 63*(2), 221-233.

Gray, C. (n.d.). Carol Gray - Social Stories: Home. Retrieved January 14, 2023, from http://carolgraysocialstories.com

Greenberg, M. (2021, June 30). *Understanding the Trauma Brain*. Psychology Today. Retrieved December 4, 2022, from https://www.psychologytoday.com/us/blog/the-mindful-self-express/202106/understanding-the-trauma-brain

Greene, R. W. (2005). *The Explosive Child*. Harper.

Greene, R. W. (2014). *Lost at School: Why Our Kids with Behavioral Challenges are Falling Through the Cracks and How We Can Help Them*. Scribner.

Henry, D. A. (n.d.). *Tool Chest*. ateachabout.com. http://www.henryot.com/index.asp

Hoppe, G., & Rankin, T. (n.d.). *Refocus, Reset & Re-Enter Form*. Carson City School District, Carson City, NV.

Horeis, M. (2020, June 23). *The vagus nerve: your secret weapon in fighting stress*. Allied Services Integrated Health System. Retrieved January 15, 2023, from https://www.allied-services.org/news/2020/june/the-vagus-nerve-your-secret-weapon-in-fighting-s/

Houskamp, B. .. (2021, October 22). *Sensory Issues in Gifted Kids*. Davidson Institute. Retrieved February 28, 2023, from https://www.davidsongifted.org/gifted-blog/sensory-issues-in-gifted-kids/

Houting, J. d. (2019, November 1). *Why everything you know about autism is wrong*. ted.com. https://www.ted.com/talks/jac_den_houting_why_everything_you_know_about_autism_is_wrong?language=en

Huebner, D. (2005). *What to Do when You Worry Too Much: A Kid's Guide to Overcoming Anxiety*. Magination Press.

*The Impact of Attention Deficit Hyperactivity Disorder on the Health of America's Children*. (2019, March 28). Blue Cross Blue Shield. Retrieved February 27, 2023, from https://www.bcbs.com/the-health-of-america/reports/impact-of-adhd-attention-deficit-hyperactivity-disorder-on-health-of-americas-children

Jacobson, R. (2023, January 23). *How Girls With ADHD Are Different*. Child Mind Institute. Retrieved February 27, 2023, from https://childmind.org/article/how-girls-with-adhd-are-different/

Jain, R. (n.d.). Online Programs for Helping Kids With Anxiety | GoZen. Retrieved November 20, 2023, from https://gozen.com/

Koch, S. B. J., Klumoers, F., Zhang, W., Hashemi, M. M., Kaldewaij, R., van Ast, V. A., Smit, A. S., & Roelofs, K. (2017). The role of automatic defensive responses in the development of posttraumatic stress symptoms in police recruits: protocol of a prospective study. *European Journal of Psychotraumatology, 8(1)*(Dec 20), 1412226. https://pubmed.ncbi.nlm.nih.gov/29321826/

Kutscher, M. L. (2008). *ADHD- Living without Brakes*. Jessica Kingsley Publishers.

Kuypers, L. (n.d.). THE ZONES OF REGULATION: A SOCIAL EMOTIONAL LEARNING PATHWAY TO REGULATION. Retrieved January 15, 2023, from https://zonesofregulation.com/index.html

Kuypers, L. M. (2011). *The Zones of Regulation: A Curriculum Designed to Foster Self-regulation and Emotional Control*. Think Social Publishing, Incorporated.

Larry. (2022, January 19). *Face It- People with ADHD are Wired Differently.* ADDitudemag.com. https://www.additudemag.com/current-research-on-adhd-breakdown-of-the-adhd-brain/

Lebrun-Harris, L. A., Ghandour, R. M., Kogan, M. D., & Warren, M. D. (2022). Five-Year Trends in US Children's Health and Well-being, 2016-2020. *JAMA Pediatrics, 176*(7), 11. https://www.webofscience.com/wos/woscc/full-record/WOS:000770397300004?SID=USW2EC0FACzd5VAQ920XRkehk8BZA

Lin, T.-W., & Kuo, Y.-M. (2013). Exercise Benefits Brain Function. *Brain Sci, 11*(3(1)), 39-53. https://www.ncbi.nlm.nih.gov/pmc/articles/PMC4061837/

Lind, S. (2011, September 14). *Overexcitability and the Gifted.* Supporting Emotional Needs of the Gifted. Retrieved February 28, 2023, from https://www.sengifted.org/post/overexcitability-and-the-gifted

Lind, S., Lind, S. .., & Rimm, S. (2000, November 3). *Overexcitability and the highly gifted child.* Davidson Institute. Retrieved December 4, 2022, from https://www.davidsongifted.org/gifted-blog/overexcitability-and-the-highly-gifted-child/

McCabe, J. (n.d.). How To ADHD: Home. Retrieved February 27, 2023, from https://howtoadhd.com/

McFarling, U. L. (2023, February 1). *MRI scans reveal disparate impact of poverty and other 'toxic stress' on brains of Black children.* STAT News. Retrieved April 12, 2023, from https://www.statnews.com/2023/02/01/brain-scans-reveal-disparate-impact-of-poverty-toxic-stress-on-black-children/

Metz, A. E., Boling, D., DeVore, A., Holladay, H., Liao, J. F., & Vander Vlutch, K. (2019). Dunn's Model of Sensory Processing: An Investigation of the Axes of the Four-Quadrant Model in Healthy Adults. *Brain Sci, 9*(2) (Feb 7), 35. https://www.ncbi.nlm.nih.gov/pmc/articles/PMC6406387/

Mickley Steinmetz, K. R., Scott, L. A., Smith, D., & Kensinger, E. A. (2012). The effects of trauma exposure and posttraumatic stress disorder (PTSD) on the emotion-induced memory trade-off. *Frontiers in Integrative Neuroscience, 6.* https://doi.org/10.3389/fnint.2012.00034

Miller, L. (2007). *In Gifted.* STAR Institute. Retrieved 12 04, 2022, from https://sensoryhealth.org/basic/gifted

Missimer, A. (2021, August 24). *Vagus Nerve Hack Hand Reflexology.* The Movement Paradigm - The Movement Paradigm. Retrieved January 15, 2023, from https://themovementparadigm.com/

Murray, G., & Robison, K. (2023). *Interactive Regulation Tool-Box* [Cycle of Regulation].

Neville, C. (2021, October 6). *Types of Behavioral Problems Gifted Children Face.* Davidson Academy. Retrieved February 28, 2023, from https://www.davidsonacademy.unr.edu/blog/challenges-gifted-students-face/

Pradhan, R. (2022, November 5). *How Fast Can The Human Brain Process Images?* Science ABC. Retrieved February 28, 2023, from https://www.scienceabc.com/humans/how-fast-can-the-human-brain-process-images.html

Roberts, W. ". (n.d.). *Focused Mind ADHD Counseling.* https://focusedmindadhdcounseling.com/

Robison, K. M. (2021). *The Secret to Happy: Understanding Your Child's Behavior: a Parent's Guide to Helping a Unique Child Thrive.* iUniverse.

Ross, G. (n.d.). LIVES IN THE BALANCE. Retrieved January 22, 2023, from https://livesinthebalance.org

Rowe, M. B. (1972). *Wait-Time and Rewards as Instructional Variables: Their Influence on Language, Logic, and Fate Control* (April ed.). ERIC. ed.gov. https://eric.ed.gov/?id=ED061103

Schneiderman, I., Zagoory-Sharon, O., Leckman, J. F., & Feldman, R. (2012). Oxytocin during the initial stages of romantic attachment. *Psychoneuroendocrinology*, *37*(8), 1277-1285. https://www.ncbi.nlm.nih.gov/pmc/articles/PMC3936960/

Shaw, P., Eckstrand, K., Sharp, W., Blumenthal, J., Lerch, J.P., Greenstein, D., Clasen, L., Evans, A., & Rapoport, J.L. (2007). Attention-deficit/hyperactivity disorder is characterized by a delay in cortical maturation. *PNAS*, *104(49)*(December 4, 2007), 19649-19654. https://www.pnas.org/doi/full/10.1073/pnas.0707741104

Shaw, P., Malek, M., Watson, B., Sharp, W., Evans, A., & Greenstein, D. (2012). Development of cortical surface area and gyrification in attention-deficit/hyperactivity disorder. *Biological Psychiatry*, *72 (3)*(August 1, 2012), 191-197. https://pubmed.ncbi.nlm.nih.gov/22418014/

Sherman, C. (2022, December 27). *What Causes ADHD? Genes, Culture, Environment, Biology*. ADDitude. Retrieved February 27, 2023, from https://www.additudemag.com/what-causes-adhd-symptoms/

Sibley, M. H., Arnold, E., Swanson, J. M., Hechtman, L. T., Kennedy, T. M., Owens, E., Molina, B. S.G., Jensen, P. S., Hinshaw, S. P., Roy, A., Chronis-Tuscano, A., Newcorn, J. H., & Rohde, L. A. (2021). Variable Patterns of Remission from ADHD in the Multimodal Treatment Study of ADHD. *American Journal of Psychiatry*, *179*(2), 142-151. appiajp202121010032. doi:10.1176/appi.ajp.2021.21010032. https://ajp.psychiatryonline.org/doi/pdf/10.1176/appi.ajp.2021.21010032

Smith, I. (2020, June 29). *How Does Trauma Affect the Brain? - And what it means for you*. Whole Wellness Therapy. Retrieved December 4, 2022, from https://www.wholewellnesstherapy.com/post/trauma-and-the-brain

SPD Foundation. (2007, July). *Understanding sensory processing disorder and recent research in ASD*. [Presentation at Progress through Partnership: PA 10th Annual National Autism Conference, State College, PA]. Sensoryhealth.org. https://sensoryhealth.org/sites/default/files/publications/SensoryissuesinGiftedChildren.pdf

Spinasanta, S. (2021). *What is Adrenaline?* EndocrineWeb. Retrieved February 21, 2023, from https://www.endocrineweb.com/adrenaline

Stahl, R. J. (1994, May). *Using "Think-time" and "Wait-time" Skillfully in the Classroom.* Eric Digests. https://files.eric.ed.gov/fulltext/ED370885.pdf

Tamana, S. K., Ezeugwu, V., Chikuma, J., Lefebvre, D. L., Azad, M. B., Moraes, T. J., Subbarao, P., Becker, A. B., Turvey, S. E., Sears, M. R., Dick, B. D., Carson, V., & Rasmussen, C. (2019). Screen-time is associated with inattention problems in preschoolers: Results from the CHILD birth cohort study. *PLOS One, 14(4)*(April 17, 2019), e0213995. https://journals. plos.org/plosone/article/citation?id=10.1371/journal.pone.0213995

Thomas, C. G. (2021). Study Shows how taking short breaks may help our brains learn new skills. *National Institutes of Health, News Releases*(June 8). https://www.nih.gov/news-events/news-releases/study-shows-how-taking-short-breaks-may-help-our-brains-learn-new-skills

*2018 Children's Mental Health Report: Understanding Anxiety in Children and Teens.* (2018). Child Mind Institute. Retrieved February 27, 2023, from https://childmind.org/awareness-campaigns/childrens-mental-health-report/2018-childrens-mental-health-report/

Ward, S., & Jacobsen, K. (2021). *Cognitive Connections.* Cognitive Connections: Executive Function. Retrieved January 15, 2023, from http://efpractice.com

Webb, J. T., Gore, J. L., Amend, E. R., & DeVries, A. R. (2008). A Parent's Guide to Gifted Children. *Gifted and Talented International, 23*(1), 155-158. https://www.researchgate.net/publication/308956718_A_Parent's_Guide_to_Gifted_Children#:~:text=Giftedness%20is%20asynchronous%20development%20where,Amend%20%26%20DeVries%2C%202007)%20.

*What is Autism Spectrum Disorder? | CDC.* (2022, December 9). Centers for Disease Control and Prevention. Retrieved February 27, 2023, from https://www.cdc.gov/ncbddd/autism/facts.html

Wilbarger, P., & Wilbarger, J. (2002). *Wilbarger approach to treating sensory defensiveness and clinical application of the sensory diet. Sections in alternative and complementary programs for intervention* (2nd Ed. ed.). F.A. Davis.

Williams, M. S., & Shellenberger, S. (n.d.). *The Alert Program Self-Regulation Made Easy.* Self-Regulation Alert Program® Online | AOTA Approved Provider. Retrieved January 15, 2023, from https://www.alertprogram.com/

Williams, M. S., & Shellenberger, S. (1996). *How Does Your Engine Run? A Leader's Guide to the Alert Program for Self-regulation.* TherapyWorks, Incorporated.

Wooll, M. (2021, November 10). *The Benefits of Microlearning: Learn Big, Study Small.* BetterUp. Retrieved February 20, 2023, from https://www.betterup.com/blog/microlearning

Zur, O. (n.d.). *Autism and the Neurodiversity Paradigm – Zur Institute.* Zur Institute. Retrieved May 8, 2023, from https://www.zurinstitute.com/clinical-updates/autism-and-the-neurodiversity-paradigm/

Printed in the United States
by Baker & Taylor Publisher Services